CRITICAL REFL
ON DISTANCE EDUCATION

Deakin Studies in Education Series

General Editors: Professor Rob Walker and Professor Stephen Kemmis,
Deakin University, Victoria, Australia

Deakin Studies in Education Series: 2

CRITICAL REFLECTIONS ON DISTANCE EDUCATION

Edited by
Terry Evans and Daryl Nation

 The Falmer Press

(A member of the Taylor & Francis Group)
London, New York and Philadelphia

UK   The Falmer Press, Falmer House, Barcombe, Lewes, East Sussex, BN8 5DL

USA   The Falmer Press, Taylor & Francis Inc., 242 Cherry Street, Philadelphia, PA 19106-1906

First published 1989

British Library Cataloguing in Publication Data

Critical reflections on distance education.—
(Deakin studies in education series).
   1. Adult education. Distance study.
I. Evans, Terry. II. Nation, Daryl. III. Series.
374′.02
ISBN 1-85000-462-5
ISBN 1-85000-463-3 (pbk.)

Library of Congress Cataloging-in-Publication Data

Critical reflections on distance education / Terry Evans and Daryl Nation, editors.

    p. cm.
   Bibliography: p.
   Includes index.
   ISBN 1-85000-462-5. ISBN (invalid) 1-85000-463-3 (pbk.)
   1. Distance education. I. Evans, Terry (Terry Denis).
II. Nation, Daryl.
LC5800.C75 1989
378′.03—dc 19 88-27331

Typeset in 12/13 Garamond by
The FD Group Ltd, Fleet, Hampshire

Jacket design by Caroline Archer

Printed in Great Britain by Taylor & Francis (Printers) Ltd, Basingstoke

Contents

Acknowledgments

On behalf of the contributors to the project we would like to acknowledge the support, assistance and encouragement of the following people: Mandie Beveridge, Malcolm Clarkson, John Evans, Lyn Gorman, Peter Harwood, Kathy Martyniuk, Angie Muccillo, Lynn Sceney and Rob Walker. We would also like to acknowledge the financial support provided to the project by the Institute of Distance Education at Deakin University and the School of Social Sciences at the Gippsland Institute of Advanced Education.

Terry Evans and Daryl Nation

General Editors' Introduction

The Deakin Studies in Education Series aims to present a broad critical perspective across a range of interrelated fields in education. The intention is to develop what might be called a 'critical educational science': critical work in the philosophy of education, curriculum, educational and public administration, language education, and educational action research and clinical supervision. The series strives to present the writings of a rising generation of scholars and researchers in education.

A number of researchers based at Deakin University have been closely associated with the development of the critical perspective across these fields. For such reasons, people in the field have sometimes spoken of a 'Deakin perspective'. We do share some common views from which we hope to contribute to contemporary debates about the future development of educational enquiry; at the same time, our disagreements seem as fruitful for us as our agreements.

The Deakin Studies in Education Series provides an opportunity for extending this debate about the nature and future development of education and educational enquiry. It will include the writings of a variety of educational researchers around the world who, like ourselves, are interested in exploring the power and limitations of the critical perspective in the analysis of educational theory, policy and practice.

The central themes of the series will not be dictated by the alleged boundaries between 'foundational' disciplines in education, nor by an unexamined division of the tasks of education and educational research between 'practitioners' and 'theorists', or between 'practitioners' and 'policy-makers'. On the contrary, one of the tasks of the series is to demonstrate, through careful research and scholarship across a range of fields of practical, political and theoretical endeavour, just how outmoded, unproductive, and ultimately destructive these divisions are both for education and for educational research. Put positively, the central themes and questions to be addressed in the series include:

the unity of educational theory and practice — expressed, for example, in the work of educational practitioners who research their practice as a basis for improving it, and in the notion of collaborative, participatory educational research, for example, in educational action research;

the historical formation, social construction and continual reconstruction of education and educational institutions and reforms through processes of contestation and institutionalization — expressed, for example, in the work of critical researchers into the curriculum and educational reform; and

the possibilities of education for emancipation and active and productive participation in a democratic society — expressed, for example, in the development of critical pedagogy and the development of communitarian perspectives in the organization of education.

These are enduring themes, touching upon some of the central questions confronting our contemporary culture and, some would say, upon the central pathologies of contemporary society. They are all too easily neglected or obscured in the narrow and fragmented views of education and educational research characteristic of our times. Yet education is one of the key resources in what Raymond Williams once described as our societies' 'journey of hope' — the journey towards a better, more just, more rational and more rewarding society. Education has always aimed to nurture, represent, vivify and extend the values and modes of life which promise to make the best in our culture better. Finding out how this can be done, interpreting our progress, and appraising and reappraising the quality of our efforts at educational improvement are the tasks of critical educational research. They are the tasks of this series.

Stephen Kemmis and Rob Walker

PART 1

THE PROJECT

Overture

What do Mikhail Gorbachev, Robert Mugabe and Harold Wilson have in common? Despite their manifest political differences, each has stood under a banner branded *socialism*. In varying degrees they have played important roles in Southern African politics. Doubtless there are many other interests and activities in which these powerful men have shared. *Distance education* has played an important part in the political career of each: as students for Gorbachev and Mugabe and as a political instigator for Wilson.

In 1962, at the age of 31, Mikhail Gorbachev's career moved sideways and upwards; he had begun the relatively rapid rise to ultimate power in the Soviet Union. During the previous seven years he had worked his way up within the Komsomol organization in his native region of Stavropol, almost 1600 kilometres from Moscow. His work was related to ideological consciousness raising among the region's youth. His long involvement with the Communist Party and his law degree from the prestigious Moscow State University had equipped him well for the work. His new position of district party organizer, in a region based economically on agriculture, demanded new skills. Thus in September 1962 Gorbachev enrolled in an agricultural economy course, as an external student, at the Stavropol Agricultural Institute. It was a broad course which covered the scientific, technical and practical aspects of plant and livestock farming, finance and management, and gave him even more education in Marxist-Leninist philosophy and economics. Upon graduating in 1967 his career prospects were enhanced considerably. It provided him with a small but significant portion of the knowledge which assisted his promotion back to Moscow in 1978.[1]

After training as a teacher in his native village of Kutama in the mid-1940s, in 1945 Robert Mugabe set off to pursue a career as a rural teacher in Southern Rhodesia. In 1949 a scholarship took him to Fort

1

Hare University in South Africa. Here he pursued a Bachelor of Arts and became involved for the first time in African Nationalist politics. Upon graduating he returned to teach in Rhodesia. He embarked upon the twin aspects of his life's work: a rigorous programme of self-education and an active interest in politics. His political activities forced him to leave his country for Zambia and Ghana in the mid- and late 1950s. His decision to return home in the early 1960s led to his periodic detention in prison from December 1964 to late 1974. Mugabe and his fellow political prisoners took the opportunity to plan their revolution from the 'inside', and education occupied a central place in their programme. Mugabe worked as both a teacher and a political leader. However, he did not neglect the opportunity to further his own academic training. Working through a correspondence course from the University of London, he obtained a law degree in eighteen months, a course which normally took three to four years to complete. According to his tutors he took independent learning to extremes.[2]

Britain's Opposition leader, Harold Wilson, had become interested in the possibilities of applying educational technology to higher education in his country, following a trip to the Soviet Union where he had observed the effectiveness of part-time correspondence courses in technical education and an experience with educational films through *Encyclopedia Britannica*. Seeking government and constantly vigilant for ideas with electoral appeal, while puffing on his pipe in his study after church one Sunday in the summer of 1963, he lit on the concept of a *university of the air*. Without seeking party approval he offered a version of the proposal to the British people in September of that year. After the Labour Party's election victory in October 1964 he handed the responsibility to Jennie Lee, a junior minister. *The Open University* was born.[3] The rest is history — a history so important for contemporary distance education that we will deal with it in detail in our final chapter.

We do not wish to make a detailed case here, but we suggest that these apparently unrelated vignettes are closely connected. Indeed, they illustrate Geoffrey Bolton's observation 'that the concept of distance education may be seen as one of those innovations which was forged on the frontier of European expansion overseas; and that the history of distance education is to a considerable extent an example of the process by which ideas and techniques developed on the periphery have gradually been accepted and absorbed into the old heartland of European culture.'[4] They are related also to an important theme for the project behind this book: things are not always what they seem!

Notes

1 Medvedev (1986), pp. 32-3, 56, 62-3; Morrison (1988), pp. 90-3.
2 Smith and Simpson (1981), pp. 15-20, 54-7.
3 MacArthur (1974), pp. 4-6; Perry (1976), pp. 10-11.
4 Bolton (1986), p. 11.

Chapter 1

Introduction

Terry Evans and Daryl Nation

This book has two fundamental purposes: it offers nine critical reflections upon distance teaching practices in a variety of settings in Australian colleges and universities; and it argues a more general case for the adoption of approaches based upon critical reflection within research, theory and practice in distance education. In Chapter 2 we introduce *critical reflection* and discuss the development of the project. In the chapters in Part 2 individuals and teams critically reflect on aspects of their practice. In Part 3 we offer a more substantial critical discussion which places our approach within the context of developments of scholarship in distance education and makes links to other relevant areas of theory and research which have hitherto been neglected.

In choosing to structure our knowledge in this way, our aim has been to sketch in the essentials of our approach; and thus to enable those readers whose primary ambition is to come to grips with one or other of the chapters in Part 2 to get on with their reading and reflection. Those who cannot proceed intellectually (academically?) without a substantial dose of theory, can exercise their right to begin with Part 3. Our approach emphasizes the importance of socio-historical factors in the development of practice, research and theory in distance education. Accordingly, we now turn to a more detailed discussion of three issues relating to recent developments in the field: institutional provision for adults requiring post-secondary education, the professional organization of individuals and institutions interested in distance education and the growth of scholarship in the field. But all this presupposes some knowledge of the phenomenon itself. At this juncture some may feel it appropriate for us to launch into a definitional discussion. We prefer to move more empirically; we wish to orient you towards an understanding, or to engage your current understanding, by discussing some concrete examples associated with the issues identified.

In the last three decades there has been a world-wide development of institutions which have applied distance education to the provision of post-secondary education for part-time students. Few would quibble with the claim that the Open University (OU) of the United Kingdom is the most influential achievement in this regard. This vast institution, with over 100,000 students, captured the minds of politicians and educational administrators internationally in the 1970s. Indeed, a diverse range of institutions styled as *open universities* began to pop up all over the world; at the very least governments were expected to hold an enquiry into establishing one. Let us hasten to add: we are not suggesting that the OU was the single *cause* of this outbreak of educational development. Two very enduring trends emerged amongst all this political and administrative activity: the *open university* concept was rarely adopted slavishly, generally local factors have had considerable influence; and those institutions which had pioneered distance education long before the 'open university fad' were given both recognition and resources for new development.

In Australia, for example, external studies in higher education have continued to progress on the courses charted within the pioneering institutions: the Universities of Queensland and New England. Without exception, all distance teaching colleges and universities in Australia are 'dual-mode' organizations which offer their courses to both on-campus and off-campus students. While there have been influences from research and practice overseas, the enduring influences have been very local: Australian distance educators have done it their way, endeavouring to translate conventional techniques into distance teaching. By world standards the Australian distance education providers are quite small; the University of New England and Deakin University, which have the highest enrolments, had about 6000 and 4200 external students respectively in 1988.

Australia will never have an *open university* on the British model. History, vast spatial distances and a federal political system will guarantee that. The Australian response was to develop external studies sections with varying levels of institutional commitment in many colleges and universities. The number of institutions involved grew from six in 1970 to forty by the late 1980s, with student enrolments growing from about 8000 in the mid-1970s to over 45,000 in the late 1980s, which is about 12 per cent of all students enrolled in higher education. From the early 1980s governments have been attempting to 'rationalize' external studies, and as we write it has been proposed to cut back the number of institutions involved to six.

While we cannot offer a detailed review of the international situation, we are confident that readers will be familiar with local versions of these developments which have occurred in many countries, on all continents, with varying degrees of intensity in the last three decades. Of course, although distance education has undergone this resurgence, in no sense has it become the dominant form of part-time post-secondary education; rather, it has moved in from the margins and established itself as one of the very attractive options for contemporary developments in this field. However, it is possible to assert that institutions practising distance education have proved their viability in a diverse range of societies, from the sparsely to the densely populated, in the economically wealthy and the very poor and with governments of various political colours. It is no longer a marginal activity!

Distance education has proved to be a mutating virus within the bodies of education systems. It has been able to rise to new challenges, to reshape itself to meet social changes and to transform itself for adoption to new contexts. In the United Kingdom the 'downstream' developments from the OU are well known: the move into *continuing education*, the recent reformulation into *open learning*, the creation of Open Tech and the Open College. Similar reforms are occurring in other parts of the world. Distance educators no longer apologize for their institutional existence; rather, they are in demand to explain a fashionable concept to eager new adherents. This trend looks set to continue. Those involved in distance education have an obligation to share their experiences with those who wish to enter the field. Our concern is to demonstrate the importance of local factors upon practice, so that experiences can be shared and reshaped for local practice. Education, like technology, has to be adapted to local circumstances.

Accompanying these institutional developments there has been an associated growth in professional organizations. The history of the International Council for Distance Education (ICDE) illustrates this well. The International Council for Correspondence Education (ICCE) was founded in 1938 at Vancouver. The ICCE was created by the pioneers of correspondence education in schools, colleges and private academies, the adult and continuing educators and the university extension movement. In the 1970s and 1980s these hardy pioneers were joined by a larger 'new crowd' from the distance education renaissance in the post-secondary institutions. As a symbolic recognition that the 'hard times' and/or the 'bad old days' were over, the organization incorporated *distance education* into its title in Vancouver in 1982. The broad consensus between members older and newer was that the name change recognized the rising of the sun upon a new era.

As its name suggests, the ICDE is a world-wide organization and it has offered an excellent basis for the exchange of ideas in the field. It has fostered the dissemination of knowledge based upon practice, the fruits of research and the discussion of concepts and theories. Its thrice-yearly *Bulletin* and its periodic World Conferences play vital roles in this regard. The ICDE has provided an international forum in which distance educators who may feel marginalized on the local or national scene can remind themselves that they are part of an educational endeavour that has world-wide significance. The organization has also been very successful in addressing the difficult problem of maintaining interest and harmony among administrators, teachers and researchers. The 1970s and 1980s have also witnessed the creation of some national and regional associations interested in the promotion of distance education. These associations have allowed the ideas and practices just discussed to flourish on these levels, particularly through the publication of newsletters.

The growth of scholarship in distance education is related to the developments in both institutions and professional associations. Until the mid-1970s most of the scholarly publication was devoted to practitioners discussing their work. Newsletters were the main vehicles for the distribution of these ideas. About that time reports on research began to appear with increasing frequency, and many people started to explore theory, particularly as it related to the notion of 'distance education as a discipline'. Indeed, much ink and paper was expended asking and answering the question: what is distance education? Clearly, theorists and researchers had been incorporated into the distance education fold.

More recently the range of research work and theoretical endeavour has increased significantly. There are now five international journals devoted to the publication of research reviews and scholarly debate. Scholars working in the field have made considerable impact upon 'neighbouring' disciplines. This applies particularly to the various areas concerned with educational technology, student learning, adult education and the administrative organization of education. At least two internationally recognized courses exist which offer an introducton to the field for practitioners.

This book emerges from a tradition of scholarship which has not been dominant in distance education. In the next chapter we offer an introduction to its claims for recognition along with a discussion of the genesis of the project. In the final chapter we will attempt to stake the claim for our approach in more detail. The chapters in between do this by example.

Chapter 2

Reflecting on the Project

Terry Evans and Daryl Nation

As a text, this book reflects several images of distance education; but these images, when seen through the eyes of you, the reader, are partly of your own making: we intend it to be this way. Much distance education seems to be based on selecting images for our students, giving them 'the' perspective and then assessing their reflective accuracy. Yet we know, through common sense if nothing else, that our students have to make sense of their course materials for themselves; they may contrive their assessment to conform to what we expect of them, but even this, within limitations, is of their own making. This book presents practices in distance education which explicitly engage people in shaping their own learning experiences and which also involve the practitioners in probing, questioning and debating their work in the pursuit of improvement. In a simple form this is what we call *critical reflection.*

We explain *critical reflection* a little more fully below and deal with it more substantially in the final chapter, however, we also wish to build it into the text of this book by reflecting critically on the *project* itself. The *project* is the making of the book and, rather like developing a distance education course, it has its own history, critical incidents and ideologies. We would like to share with you our *critical reflection* on the *project*, both as an example of the sort of process we are advocating for distance education more generally, and also as an entrée into the contributors' reflections in Part 2. This means telling you something about ourselves and about how things developed with the book. As you can imagine, such things are not without their difficulties and it is important that you share them too. We would like you to read this text in different ways; it says things as much through its nature, form and style as it does through its content; the content also has various seams which can be mined by you at will.

Critical Reflection

At the heart of our understanding of *critical reflection* is a view about the nature of social life and how it is constituted. In essence, this view embodies a recognition that culture and social structure are constructed and reconstructed through history by the people who share and occupy them, and that people are themselves shaped as social beings by the cultural and structural conditions which surround them. Such a view draws upon the work of the social theorist, Anthony Giddens, in its espousal of a fundamental reflexive link between human agency and social structure.[1] *Critical reflection* is the process through which human beings use their analytical powers to assess elements of their lives against their explanatory frameworks (theories). *Critical reflection* is a precursor to change because, through the recognition of human agency, it encourages people to seek to improve their lives in their own terms.

Critical reflection requires that social life be understood as problematic. In education this means that there is no perfect way to teach, in the same way that there is no one truth to teach. In this sense teaching — and it goes without saying that we include teaching at a distance — is a problematic field of practice which is riddled with contradictions. For us, being a good teacher requires recognizing both the problematic nature of teaching and that teachers have power to change their practices. Such power is circumscribed by the prevailing conditions, but the contradictions embedded within those conditions mean that their circumscription fluctuates and is never absolute. One of the most problematic arenas of conflict and contradiction in teaching is the relations between teachers and their students. In distance education — particularly higher education — these relations are substantially fractured by distance, in its temporal and spatial forms, and often exacerbated by the diversity of students involved. As distance educators, we believe that the *critical reflection* process requires that students and teachers share collaboratively in the educational experience. Hence *critical reflection* is embodied within, and also contributes to, the development of the pedagogy and curriculum.

When *critical reflection* is incorporated into the educational process, we find that the power relations in traditional student-teacher relations mitigate against its use. In distance education this is particularly ironic because so many students come to their studies with considerable knowledge, experience and power. Perhaps one of the most important elements of *critical reflection* is that the persons involved believe in the fundamental equality of the participants. In our view issues such as class, gender, race, ethnicity and age can contribute serious impediments to the enactment of equality in any social setting. Distance teachers, therefore, need to be critically aware of such issues in order to sustain *critical reflection* in their work.

In a sense our project was concerned with providing a group of distance educators, including ourselves, with a context in which *critical reflection* could be pursued, both individually and collectively. We believe that everyone reflects on aspects of their lives for all sorts of reasons, hence *critical reflection* is drawing on this human capacity in a systematic way to provide a basis not only for critical analysis, but also for constructive change. The project provided a context for the contributors to stand aside from their practices and to *reflect critically* on them. A difficulty for so many teachers is that they are deprived of, or are unable to make, the time to reflect. In distance education, especially in Australia, this is particularly prevalent due to the overlapping and competition between teaching and production schedules, especially when overlaid with on-campus and off-campus responsibilities. We all know the feeling of not having the time and opportunity to take stock of our work and make improvements to it. Instructional industrialism requires sustained production of the instructional product!

Although the project was itself a demand on everyone's time — and some people found this to be a big difficulty — it provided a context through which people could justify a claim on their time for *critical reflection*. It was seen as a legitimate activity to which people could devote time and from which they gained significant support from other contributors. In effect, the project helped the contributors reclaim time for their own *critical reflection.* Is this a lesson in itself? Do reflexive educators need to address the issue of the legitimacy of the reflection process in their own practices, and thereby make a claim on their own time for this purpose? Many of the contributors tell how the pressure of schedules mitigates against their practice as distance educators; we expect you may find things much the same.

Genesis

Nowadays we work in different places: Daryl at Gippsland Institute in the Latrobe Valley east of Melbourne and Terry at Deakin University to Melbourne's south-west. It is about a three-and-a-half hour drive between our two work places. However, from late 1979 we worked together for over five years, teaching sociology and the sociology of education at Gippsland Institute. This was a formative period for us both because, although our previous experiences were often quite different and far removed from one another, there emerged a kind of kindred spirit.

Partly this was due to our mutual interests in sociology and particularly the sociology of education, but it also centred on a concern for our own teaching. We had both been school teachers and were sharply aware of the theory-practice division which pervades teachers' views about teacher education and teacher educators. The students on one of our off-campus courses were 'upgrading' teachers who earned their living at the 'chalkface' and, although we had a keen desire to help them learn what sociology could contribute to understanding their work, we did not ever want to pretend to tell them how to do their jobs. We decided to bring the curriculum of the course to them by using our skills as teachers and sociologists to provide a framework of analysis, together with some course materials, which would help them to look at themselves as teachers within contemporary Australian society. Thinking about it now, we often addressed our analysis to issues within schooling at the time, including their own position within occupational hierarchies and systems of accreditation and registration, which either required them or encouraged them to 'upgrade' their qualifications: that is, study our course. It was *critical reflection,* but we never called it that.

To us sociology is very important. We believe that sociological forms of thinking about social life are a powerful way of addressing practical issues in society. Of course, sociology is not a static, monolithic body of theory. There are debates and divisions within sociology which can make outsiders wonder if there is such a thing as *a* sociology at all. Certainly our own location within sociology — and we occupy much the same one — is commensurate with our approach to teaching. If you read the final chapter you will find a version of our sociology put into a critique of distance education; if you are acquainted with the broad divisions and changes within sociology: we were suckled on functionalism, supped contentedly on interactionism, chewed on conflict structuralism, and have been digesting and cooking up recipes of the last two ever since.

Distance education is also very important to us, although we find the term itself highly problematic. In our teaching together we have had to face the task of teaching sociology *at a distance,* and quite often to 'traditional face-to-face teachers'. It was through teaching sociology to teachers that we became involved in reflecting critically on our own practice, in terms of both curriculum and pedagogy. Whilst teaching teachers we learned as much about our own teaching as we taught them about theirs. Does this happen to other people who teach reflexively, especially when teaching other professional people? It was not very easy — some teachers can be soul-destroying, credential chasers or anti-theoretical charlatans! But it was interesting, so much so that we now have a research project entitled 'Distance Education and the Continuing Education of Teachers' which consumes a lot of our time. We were not especially innovative in our teaching, but we were always changing parts of the curriculum or our methods of teaching due to our reflections on the course, our discussions with students and the changing nature of teaching in Victoria.

Critical reflection is at the core of this book in other ways; it has been produced through a structure of *critical reflection* processes which we, as editors, planned and then asked the contributors to comment upon. But first, let's share with you the genesis of the book, and then we shall tell you more about how the text took shape and who the contributors are.

In January 1987 we were on a flight from Melbourne to Wellington to attend the Australian and New Zealand Association for the Advancement of Science (ANZAAS) Congress. The flight was a chance to discuss various matters concerning the papers we were giving and our work in distance education. We had nearly a day to spend in Wellington before heading to Palmerston North for the conference; it was during this time that we considered seriously writing a book 'on distance education'. We knew of several people in distance education around the world who were addressing matters of interest to us as sociologists and distance educators. Our plan was to assist by synthesizing some related social and educational theory and linking this to work in distance education. The final chapter of this book represents a form of this intention, but our experience at ANZAAS deflected us from our original plan.

Usually ANZAAS congresses have a substantial section for the educational sciences, but distance education is rarely mentioned. However, the 1987 congress was centred at Massey University which is the major distance higher education institution in New Zealand.[2] Therefore, appropriately, a sub-section on distance education was included within educational sciences. Jackie Cook presented a paper in this sub-section which reflected on her teaching of women's studies in terms of theory embedded within her understanding of literature. This stimulated a change in direction toward editing this book. Later in the conference we presented a joint paper which addressed some issues about the nature of theory and theorizing in distance education. Several people, including Jackie, contributed to the discussion. One important theme concerned the ways distance educational practice and institutions shaped the relationships between teachers and students, and between the students themselves. It was suggested that we should be striving for new forms of practice and for ways of sharing such practices with other distance educators.

On the bus back from Palmerston North we discussed the idea of changing our plan in favour of producing a book of reflections on practice in distance education. As the outskirts of Wellington appeared through the rain-spotted bus windows, we were settling on the approach we would take to developing this book. We felt it was important that the book should reflect the issues embedded in it. Therefore, the project should engage the contributors in working on the text collaboratively and yet preserve the heterogeneity of people contributing from a variety of different backgrounds, interests and concerns.

Our first problem was to think of possible contributors, and here the nature of the book was already being imprinted with our own particular marks. We decided to keep to contributors who worked in Australia principally because, even with its vast distances, we thought we could maintain some dialogue among us all — something which was crucial to the process of producing the book. Beyond that it came down to people we knew who were doing something innovative in distance education. We looked for a range of different practices and circumstances through our network of personal contacts. Eventually we found that we had contributions based on distance education practices from every mainland state, although most authors were currently living in Victoria. In this sense the book represents nothing more than our personal selection of a series of quite different contributions to distance education. The forms of practice involved are not exclusively about teaching, but they include a range of practices which help comprise distance education.

Creating the Text

When we invited each of the contributors, their replies were very encouraging: everyone accepted and expressed their own enthusiasm for the project.[3] We asked each of them to write a chapter which explained their practice and its context; they were asked to explain their reasons, in both practical and theoretical terms, for developing their particular practice. The contributors were asked to prepare draft chapters which pushed beyond mere description of their practices and which reflected critically in their own theoretical terms. You will see that for some of the contributors their theoretical positions are writ large and rooted in established educational, social or literary theories; others bring more personal explanations to bear. People were not asked to present themselves as experts for you to follow, but rather they were to share their work with you as problematic entities with histories, contexts and actions. When you read their chapters, please do so with these details in mind and also be inclined to use the opportunities provided by the contributors to reflect on your own work or interests in distance education or education more generally.

The process through which this book was developed is different from the way most such books are prepared. In order to sustain *critical reflection* throughout the preparation of the book we had to face the perennial problem of distance educators: communication at a distance. In addition, an equal and open form of communication was necessary, and here we had to deal with the editor-contributor relationship as well as others concerning the relative academic status of the contributors (and our contributors span the entire range of the academic hierarchy), the university-college 'distinction' (which is undergoing its own change) and various other concerns. Our aim was to make the 'core' Part 2 of the book as the focus because here everyone could be seen to be contributing on equal terms. As editors, we recognized that we not only shared the responsibility for establishing and maintaining communication among the contributors, but we also held the responsibility for writing this and two other chapters outside Part 2 and for managing the negotiations with publishers, series editors, etc.

With Part 2 as the focus for the *critical reflection* process we asked each contributor if they would provide a first draft for everyone to review and then to participate in a two-day contributors' seminar at Deakin University. The demands of this process were more complex than one might first imagine. We envisaged a four-stage process. The first stage required contributors to send us a brief outline of their chapter which we then copied and distributed to everyone involved. Thereby, we all understood what the others were writing as we prepared our own first drafts. Preparing the first drafts was the second stage. We set a date for submitting two copies of the first drafts to whomever of us had been designated as their 'contact editor'; it was the contact editor's responsibility to monitor progress and to distribute two copies of drafts to the other contributors.

The third stage represented the onset of *critical reflection* in earnest. Each contributor was asked to read all the other drafts and to make critical comments on one of the two copies provided; they could retain the unmarked copy but were to return the marked copy to the author at the contributors' seminar. Meeting together at the seminar was very important to the establishment of a community within which *critical reflection* was to take place: in effect, a *critical community*. Most people paid their own travel costs to attend, and the local contributors were asked to provide accommodation in their homes for the visitors. The sharing of costs and staying in other contributors' homes helped toward establishing the 'critical community'.

The first day consisted of a series of discussions of each first draft chaired by the particular author. The idea of each contributor chairing their own discussion was partly to emphasize their centrality to the *critical reflection* process for their chapter and partly to reduce the profile that we as editors were playing; we wanted to be viewed as contributors. It was intended that each contributor receive several copies of their draft annotated with contributors' comments, and they would have the comments from the discussion at the seminar. The second day of the seminar was given over to discussing the draft of Chapter 12, which we distributed at the end of the first day, and to general issues concerning the book's production and contents. This led to the final stage of the process which commenced with each contributor nominating the date by which they would complete their final draft and send it to the editors. In most cases people revised their chapters and submitted them without further ado. However, some sought further advice about changes before they settled on their final versions.

Reflecting on the Making of the Book

Producing an edited collection of chapters, rather like any form of collaborative work — such as course team work in distance education — relies heavily on the personal circumstances and capacities of the people involved. Sometimes differences of personality, ideology and commitment can lead to rifts between people which are impossible to bridge and which serve to destroy the whole collaborative venture. Broader social and cultural divisions, especially gender, can contribute to differences in perceptions and power which further distort the nature of group work. As teachers of sociology and sociology of education, where such issues have been grist for the academic mill, we have a commitment to 'social justice' which interacts in both our personal and public lives. This consciously, and probably subconsciously, flowed into our production of the book. Of the contributors we invited to participate, four are women and five are men; this was not a deliberate attempt to strike what some people call a 'gender balance': it just worked out that way.

We tried deliberately to ensure that everyone saw themselves as having an equally important contribution to make and we moved to minimize our own control over events. This proved to be a compromise because, not only were we the editors and hosts/organizers of the contributors' seminar, but also everyone had considerable experience of the academic game of (patriarchal?) intellectual jousting. The matter of the organization of meals, and to a lesser extent accommodation, we considered to be very important because these are social occurrences through which people experience feelings of welcome and well-being, and in which they cement the bonds of (critical) community membership. We arranged dinner at one of our homes because we felt that a more convivial arrangement than attending a restaurant; it also enabled us to meet the costs, which would have been impossible otherwise. The seminar finished at lunch on the final day which provided a fairly open-ended social event that people could leave when they needed to. It may seem strange to recount such ordinary 'housekeeping' matters. However, these steps *are* important to the success of such events, especially if they are to work as critical communities. Kevin Hince, an ex-colleague of ours at Gippsland Institute, demonstrated this to us and our students when he explained the procedures he adopted in industrial relations to bring about agreements between disputing parties, especially in educational occupations.[4] We would go further and argue that these steps are also important to distance education, whether organizing course team meetings or when students are brought together for tutorials, weekend or summer schools, laboratory work, etc.

Let us return to the beginning and discuss how each of the stages went. The first stage of having people produce a summary of their intended chapter proceeded quite smoothly. It was probably more useful for us, as editors, than for the contributors, in that it enabled us to produce an outline of the book for the publisher's editorial board. However, for the contributors the procedure represented small, equal and unthreatening (we think!) steps on a path towards the critical community. It represented a sign of membership which was duly recognized as such when the copies were distributed. Three of the contributors, working on two chapters, were very late with submitting their summaries, and it was here that we first encountered difficulties. The competing interests and commitments of these three people were to impinge increasingly on the book's development.

The first draft stage proceeded according to plan, although one or two more people found it difficult to keep to schedule. The deadline was predetermined by the seminar dates which had been agreed with everyone in advance. The three contributors with whom we had shared difficulties since the beginning were unable to produce a draft in time for distribution to the other contributors; they eventually dropped out of the seminar.

The contributors' seminar made a very bad start because of the late withdrawal of the three contributors from the seminar. This was particularly embarrassing because the persons involved were all 'locals', whereas others had travelled a long way, largely at their own expense.

There was an air of tension which was only submerged, rather than dissipated, during the discussions of the drafts. However, in another way the feeling of disappointment amongst the contributors was an important shared experience for a new group of people. It did serve to bond people together prior to the important part of the process: the critical review of the first drafts.

The first day was given over to spending a half hour on each draft chapter. The time passed quickly with a complete absence of the academic jousting one can expect when people from different institutions and perspectives meet to discuss their work. By the end of the day there was some strong, but friendly, debate about the nature of critical reflection and the capacity of individuals to shape their own lives. A Marxist-structuralist member had to contend with several others attempting to exhibit the power of human agency! We could have spent more time in discussing each contribution, however, any increase in the time spent would have taken us into the second day. It was important to complete everyone's chapter review on the first day because we wanted everyone to have dinner together on equal terms with no one (other than the editors!) worrying about the next day. The discussion of each contribution was always positive and constructive, to the extent that we wondered afterwards if people had resisted saying things which they felt might be negative or destructive: perhaps you can decide this better than us. It certainly is an important point for a critical community; in a sense traditional Western academic values of 'criticism' conflict with those of 'community'. In establishing a community at a distance and then bringing it together at Deakin we had concentrated on the latter, but did this mean that we blunted our critical faculties to sustain the community?

The final day of the seminar commenced with the discussion of the final chapter. There followed what for us was a most useful discussion which led to us refining the chapter. It was encouraging that everyone broadly agreed with our critique and pushed us forward to make more powerful connections between distance education practice and educational and social theories. The discussion broadened into a consideration of the entire book and its underlying principles. It was from this debate that the suggestion was made that we write the type of beginning to the book which is consistent with the notion of *critical reflection* and which is consistent with the approach to distance education which we all, in various ways, are advocating. This final session demonstrated to us that the contributors were discussing *their* book and were helping to shape its overall nature and purpose. The particular significance of *critical reflection* emerged and was symbolized in the book's title being generated from the group.

The final session of the seminar was given to discussing practical matters concerning the preparation of the final drafts and the book's structure and style. Two of the three contributors who were unable to participate in the contributors' seminar joined the group and spoke about their chapters and the book. Some of the original resentment returned and this was discussed openly. The group agreed that the two remaining chapters should be circulated as drafts for all contributors to review. In the following months the drafts were circulated and revised; the book is created!

The Contributors

Jackie Cook was the first person we wanted to contribute to the book because of her interesting paper at ANZAAS which, in a way, had started the whole project. Jackie's chapter, in both its form and content, provides a *critical reflection* on the distance teaching of any course, especially in terms of the patriarchal institutional structures which shape distance education. Jackie teaches literature at the South Australian College of Advanced Education, and it was her secondment to work in China which provoked her particular *critical reflection* on her practice. Also from the same institution is Bruce King who is Head of External Studies. Bruce writes about the Graduate Diploma course in distance education from his viewpoint as one of the originators. Bruce's chapter represents a powerful insight into the difficulties of trying to develop a course which pushes beyond the traditional boundaries of distance education practice.

Helen Modra provides a *critical reflection* on her practice as a distance teacher of librarianship at a country college; she is currently teaching and is a postgraduate student at Deakin University. Helen brings the ideas of Paulo Freire into her analysis of her distance teaching, which provides a rich vein of thinking for other distance educators. Lindsay Fitzclarence and Stephen Kemmis have spent several years teaching a course about curriculum theorizing at Deakin University. In their chapter they address the fundamental problems of creating a critical community at a distance. John Smyth discusses a part of his work at Deakin University concerning a course which encourages teachers to reflect critically on their practice. You can see John's chapter as a *critical reflection* on teaching at a distance about *critical reflection*! Similarly, one of our contributions, by Daryl Nation, looks at the use of personal reflections in the teaching of introductory undergraduate sociology courses.

Each of these contributions deals with approaches to teaching at a distance which actively involve the students in their courses; other contributions concern different aspects of distance education practice. Geoff Arger, who is course development adviser at the University of New England, reflects on a project which brings the techniques and effects of 'talkback' radio to the teaching of distance students in the Sydney area. This represents another innovative form of distance education practice which helps to bring the students and staff into a closer relationship with one another. Frances Bonning, who is a postgraduate student at Deakin University and a primary school teacher, contributes a chapter with one of us — Terry Evans. This contribution reflects on the practices of some novices in distance education who wanted to use a democratic curriculum development process. In this case the prospective learners were being asked to shape their own course. Margaret Grace, who currently works and is a postgraduate student at Deakin University, provides a *critical reflection* on her experience as the External Students' Liaison Officer for the University of Queensland Students' Union.

The chapters in Part 2 can be read in any particular order. We have placed them in a sequence which links the various chapters and parts. However, your particular interests and knowledge may mean that you want to read things in a different order. Part 3 deals with our critique of distance education. It reflects ideas in progress, because we are hoping, as distance education becomes an increasingly popular area of critical scrutiny and research activity, that there will be a broadening and enhancing of the critiques of distance education. We hope that we and the other contributors are helping in this process.

Notes

1 See Giddens (1979, 1984).
2 Like its other Australasian counterparts, but unlike many others internationally, it also has 'on-campus' students.
3 Later one contributor withdrew because a change of job created its own extra demands.
4 Kevin Hince is now Professor and Director of the Industrial Relations Centre at Victoria University of Wellington, New Zealand.

PART 2

THE PRACTICES

Chapter 3

The Liberation of Distance:
Teaching Women's Studies from China

Jackie Cook

In the beginning is my end . . . .

> I must, as a conclusion, say a few words about the mythologist
> himself [sic] . . . mythology *harmonizes* with the world, not as it
> is, but as it wants to create itself. . . . This harmony justifies
> the mythologist but does not fulfil him: his status still remains
> basically one of being excluded. . . . His speech is a
> metalanguage; it 'acts' nothing; at the most, it unveils — or does
> it? To whom?

> . . . He can live revolutionary action only vicariously: hence the
> self-conscious character of his function, this something a little
> stiff, and painstaking, muddled and excessively simplified which
> brands any intellectual behaviour with an openly political
> foundation ('uncommitted' types of literature are infinitely more
> 'elegant'; they are in their place in metalanguage). (Barthes,
> 1973, p.156)

> . . . when a subject is highly controversial . . . one [sic] cannot
> hope to tell the truth. One can only show how one came to hold
> whatever opinion one does hold. One can only give one's
> audience the chance of drawing their own conclusions as they
> observe the limitations, the prejudices, the idiosyncracies of the
> speaker. Fiction here is likely to contain more truth than fact.
> Therefore I propose making use of all the liberties and licences of
> a novelist . . . . (Woolf, 1975, p.6)

What follows is an experiment in mythology: an account of an
experience, and an attempt at not drawing from but seeing through it to
some conclusions. Like most or all such attempts, the process is both

narrative and analytic, produced and so controlled from and by me. Partially at least to moderate this authorial tyranny, and to anticipate in myself an attraction to the personal 'truth' of narrative and suspicion of the ease of abstraction of patterning in analysis, I have reversed the conventions of subjective/objective discourse: narrative of personal experience is in the third person past tense, analysis in the first person present.

Towards the end the dual system ceases — or perhaps has merged; either I as producer began to lose the distinction, becoming more interested in the 'conclusions' which were appearing, or there was/is no distinction.

Jackie Cook, Lecturer in English/Women's Studies at the South Australian College of Advanced Education (SACAE), was sent in 1986 as exchange fellow to teach in the Foreign Languages Department of Shaanxi Teacher's University, Xi'an, China. There she was to work with faculty members and senior students on English language and literature, to improve the training of prospective middle school (high school) English teachers for China's north-western provinces, as part of a continuing staff exchange development scheme between the two institutions.

Meanwhile, back in Adelaide the Women's Studies Course Team in SACAE was packaging course units from its Graduate Diploma in Women's Studies for the external mode. In its seventh year in the internal mode, and its second year in distance education, the women's studies course was confronting the usual problems, ideological, methodological, pragmatic, of the transition. These were exacerbated by staffing shortages, heavy teaching loads and inadequate lead-times. In the first semester of 1986 students were enrolled in an external unit which had run only once before in the distance education mode, a unit called 'Women Writers and the Literary Tradition', developed and taught by Jackie Cook.

Crisis:	How to be in two places at one time?
Problem:	Which of these two college programmes took priority?
Suggestion:	Why couldn't an external studies teacher be *external*?
Solution:	'Women Writers and the Literary Tradition' would be taught in 1986 by Jackie Cook from China.

As a tertiary teacher of fifteen years' experience, all in the conventional 'internal' mode, I approach the development of external packaging and teaching of my women's studies units with some trepidation. My inexperience in the external mode is probably primary; my nervousness at 'fooling around with' a new and still half-defined methodology in women's studies secondary, but equally strong. A continued heavy internal teaching load leaves no lead-time for slow and considered development or piloting: it is to be my usual deadline/breadline existence . . . . Despite the pressures in these development years of the mid-1980s, I take time for induction into the mysteries of external studies. I read. I attend seminars. Best training of all, I teach courses. During these processes I realize that my nervousness is, if anything, increasing.

Current discussion of distance education seems obsessed by the 'technological fix' — the issues are pragmatic and technical, centring on delivery, materials production, hardware, student contact mechanisms. Theoretical perspectives are suspended — or even subsumed — into 'process' definitions. We (notice how glibly she already claims kinship with other external educators . . .) are presumably to pause, pending some semi-mystical organic development of the distance education philosophy.

Despite the cynical tone (my mother speech), I'm prepared to accept that there are excellent reasons for this ideological hiatus. The global dimension of distance education — itself one of its charms — gives it a cross-cultural element not previously prominent in educational design, and a comparative basis, which slows down definition. The lateness of emergence into the education field has brought distance education into an age of more complex theory, more readily accepting of variability, of difference. Since as a women's studies teacher, that is a political stance I endorse, I cannot help but be approving, as well as seeing the advantage of integrating the new technologies as we (there I go again) design materials and teaching/learning strategies. The longer an overview is delayed, the wider we extend it, the more good practices we find, the wider our theory base.

But 'waiting' in education is no more passive in truth than the verbal mode into which I slipped above. Actions are actions: practice marches on. In the absence of a clear theoretical perspective or methodological directive, those of us in the field continue to teach, and to develop practice and process which inevitably harden into 'standard procedure'. In a myriad of instances globally there must be experiences like mine: teachers and academics who have adjusted their practice to the demands of their field and the student profile; rethinking and reshaping to the perceived differences of the distance mode. But where and what are the descriptions and reflections of these revisions? When I approach the distance education literature, why am I confronted by bureaucratic history and brochures of electronic whizzery? Why is that most problematic of issues, the teacher/student relationship, addressed in the main by Telecom, and discussion of learning bristling with behaviourist categories and reduced to statistics? In the light of my own limited experience, how can I test my perceptions against those of fellow practitioners? Most of all, for a discipline like mine — women's studies, peripheral and revisionist by definition — will any of these experiences, definitions, processes, be appropriate? I am beginning to feel much as the beginning distant student must feel: 'Is there anybody out there?', or, 'Now that I have a ticket on this bus, who's driving and where are we going?'

Jackie Cook, precariously balanced on the cultural tightrope of English teaching in China, noticed the date for commencement of the Australian academic year, and wondered whether the external studies machinery had ground into gear, and package one of 'Women Writers' was speeding out through the Australian mail system. Despite the optimism which had persuaded her to insert her Chinese telephone number in the *Study Information Booklet,* in case of some especially rich/enterprising/desperate student, naturally no one called. The usual preliminary tension was obviously going to be prolonged; she anticipated no need to visit the post office (there is no mail delivery in China) for at least a month. But then personal letters began arriving. (These had bypassed the external studies dispatch process, and arrived direct.)

> Hello, my name is X, and I'm writing because I was fascinated to see that you are in China. I visited there in 1981, but it must be amazing to be living there — what exactly are you doing? You said in the *Information Booklet* that . . . .

> I thought I would like to begin the course by telling you about myself, so that you can see where I'm coming from. Well, I live on a station North of the Flinders, so I'm as isolated as you are, although not so crowded . . . .

> I do not know if this letter will reach you, because I am writing from Indonesia where I live, and political relations with China are not clear. I have sent a copy of this letter to the External Studies address in Adelaide. It will be interesting to see which one you get . . . .

> I have so many questions about the course — I don't know where to begin! I'm doing the unit as I travel around Australia in my van — at the moment I'm in the Blue Mountains. I've enclosed a sort of 'Bulletin' about myself that I type up each month or so and send to my friends. Would you like to receive it too?

In previous experiences of teaching this course externally these personal expressions had also arrived. The relation of self to subject is basic to women's studies; for internal students classroom practice, and for external students advised study technique elicit this sort of response. But this is usually a gradual, cumulative process, requiring many inter-actions. Even internal students do not establish themselves so clearly in session one.

Even more clearly, the questions have begun:

> I haven't studied for more than ten years and it's *hard!* Most of all, I'm confused about the work required. I've read through the section where you say we can design our own work, but *do you really mean it?*

> I think I like the idea about concentrating on the areas that appeal to me most, because some parts obviously do, but I still feel uncomfortable about the bits I'm skipping. . . .

> It's the old problem of depth versus range. I enrolled to do this course to let myself just read all those books I'd always wanted to, but never had time for. Only now I want to spend all my time on each book as I get to it. . . .

> This is a *Graduate* Diploma course, but I've come in without ever going to a University (I'm a nurse). I'm not sure about what sort of level you're looking for.

> My own writing skills worry me. It wasn't so bad in the other units. Here we have all those wonderful models of women writers in front of us. I can never be that good. Is it o.k. if I do taped commentaries? I feel more relaxed if I'm just talking. . . .

Most striking in this spontaneous correspondence — apart from its very existence! — is a two-fold change from the experience in previous semesters, taught conventionally from Australia. First, there is the depth and difference of the relationship which is developing between myself and these students, and the spontaneity of their disclosures. Secondly, there is a much earlier, and more clearly defined, questioning of the work requirements of the course — a questioning which emerges as students design their own learning path, but which is usually slower in developing, and more hesitant in approaching the institutional agent who represents assessment as well as assistance — me. I attempt to unravel the difference of these two types of response.

First, the spontaneity of student disclosure: women's studies fosters this immediacy of contact: the personal is central, the whole process and intent of women's studies is to elaborate the political from the personal, redefine and reapply it. That is the purpose and justification of our adult learning/groupwork methodology, which creates my initial and continuing nervousness in the transfer into external studies. Under normal circumstances, Adelaide-based and teaching the 'Women Writers' unit, I build a 'buffer system' for myself and students. I telephone them in the first week; I place those living close to fellow students in contact with one another; I invite metropolitan Adelaide students (usually women with intense child-care demands) to attend special sessions with internal students (such as poetry readings) where possible. Conscious of the effort and energy which have gone recently into the creation of a women's studies methodology, I want to preserve it, duplicate it somehow, for the external student — the student I persist in seeing as 'underprivileged' by isolation; 'shut out' from the circle of learning carefully set up and fostered in internal classes.

Induction into this 'circle of learning' is itself time consuming. Women's studies begins with intensive group establishment techniques, as we relearn techniques of listening, trusting our own and others' opinions, building confidence in present skills of insight, elaboration, analysis, and presentation, before improving them; then applying all of these to the business of what Adrienne Rich (1972) calls RE/VISION: the redefinition of the conventional codes of knowledge which are called — itself a problematic concept — 'academic disciplines'.

Worse, and yet another explanation of the ferocity of my defence of it, the creation of this methodology and its introduction into the educational institution have been acrimonious. (It is a truism among women's studies academics that the establishment of coursework, and especially of complete programmes such as those in SACAE, receives strongest opposition from academic colleagues.)

What is hard-won is precious: external studies has me on the defensive, worried by the concretization of the written word, the standardization of student learning inevitable even in open-ended 'guidance questions', the 'telling' required by time constraints when reading dominates; the guilty tendency towards the 'oracular' in my role as organizer and selector of the *Study Guides* and *Readers*. My defensive anticipation has led me to 'open' the 'Women Writers' external unit as far as possible. Structurally the parallel with the unit's aim has been helpful. In 'Women Writers' we retrace the evolution of women's poetry and prose narrative from 1500, relocating 'lost' authors and texts, examining critically the 'accepted' valuations of women's writing, and seeking patterns of 'difference' in theme or style, which might suggest the existence of a female tradition. To design learning strategies which close off such a vastly open critical revisionism would be self-defeating: opinion here has to be produced, not consumed (in Barthes' terms 'scriptible', not 'lisible'). Even newly emergent 'authorities' of feminist literary studies (Ellen Moers, Elaine Showalter, Dale Spender, Annis Pratt, Mary Ellman, Mary Jacobus) are careful, as was Virginia Woolf, fifty years before, to display the processes of their own revisionist judgments. I can suggest but not command activities, offer but not insist, and trust that the 'overprovision' of readings and activities I offer to prevent compulsion will democratize rather than daunt.

Add to this the comparative (again, hard-won) 'opening' of admission into a Graduate Diploma in Women's Studies course, which means that, although students have equivalent undergraduate degree status, their backgrounds are highly diverse: education, fine arts, social sciences, law, religion, medicine, public administration, business, languages, sports and recreation, media, science and technology, commerce, defence training. Women studying 'Women Writers' with me can have any level of background in literary study, from primary school to postdoctoral, including students from non-English cultural backgrounds. Students gain from the course by establishing their own level, and extending down the line of their own potential and needs — a system which happily strings with other design parameters.

So far so good: within my external as within my internal women's studies units I have to some degree at least created and preserved a feminist integrity. I provide the right to choose; to fit and test ideas against the self; to practise within a field of support: the speech of fellow students, or the writings of other thinkers. I pride myself that ingenuity and the strength of women's studies practice has resisted a 'pull' into formalization and built a successful 'women's studies external' practice. With a constantly vigilant eye, subtle applications of the new contact technologies (teleconferencing, video exchange) and careful evaluation, I can approximate external study more and more closely to internal — spread the links wider, but maintain the learning circle.

But as I look again at the student letters to China, and try to summarize what is 'different' about them, doubts begin. First, the letters have arrived noticeably earlier than the usual 'initial contact' of external students. Partly this is because I normally telephone external students in the first week, but this is not entirely the distinction. This first week call is never the most comfortable of contacts. Although students always end by stating how much happier they feel about the course and their direction of it, initial responses are for the most part nervous and tense — who isn't, when 'teacher' phones? Is it only time constraint that usually leaves follow-up written contact, this time student initiated, until several weeks later? Secondly, the China letters produce a markedly more spontaneous and enthusiastic tone. Students appear to find me 'real' — a person to be chatted to; someone involved in her own projects, so liable to be sympathetically interested in theirs; not just an institutional title, but a personality. I feel 'rehumanized', and learn more, and more quickly, about my students than ever before, even in comparison with internal students. Thirdly, there is an unprecedented clarity and focus on the student's need to decide between the demands of women's studies and the demands of the 'Graduate Diploma'. 'Women Writers' uses the traditional tools of literary study: set literary texts (from the canon and from the 'reprint' shelves of feminist publishers); critical evaluations (conventional and feminist); historical and biographical backgrounding; discussion and application of key theories; but above all personal evaluation and commentary on texts.

All literature study walks in tension down the line of received judgment and personal opinion, feminist literary study more than most, since it has to accommodate its anger at much of the received judgment, and forge new critical frameworks for the personal view. By placing these processes inside the structures of an award course, inside the requirements of a competitive educational institution, women's studies endangers its revisionist freedom — a problem for the discipline itself, and for every student who battles to come to terms simultaneously with self-direction and valuing of her own opinion, and the traditional requirements of assessment. Aware of this dilemma, I design for optimum choice, with a study program provided but not enforced, and a contract assessment scheme. However, the tensions remain. My carefully arranged structures, my careful/conscious discourse, may open opportunity, permit self-selection, even direction. But this is after all an accredited award in a tertiary institution, and students are rightly suspicious. Where are the 'traps'? the exams? the standards? the objective scales? the comparative grading? the academic requirements? the 'intellectual rigour'? where is the 'discipline' of this discipline?

For the students confronted by a teacher who has run away to China there is an added dilemma: paradoxically they have chosen to see me as 'closer': someone to whom they reveal their worst fears about themselves and their study. They are solving their problem for me: I can now pass the power of self-direction explicitly back to them, since they have expressed their disbelief in it so openly.

In the meantime, I am left with two further problems. First, my view of myself as a women's studies teacher: liberal, open, negotiating, non-directive, cooperating, has just split into paradox, and revealed itself as fraudulent. I am the authority who says 'there is no authority'. How can I be taken seriously? Secondly, why is all of this happening with such intensity in this particular context?

Back in Xi'an, Jackie Cook was fighting her way at least twice weekly onto the No. 3 public bus, to redeem at the local vegetable market Post Office the fragile receipts which kept arriving at her university work-unit, to tell her that a package had arrived from Australia. Five days out from Adelaide, the Chinese Post Office was witness to the receipt of audiotapes, videos, written and visual material in far greater bulk and diversity than 'Women Writers' had ever before elicited from its students. Projects presented included two-hour verbal 'response' tapes; original poetry and short stories; taped interviews with women writers; videotapes of TV adaptations of women's narratives with accompanying commentaries; poster displays; programmes and evaluations of short community courses in women's writing which students had organized; translations of non-English texts; bibliographies of Third World writing; written commentaries in every format, from word-processed essays to marginalia, to journals and diaries.

Each Sunday a package of responses was sent from the main Post Office, while the Chinese postal staff had their own, not irrelevant, debate over the differences between 'educational materials' and 'personal letters', and the cost differentials involved. Procedures agreed with the external studies dispatch centre in Adelaide fell into disuse, as students increasingly wrote direct, and the regular 'open letters' sent through the Women's Studies Course Team were superseded by the regularity of individual contact. The student retention rate emerged as surprisingly high: the usual up-to-one-third dropout in what is largely a non-career and totally a non-compulsory course much improved.

The activity level began to be noticed by Chinese students in Xi'an, and by foreign resident colleagues. There began to be enquiries about enrolments. The whole experiment was beginning to look dangerously like a success.

What do these experiences mean within the frames of women's studies/distance education?

When the intensity of the 'difference' of the China experience leads me to ask this question, I quickly see that, for all of my careful preparation of an 'external package' of a women's studies course unit, I am still guilty of operating without a clear perspective as to the difference between internal and external study. Worse, as an Australian academic, presumably advantaged by the dual internal/external role, who has experienced even the simultaneous internal/external teaching of the same unit, I am *overwhelmed by my anxiety to produce a 'sameness' of experience for two groups of 'my' students.* This is me, a women's studies lecturer, capable of speaking passionately in public over the need for self-direction, open-ended learning, group decision-making, insisting that 'I know best.' Worse, when confronted by examples of students seizing those very opportunities, producing work which I know to be good, I am confused by my initial analysis of the reasons.

All of the reading I have done on external studies speaks of the need for closing the external/internal student 'gap', approximating the former study experience to the latter, a project with which I, in my enthusiasm for student contact techniques, have seemed to concur. Yet by going to China I have widened that gap, separating student and teacher geographically and culturally in a way probably more extreme than any other possible, short of leaving the planet. (Foreign residents and tourists still speak of going 'in' to China; our current and indeed age-old cultural fascination with it indicates the power of a cultural difference which even the least conscious of us acknowledge.) In separating myself, however, leaving myself at the mercy of a notoriously unreliable postal service, there has somehow been produced in the students the very self-directness and independence of thought which I have always wanted.

Note at this stage the passive mode and lapse from my usual cavalier use of the possessive pronoun. 'I' in China perceive myself as too far away to be affecting all of this. How can it be that 'I' have passed my centring status to all of those other 'I's who are co-respondents? 'I' (the one my third person narrative refers to as 'Jackie Cook') knew the truth of this, as had all of those students with their week-one-of-semester letters. But this is experiential knowledge — impressionistic, intuitive. How do I redirect that into design, to duplicate in future teaching? How do I explain it, in terms of conventional knowledge which is called 'theory', for women's studies? external studies? SACAE? the future? When I try to elaborate the experience into a coherent statement, it seems paradoxical. Distance education, as I encounter it, seems to be heading in one direction (greater student contact); women's studies in another (greater student autonomy). Yet by giving less contact I have created more autonomy. ('Let them alone/And they will come home . . . .')

What was it I had done?

(My monitoring mind has just lost the battle to maintain a separation of narrative and analysis: as the two merge, the first person of agency and the past tense of mythology have forced a marriage. It is still myself I am trying to convince.)

Unaware of any existing analyses or models of distance education to frame a response around, I moved laterally, and discovered Roland Barthes (1982), experiencing the same 'unframed' field — in photography.

Like distance education, photography has a quite lengthy and healthy existence in most societies; yet, while it has an obvious history which can be studied, that study seems unable to answer the question, what is photography? As with international publications on distance education, photography texts give examples of the hundreds of variant possibilities, but no examination of what a photograph *is* or *does* or *might* do. Similarly, the discussion displaces sideways — and in the same direction — into the technical. Hardware is concrete — here we are safe. Books proliferate on cameras and 'how to'. But what *is* a photograph? What *is* distance education?

Barthes evolves the following structural frame to describe photography:

There exist	SCENES	of which we make	PHOTOGRAPHS	taken by a	PHOTOGRAPHER	to be looked at by a	VIEWER

Barthes calls these:

SPECTACLE   SPECTRUM   OPERATOR   SPECTATOR

The keys to his system are two-fold: the reintegration of the *viewer*, without whom a photograph has no being (for what is its point, locked up in an album?); and, more important still, the separation of *spectacle* and *spectrum*, and the dissolution of the old, naive idea that a photograph somehow 'is' what it shows — the 'slice of reality' theory of the camera's 'eye'. A spectrum is clearly what Barthes calls elsewhere a 'laminate': a highly selected, meaning invested, 'choice' of point-of-view (both operator's and spectator's); value-laden, culturally heavy. These seemed not unlike the keys I was seeking to a distance education 'system', as I sought to unravel the relationship between the 'discipline', the student, the institution, the teacher.

I add to the Barthes' system a grouping for distance education:

the spectacle becomes	SOCIETY is	spectrum	DISCIPLINE is the	operator	INSTITUTION the	spectator	STUDENTS

How is this helpful? In the first instance it allows me a clearer view of where I as a teacher perceive myself/am perceived to be.

In normal circumstances, for internal or external students, the identification 'teacher/institution' is strongly held. Internal students have a high degree of institutional regulation of their behaviour and expectations. The institution's 'requirements' are quickly passed on and assimilated into student behaviours and values, whether consciously or unconsciously. Formal consultation (discussion of 'models', practical and demonstration classes, reading of 'style manuals') or emulation (staff role modelling, peer-group pressure) combine to produce the individual, 'the student'. To a greater or lesser degree, according to my own 'institutional socialization' and/or politico-educational perspectives, I accede and contribute to this process.

As 'teacher', I am also *observably* a part of the institution. My statements, actions, expectations are moderated by those around me: I can easily generate surprise, even shock, by reacting otherwise than according to institutional 'norms'.

For the external student the situation is more problematic. More than 60 per cent of my external students never see the institution in which they study. Their teacher, however, remains 'within the institution', telephonable, academically titled, listed with full credentials in its handbooks, and presumably regulated by its collective behaviour.

This seems comfortable enough, but it ignores two issues:

1 *When a teacher is not only geographically but culturally separated from the institution, what happens?*
   This is presumably a rare event — attractive as the idea is of transferring all coursework onto the external mode and working thereafter from a hotel room in Bali, I am unlikely to be so 'external' again. But the experience was significant — why?

2 The second issue involves the role of 'the student' — that being we now see as 'socialized' into the role of institutional 'receptor'. The values/expectations/behaviours that 'the student' brings to study, and especially to external study, are equivalent to those the 'spectator' brings to the photograph: that is, not passive 'reception' at all, but socialized/enculturated expectation.

For the external student that 'expectation' is not generated by their current study, but by previous encounters. The external student's contact with 'the institution' is tenuous: unless the expectations and behaviours are clear in the study guide materials, and possibly even then those of previous institutionalized study will be applied — appropriate or otherwise. Therein lies the problem for women's studies, generating a feminist revisionist theory and methodology.

To build my formula one step further:

SOCIETY	DISCIPLINE	INSTITUTION	STUDENTS
Western culture	women's studies	SACAE	women graduates
is	is	is	are
patriarchal	women-centred	male-defined/dominated	female, with previous male-dominated education

Women's studies students, internal or external, themselves living and working within male-oriented systems for the most part, express a delight in and enthusiasm for the ideas and study techniques of women's studies, which enable them to see and to revalue female dimensions of their society, and of themselves, 'closed off' by traditional perceptions. Simultaneously, these same students face the problems of reintegrating this 'new view' into their lives, careers, philosophies. (Women's studies is political: it expects this reintegration to occur, at least ultimately.)

More clearly than in most cases, the integration problem is shared by the teacher, who is also caught in this concatenation of *male-female-male-female*. While she may find support from her students, and from the tenets and practice of her discipline, the women's studies teacher rarely sits easily in the institution from which she teaches. Half-in and half-out of institutional respectability, her status is ambivalent — sufficiently so to be comparatively clarified for students by the unusual act of placing herself perceivably *outside* the institution (as I have mentioned, about as far outside as seems possible).

Women's studies even, as I have attempted to show, in its external mode attempts interactive learning, where student and teacher move into a mutual relationship of learning. For the internal student this mutuality has also been signalled by some interesting 'spontaneous' developments which have shown up only later as significant, for example, the way in which women's studies 'internal' classes have progressively moved off-campus, to run in venues ranging from health centres to libraries. Something of the symbolic quality of this 'deinstitutionalization' seems to have been communicated — unconsciously on my part — to the external students, as their lecturer moved so graphically outside the academy. As with the physical shift of internal students into non-academic teaching spaces, the lifting of what is perhaps an attitudinal barrier for the 1986 external students may have created a 'free space' into which their creativity and personal direction could move. In my 'chain-link' formula one element splits away: 'teacher' splits from 'institution' into the ambivalent female/male space of the student.

At this stage the experience is resolving into a theory which fits with the development of women's studies itself, and so raises my final question for distance education. Progressively from 1950 to 1985 feminist theory and practice have developed an autonomy, a self-definition, which are now creating, in some fields at last, recognition of their primacy in theory development. From de Beauvoir to Kristeva, feminist philosophies have moved from an initially reactive position: women as 'other', as secondary or even silenced; repressed, castrated, 'shut up in the sphere of the relative', to the more recent French psychoanalytic/post-structuralist theories, which, providing their own integrity, locate themselves in play, in autonomy, in multiplicity, in plurality, in change, in self-definition, in 'difference'.

In parallel development, growing out of the consciousness raising sessions of the late 1960s women's movement (themselves, ironically for me, influenced by the 'self-criticism' of the Chinese Great Proletarian Cultural Revolution), women's studies has evolved a revisionist methodology of self-analysis/self-direction/group reflection/practical application. To return to the Barthes' inspired model, and to seek your active participation:

learning which is	SOCIALLY useful	defines and extends the	DISCIPLINE	modifies the	INSTITUTION	giving the	STUDENT impetus for
(CUT)							(PASTE)

REVOLVE . . .

By seemingly jumping off this 'circle of learning' I had paradoxically signalled the true extension of my teacher role: 'I' am everywhere/'I' am nowhere:

> I am in society/it is in me
> I am in the discipline/it is in me
> I am in the institution/it makes me
> I am a student/students teach me
> I am me/but also you

By such an aberrant act as removing myself so dramatically from my institutional frame, I had signalled both my own power to self-direct, and the validity of my claims to accept self-direction in others.

Yet it was 'distance education' which let me do this: distance education, with all of its pre-thought study 'guides', standardized pacing, written-not-spoken, desire to 'contact', with 'control' implicit . . . . What had seemed to run counter to my group learning/hands-on methodologies, had opened rather than closed possibilities: by dissociating 'I' from the institution Jackie Cook had empowered all the other 'I's into operation.

It is now her/my worry that, in well intentioned efforts to 'assist' distance education students by introducing 'the benefits' of a wider range of institutional contacts, by 'tightening' (how we love the vocabulary of control!) the procedures, we may lock students in to processes and points of view not necessarily the best for learning.

I am interested in seeing from practitioners in the distance education field more and more analysis of the student perception and reaction to our teaching and contact procedures. In 1987 I have taught the 'Women Writers' course again in the external mode, with myself 'on deck' in the conventional way — telephonable, visitable, in much closer institutional contact than in 1986. The result has been markedly *less* student initiated contact, and a more conventional range of contracted assessment styles.

When we say 'contact', what do we mean? 'Contact' with what? And for what purpose? Our efforts may be motivated by the most excellent, humane concerns. But do we really see or understand the subtleties of connection between 'contact' and control in our institutions, our students, ourselves?

Are my experiences with women's studies students, taught from China, exceptional, or do they contain insights into the subtlety of relationship between society, discipline, institution, teacher and student, which are important for us all? Is there liberation in distance?

Chapter 4

Personal Reflections in an Introductory Sociology Course

Daryl Nation

My purpose is to offer some reflections upon the *personal reflections* which I have built into the teaching texts for an introductory sociology course. Unlike 'in-text questions', 'statements of objectives', 'advance organizers' and 'lists of key concepts', personal reflections are not conventional pedagogical devices for teaching texts used in distance education. Indeed, I am unaware of any other distance teachers who use anything remotely like them.

What, then, are these personal reflections? Despite my authorship of them, I find it difficult to describe them. Despite my satisfaction with them as a teaching strategy, I find it difficult to ask you to begin this journey of exploration by asking you to consider an example. Here in a 'real book', outside the context of my course, without all my audiovisual tricks and without my authority as a teacher (*you* don't have to read this, or do you?), I have lost my nerve (no, I'm catering for individual differences). You can choose your own intellectual adventure.

Three Choices

If you are inclined not to take teachers (authors?) at their word and/or you have a sense of adventure and/or you like to begin at the beginning, you should turn to 'Some More Personal Reflections' (p.46). If you are inclined to follow authority and/or need some assistance to find the beginning and/or are wondering if you should keep reading, you should turn to the boxed section below which contains a summary of 'Some More Personal Reflections'. If you are considering the third possible choice, please don't.

In his personal reflections the teacher/sociologist narrates aspects of his own life experiences which relate to the topics under discussion in each section of the course. They are an analogue of the asides made by lecturers and the anecdotes offered by tutors which are meant to provide examples from 'real life' to which sociological concepts and theories can be applied.

Reflections upon the Personal Reflections

How do these personal reflections fit into the teaching strategies for an introductory sociology course? How and why were they developed? What were the reactions of students to them? After using them for four years, how satisfied am I with them?

In 1982 I was asked to develop an introductory sociology course which would operate for the years 1983-1986. It was to serve students from a variety of courses; some would be full-time on-campus students and others would be part-time studying through distance education. The course had to cater for students who wished to use it as a foundation for further studies in sociology and for those who would use it as an end in itself.

This was not my first experience of either introductory sociology or distance education. By 1982 I had a decade of experience in the latter and five to seven years earlier I had the major responsibility for another introductory course. Introductory sociology courses are regarded universally as difficult to teach. Students face the obstacles of sociology's notorious jaw-breaking jargon and its emphasis upon the abstract rather than the concrete. Conventional wisdom amongst teachers of sociology suggests that new students need to be encouraged constantly to relate the concepts and theories they are grappling with to their own experiences. As Don Edgar has put it: 'Students should be encouraged to write constantly about their observations of the ways people behave on railway stations, in cafes, buses, theatres, tutorials, at meals and at meetings. They should compare their own with others' ideas and experiences of family life, inequality, work and leisure' (Edgar, 1980, p.xv). Tutorial discussions in introductory sociology classes are commonly dominated by the sharing of experiences of this sort. But how is this to be achieved when students are able to attend tutorials infrequently or not at all? Our course addressed this problem in two related ways: the personal reflections and an associated assignment were developed, and the curriculum was structured to allow students to study, in the earlier sections of the course, aspects of social life with which they were likely to be familiar.

The earlier sections of the course dealt with a basic outline of the sociological approach and three areas of social life: families, schooling and work. For these sections we were fortunate in being able to set the book *Making the Difference,* which is an exceptionally clearly written research report dealing with these issues (Connell *et al.*, 1982). These sections were followed by a study of the life-cycle in society, which focused upon the social influences along the journey from the cradle to the grave. This curriculum structure is very common in introductory sociology courses and fits with the approach adopted in many of the textbooks.

I cannot be sure of the origins of the personal reflections. I can recall thinking about strategies which would support the curriculum structure outlined above. I recall thinking in terms of comparisons with conventional teaching. Certainly my own tutorials had always involved both me and my students actively relating our experiences to relevant sociological concepts, theory and data. My lectures had also included such observations. Most pertinent of all has been a 'teacher-training' which forces/allows me to look at a teaching problem in terms of the content-method dichotomy. Once you know what needs to be taught, it is a matter of searching the available resources to come up with appropriate means. Given that print is the major vehicle of our distance education programme, I had to adapt this text-form. I am sure that a few pages of Basil Bernstein's prose were influential. How?

Throughout the 1970s I had taught a series of courses relating to the sociology of education. Most of the students were either aspiring or practising teachers. Aspiring and practising teachers are very difficult for an 'academic sociologist' to teach! 'Relevance' is their watchword. They want knowledge and skills they can 'use in the classroom'. As a rule they find it difficult to see any practical significance in theoretical knowledge.

Bernstein's work, which related language use to social background, was centrally important in the sociology of education in the 1970s. The details of this work need not detain us; what is important is the complexity with which his ideas were expressed. My students found Bernstein's writing very difficult to follow, and most relied upon textbook digestions of his ideas. I was constantly searching for strategies to get the students involved with the original work. One possibility manifested itself one evening as I read the introduction to the first volume of his collected papers (Bernstein, 1974, pp.1-20). Here he offered 'a personal history which bears upon the development of the guiding ideas' of his work (Bernstein, 1974, p.2). He provided details of his work as a welfare worker in London's East End, which he had undertaken prior to his undergraduate degree in sociology. He dealt with his dropping out from higher degree studies to undertake teacher training. He offered great detail regarding his work as a technical college teacher, where he taught English, arithmetic and civics to part-time students on day-release from the Post Office. Without labouring his points he made it obvious that these experiences were the basis for his research and theory. He also outlined many of the intellectual steps he took as he knitted together various lines of theory to illuminate the practical situation he had described.

The next day I read extracts from the introduction to my sociology of education class. Eyes lit up. Wires were uncrossed. It worked! Obviously, Bernstein's uncharacteristic lucidity was important; but other factors were at work. By focusing upon the links from 'experience' Bernstein had cast a new light on his theories and concepts. I began to use this strategy with other classes. It seemed to work because teacher and students could 'see' a sociological mind travelling the paths between everyday reality and a scientific understanding of it.

I want to move on to a detailed discussion of the development of the personal reflections as teaching texts, but one other aspect of the course context, which is of vital significance, must be mentioned. In this course we were planning to require students to reflect upon their own life experiences in their first assignment. This is a logical strategy which fits with the generally conventional attempts to get students applying textbook sociology to their own experience, which I have dealt with already. Indeed, some form of sociological autobiography is a common aspect of the students' first assignment in many introductory courses; and this strategy had been used for many years at our college.

Since our distant students were required to provide us with written reflections on their own social experiences, and given that they would have no or little opportunity to hear their tutors give 'model experiences' of their own in classroom discussion, I felt obliged to provide a text version of my own. This was the real basis for the personal reflections. The experiences with Bernstein's 'personal history' were the instructive classroom examples which I was able to adapt for the teaching texts.

There was one other important model from the course context. The textbook *Making the Difference* was written in a style which emphasized the narration of the social experiences of the individuals who were its subjects. Indeed, the teachers, students, parents and children studied were all referred to by pseudonyms, like characters in a fictional work. The book was structured so the 'facts' or 'data' were reported as vignettes, which the authors then discussed in terms of sociological concepts and theory. The authors were interpreting the research subjects' accounts of their travels through family life, schooling and work. As a complement to *Making the Difference,* almost 90 per cent of our external students were able to see a television documentary, *Twenty-One,* at our first weekend school. *Twenty-One* took fourteen English boys and girls from working-class, middle-class and upper-class backgrounds and interviewed them at the ages of 7, 14 and 21. It concentrates on how their social background influences their schooling, their future occupations and their family lives. Thus our students have yet another set of experiences which they can compare with their own.

One aim of the autobiographical assignment is to teach students to be objective about their subjective social experiences. It helps them come to grips with the conventional social scientific techniques of 'standing back from the data' and developing explanations of them which have their bases in 'relevant theory'. In the earlier sections of the course students come to grips with considerable 'textbook sociological theory'. We also ask them to study extracts from C. Wright Mills' *The Sociological Imagination.* Mills' perspective suggests:

> The facts of contemporary history are also facts about the success and the failure of individual men and women. When a society is industrialized, a peasant becomes a worker; a feudal lord is liquidated or becomes a businessman. When classes rise or fall, a man is employed or unemployed; when the rate of investment goes up or down, a man takes new heart or goes broke. When wars happen, an insurance salesman becomes a rocket launcher; a store clerk, a radar man; a wife lives alone; a child grows up without a father. Neither the life of an individual nor the history of a society can be understood without understanding both . . . . The sociological imagination enables its possessor to understand the larger historical scene in terms of its meaning for the inner life and the external career of a variety of individuals . . . . We have come to know that every individual lives, from one generation to the next, in some society; that he lives out a biography, and that he lives it out within some historical sequence. By the fact of his living he contributes, however minutely, to the shaping of his society and to the course of its history, even as he is made by society and by its historical push and shove . . . . (Mills, 1970, pp. 17-19)

Mills' theory offers an ideal complement to that used in *Making the Difference.* Viewed in this context, my personal reflections are designed to give students an example which they can follow, in order to develop their own. At the close of the first personal reflection I address this issue:

> These personal reflections have been provided to give you a basis for thinking about the autobiography we are asking you to construct. As you will appreciate, if I were writing this entirely for myself and my intimates I could be considerably more frank in my observations. You will face the same problem when you have to put forward some aspects of your autobiography for the first assignment. These 'more personal' thoughts are worth exploring and we would encourage you to think about them, but we do not expect you to reveal them. In passing, it is worth noting that people who are subjected to sociological interviews are often prepared to disclose intimate details of their life experiences. You will see evidence of this when you read *Making the Difference*. Social researchers have an important obligation not to disclose such information in a form in which it can embarrass their subjects.

Writing the personal reflections proved difficult. Bernstein's 'personal history' provided a useful model. The content of each piece was controlled by its context in the course: I had to discuss experiences which related to the topics under discussion. Many of the influences on the actual style of discourse have been subliminal. Did Donald Horne's *The Education of Young Donald* have any influence? Probably — as did many other autobiographies I have read. One book which stands out, on reflection, is *On Loving Men* by the New York artist, Jane Lazarre (1981). I had read this book not long before beginning the project. Its theme, gender relations, was an important one in the earlier sections of the course. Lazarre's style, which was a combination of directness and intimacy (which stopped short of exposing the justifiable secrets of others), had an important influence on my own. I always felt, even though I was writing for an audience of student conscripts, that the reflections had to be interesting in themselves if they were to work. Further, they had to have an air of confidentiality, despite their real public existence. They needed to be an analogue for the semi-confidential exchanges which take place in the sociological classroom, which give an important place to personal experiences.

How did our students react to the personal reflections? We have carried out extensive research on students' reactions to the course and this question has been addressed in that context. Elsewhere I have offered detailed discussions of the research results relating to the personal reflections and I do not wish to repeat much of these here (Nation,

1987a, 1987b). Another source of students' responses is their attempts at the first assignment. One clear message comes from this source: students have been assisted in the expression of their relevant social experiences, without falling into the pitfall of overemphasis upon subjectivity. Had this occurred, I would have regarded the reflections as more than a failure, indeed, as counterproductive.

While not all students believed that the reflections had helped them to make the links between their own experiences and 'the sociology', most did. Indeed, many were emphatic in their recognition of the value of the reflections in this regard. Another clear message from the research is that the reflections make the distant teacher 'more human'. By this they mean that they feel they know something about their teacher's personality and background. The common desire of students to know these simple things is satisfied. For many this is of great educational value. I am not sure whether I was trying to achieve this with the reflections or not. As I have said in another paper, this was certainly my motive in the audio-tapes and in the use of a 'conversational style' elsewhere in the teaching texts, my motive being to engender in students a feeling that they could approach their teachers, especially by telephone (Nation, 1985). It appears that the reflections have complemented these strategies.

In writing the reflections I had anticipated one problem, the possibility of me being regarded as an 'ego-tripper'. This was something which I addressed very directly in the writing stage. Thankfully, students do not seem to have perceived the exercise in this way. One likely reason for this was the constant attempt to keep the reflections relevant to the topics at hand.

I will be using this technique in my future courses. It appears to be particularly appropriate in contexts where the students are expected to offer their experiences, and all of my courses have this component. I am puzzled why none of my immediate colleagues has adopted their own version of this teaching strategy. Indeed, I find it difficult to talk to them about it. The issue seems to revolve around the 'confidentiality' of classroom discourse mentioned above. This reflection is addressed to those others in the distance education world, who may be interested in using personal reflections in their teaching texts.

An Example

Did you take the long or the short route? A slightly edited version of the second personal reflections piece from the teaching texts of the introductory sociology course appears below. It and its predecessor relate to the topics which occupy students for the first eight weeks of the course: schooling, family life, gender relations and class divisions in society.

Some More Personal Reflections

The following remarks are meant to be read in conjunction with my previous personal reflections upon families, schooling, work and gender, which you will have considered in Section II (Book 1: 21-23). That earlier discussion was offered from the perspective of a masculine-child-student; the present discussion has been written from the perspective of a masculine-teacher-parent. You should use this discussion as a stimulus to a further consideration of your own autobiographical deliberations upon gender, schooling, families and work.

Three significant events in my life occurred in 1968: I took up my first teaching appointment, I got married and our first son was born. Full adult responsibility arrived with a rush!

Things were going very well for me as 1967 drew to its close: I had been in love for over a year; and I had just completed a successful year of studies, which had certified me as a secondary school teacher of geography and history. My career ambitions had already moved beyond being 'merely a successful classroom teacher'. I felt that I would one day be able to teach teachers, or, at worst, become some form of respected educational administrator or adviser. Consequently, there were two reasons why I wanted to obtain a teaching position in Melbourne: my girlfriend would be working there in the fashion industry, and I intended to further my university studies.

Even during the 'teacher shortages' of the late sixties it was difficult for first year teachers to get appointments in Melbourne. According to rumour, there were only two ways one could be guaranteed an appointment in a metropolitan school: to be a woman who was married to a man working in Melbourne, or to be a man who played 'League' football. Despite my performance upon the MMPI (a personality test) neither of these options was open to me. Rumour suggested another possible, but riskier, course — one could apply for technical schools in the 'western suburbs', apparently there were many vacancies. I had also heard that there were some interesting jobs teaching senior students in the technical colleges; a geographer/historian would be able to teach 'social science' to budding engineers, accountants and applied scientists. Armed with this knowledge my strategy was to apply for metropolitan technical colleges, metropolitan technical schools, and high schools in Gippsland, in that order of preference. The Education Department sent me to the technical college in my home-town in the Latrobe Valley!

After some reflection, I was not unhappy about the prospects of the appointment; anyway there was nothing I could do about it, as I had signed a contract with the Education Department to accept any position they chose to offer to me. However, my girlfriend and I were quite distressed at the likely effects of our 80 mile separation during the week, and I was rather unsure about the real nature of technical education. Within an hour of receiving the offer I had telephoned the Principal, who wished to see me immediately. With my ambitions rekindled, and dressed rather casually, I drove to the college.

The Principal received me with cool efficiency. I was soon informed that social studies had a rather humble place in technical education, and that I would be assigned to the junior school. (Later, I found that two new teachers with university qualifications in mathematics were assigned to the senior school.) As a parting remark the principal suggested that I should get a haircut and turn up for the first day of school with a tie on.

One of his old college lecturers had told him, he recalled, that teachers should dress and act inconspicuously. This advice was rather at odds with my limited classroom experience which had confirmed the utility of showmanship. The fiery little man who was 'headmaster' in charge of the secondary school had also neglected this advice — he was loud, conspicuous and engaging. He made me very welcome, perhaps because the school was short of humanities teachers; but he could not make me feel entirely at home.

There was much which was alien to me in the technical school. The fundamental difference between this school and those which I had been involved in before was related to the place of 'industry' in the curriculum. The school was oriented towards training young men for skilled trades, engineering and applied science; except for the humanities teachers and a few of the mathematics teachers, all of the staff had experienced some form of 'industrial experience'. Indeed, many of the 'tradies' (as they liked to be called) had worked for more than ten years as carpenters, plumbers, jewellers, fitters and so on. The 'cultural balance' between the sciences and the humanities, which existed in 'academic' secondary schools and the universities, was loaded heavily in favour of a peculiar version of the scientific approach. Other distinguishing characteristics were: the preponderance of students from working class families; strict discipline, which was based upon the strap; small classes (called sections) for science and workshop subjects, which were doubled-up for other subjects (namely English and social studies); rigid streaming based on ability in maths and science; and a significant number of students who were uninterested in schooling.

An illustrative example of my naive alienation is demonstrated by my experience of taking an 'extra' class in art in my first weeks at the school. Since the school was one teacher short in art (we seemed to be one short in most areas) some art classes had to be taken by teachers from other areas. I expected that my job would be merely to watch over the creative activity of the art class. The instructions from the Head of the Art Department soon confounded my stereotypical visions of creative art. My job would be to supervise the class carrying out a set task. I was to check the following: each student would sit in a numbered seat, according to a set plan which I was given; I would check each student's bench before and after the work period for any marks, etc.; I was to prevent any boy without an apron from working and then belt him; I was to collect students' money for art supplies, those without money were to be belted. This was industrial art! Before experiencing it, I had thought such activities would be confined to prisons and Dickens.

Like most inexperienced teachers, my major problems were related to classroom discipline and maintaining the students' interest in social studies. My strategy for confronting this problem rested upon the development of assignment work based upon 'enquiry-learning', which was the current fad during my teacher training year. It was not very successful. The students wanted to know why I could not write all 'the work' on the blackboard like the other teachers. Most of the students who took 'Social' seriously seemed more interested in producing well illustrated note-books than in grappling with the questions posed in the assignments and their answers locked into the dull textbooks. Eventually I realized that plagiarism was better than nothing. Therapeutic talks, humour and other forms of 'humanistic' social control just did not work, with many regrets I had to resort to the belt to deal with disruptive students. The few really satisfactory learning experiences which occurred seemed to be accidental; such as the project on motor cars and society which grew out of my observation that most students 'hawk-eyed' all cars which passed by the school. [The fantasy car of the time was the Monaro, which turned out to be the foundation of *Mad Max's (The Road Warrior)* customized death wagon.] By Easter I had accepted what should have been self-evident much earlier: the curriculum and our resource materials were only of marginal relevance to the present and future lives of working class adolescents. I needed my own fantasies to keep me going, as I was already hoping I could pick up a position in a high school in the following year, and I was searching for some students who wanted to learn what I could teach. My prayers seemed to be answered when the Headmaster told me that he had recommended me for a job in the senior school teaching an evening class of diploma students.

The students in the evening class were enrolled in the first year of a four year diploma course which would train them to be accountants. This level of study is equivalent to what is now called the TOP (Tertiary Orientation Programme) and is taught in TAFE colleges. I was to teach these students Social Studies. The college authorities gave me a course outline, a room, a class time (6.00-9.00 p.m.), and assumed that I was competent to take things from there. The course seemed interesting enough, it was based upon the contemporary HSC Social Studies syllabus and involved a study of Australian political institutions and foreign affairs. There were eight students, all men, seven of whom had come from technical, high and private schools, in the Latrobe Valley; one student, who had been a contemporary of mine at secondary school, had returned to study after four years' work as a clerk.

There was a sharp contrast in the approach to schooling of my day and evening students. 'Discipline problems' were non-existent in the evening class. Indeed, the business studies students had a contractual approach to learning: I was to supply knowledge and they would supply the attempt to understand it — the volume of the latter was dependent upon the volume of the former. Despite their cooperation and earnest studentship the evening class still posed a rather fundamental intellectual problem: their interest in politics and its academic study was not genuine. However, their compliance with organized schooling gave me a good start in my quest to give them a real interest.

The evening class were quite happy for me to indulge myself intellectually and pedagogically. I used to tape-record ABC radio public affairs programs, which were relevant to the course, and we would listen to these in class and discuss them. The students were asked to prepare and present 'papers', which were also tape-recorded; we discussed and analysed each student's presentation not just for its 'content', but also for its 'manner of presentation'. I used to play them recordings of parliamentary speeches by good performers like Fred Daly, Gordon Bryant and Gough Whitlam, unfortunately Bob Menzies had retired. I can even remember kidding them and myself that I would treat them to a 'series of lectures', I cannot even recall the topic. It was no Oxbridge common room, but we had great fun and the standard of their 'assessed work' was very good. I am not sure that they became deeply interested in politics; I am sure that they will be better accountants for the experience. They did attempt to teach me that academic social science has a more humble place in society than its practitioners believe: it is a lesson which I have never learned.

After re-reading the above discussion I can see that my opening remarks were somewhat misleading: I have emphasized my early teaching experiences, said little directly about 'masculinity' and almost nothing about my family life. I intend to redress this balance in my 'personal reflections' in the next section which deals with gender and generation. In closing I would merely add that late in the year which I have just been discussing (1968), I was offered positions at a high school in outer metropolitan Melbourne and in the senior technical college where I had worked as a part-timer. I accepted the tech. college position. My son currently attends a technical school, and I am a member of a technical school council. I have enjoyed my experience with technical education, but I am still an alien. My experiences in technical schools have shaped my working career and my identity, as will be revealed (partially) in the discussion below.

Sociology and the Personal. It is time to clarify the place which my 'personal reflections' have in this course. You will **not** learn a great deal about sociology from an understanding of aspects of my biography and your own biography. However, experience suggests that students can understand sociological subject matter and the sociological perspective if they can address these in terms of their own personal experience. Consequently, my personal reflections are put forward to provide you with a basis for thinking about similar social experiences of your own. The autobiographical exercises in the early sections of the course are designed to foster these skills. But, to understand sociology we have to go beyond the personal social experiences of a few individuals. Sociologists attempt to study the collective social experience of many individuals. From a sociological perspective we must understand biographies in the sense that C. Wright Mills has expressed. As *Making the Difference* demonstrates, sociologists are interested in how individuals construct their biographies within institutions like families, schools, classes and neighbourhoods. So while my revealed social experiences and your own reflections upon your social experiences are not in themselves *sociology,* they will give you a useful intellectual pathway into the lives of others as they are reflected in sociologists' data.

Personal experiences can often serve as starting-points for social scientific investigation, and my experiences in technical education provided the beginnings of the research project which eventually became the topic for my masters thesis. This is revealed by the introduction to a preliminary essay in this project which was written in 1970 and is printed below.

> When I was eleven and in sixth grade I had to decide whether to go next year to the 'high' or the 'tech' school. As my father was a retailer and I was 'smart' I went to the high school. But when I was twenty-one, and finished a university course, the Victorian Education Department sent me to a 'tech', as a teacher.

> As a result of this I have confronted two educational worlds which are in many ways quite different. For three years I wondered. Why is this so?

> To find the answers to this question, like so many others which concern the present, we must turn to the past. I did. The results of my explorations have created the discussions in future chapters. I believe these explorations and analyses have answered, to a large degree, the question posed. However, my journey through the records has made me aware of a much grander theme: the

attempt to realize a vision. At the turn of the century there was no state post-primary system of education in Victoria. In 1902 Frank Tate was appointed Director of Education. The politicians and the ideological climate of the time had written his charter. One of his tasks was to build a state post-primary system of schools to cater for the needs for vocational training of the lower classes. But Tate had a vision of a much grander scheme: a 'national system' of education; state post-primary schools to cater for all.

We shall see now how this vision, which became ever sharper and clearer to Tate and his supporters, became blurred and bastardized as countervailing forces resisted its translation into educational policy and practice.

In this project I was concerned with tracing the nature of the structure of state secondary schooling which was developed in Victoria in the twentieth century. Conveniently, this study has provided me with a good deal of the knowledge required in the writing of the succeeding discussion which deals with structure of the education system in Australia.

Some Further Reflections

At the contributors' seminar there was general acceptance of the draft which I presented. It was very much as it appears above. In fact I was counselled to make only one change: to delete a reference to the summary of 'Some More Personal Reflections', which appeared near the beginning. I had referred to it as a 'readers' digest' version of the 'real thing'. This was regarded as a patronizing remark which could be seen as a slur upon both an important literary institution and some of my readers. My plea that *The Reader's Digest* was a major source of ideas and comment for me in my youth was not accepted as a defence. Consequently I felt obliged to initiate the changes which now constitute the text.

As I told my fellow contributors, I had always been worried about the 'problem' of bringing the personal reflections to the readers' attention. I had never deviated from the course which would require an example to appear in full in this chapter. But where best to put it? In the earlier drafts I had it at the beginning. Colleagues had convinced me that this would 'turn off' my readers. 'Don't forget they're academics!' A compromise was struck between a summary near the start (to give them some idea of the nature of the reflections) and a complete example as an appendix.

The 'readers' digest' reference came from my attempt to put into words an invitation to readers that they had a choice: they could begin with a summary of the text under critical review or with the real thing. Thus to conform with my colleagues' suggestions I had to invent a new device for this purpose. The solution came from two sources: instructional design and children's story books. (Maybe they are a single source.) One of our children used to get me to read him *Choose Your Own Adventure Books*. These operated on a principle common in instructional design called branching programming. At key points in the story readers are confronted with choices (created by the author), their selection from the alternatives takes their adventure in different directions. You get four stories for the price of one. I could only offer you two, but I hoped you liked your adventure.

To make these changes I had to reread the draft. This allowed me to see all sorts of problems which needed attention. There was one glaring factual error: I had neglected to refer to two books which have been just as influential in my endeavours as Bernstein's work. (I think they only came to mind because I had been using them recently in another course. Ah, well, I did mention subliminal influences.) The books in question are: Bell and Encel's (1978) *Inside the Whale* and Bell and Newby's (1977) *Doing Sociological Research.* Both contain a series of reflections from sociologists which relate to research projects they have undertaken. Each contribution follows a format: some personal background, an outline of the project under review, some details of sociological influences and the connective tissue in which each of the sociologists reflects upon 'how it happened for them'.

I had used *Inside the Whale* and *Doing Sociological Research* with research methods students for some years before I wrote the introductory course. Those experiences demonstrated to me the value students see in getting behind the academic scenes. Particularly important was the effect upon them of reading about the relationships which personal experience have upon scientific research. The reflecting researchers had made many of Mills' abstract points more concretely, more personally. For me the books themselves had made *publishing* about the influence of personal experiences upon social science legitimate; it did not just have to go on behind closed doors. The editors of these books were distinguished professors!

Since I finished writing the texts for the introductory course Ann Oakley, the English sociologist, has published her sociological auto-biography, *Taking It Like a Woman.* This book shares much with

Lazarre's work. It adds further 'legitimacy' to my own efforts, but more importantly as a text it demonstrates that travelling between objectivity and subjectivity is valuable in sociology. I am confident that more sociologists will publish comparable work. Also I have to retract (partially) my observation that my colleagues have not been interested in adopting their own versions of personal reflections; many have and they are doing it 'their way' — which is, of course, of vital importance.

I hope you have noticed some stylistic changes which have crept in to this text following my post-contributors' seminar reflections. (What am I going to call them? I have never had to write about them before. [Well, what have you been saying in conversation?]) This form of text, which includes internal dialogue using three 'voices', has come from the reflective processes regarding the personal reflections and from the influences of the ideas in two sources, an article by Gary Gillard (1981) and a book by Michael Mulkay (1985).

Chapter 5

'Is the University Awful?':
Political Activism and Consciousness Raising
among External University Students

Margaret Grace

For some people on the University of Queensland campus September is the silly season. This is when the annual ritual of the Student Union elections is in full swing. The Union is a large organization representing 18,000 students. As well as providing a forum for political debate, it is responsible for the management of many services including three refectories, a creche, a cinema and a legal service. A position on its executive offers opportunities to exercise considerable power and gain valuable managerial experience. For two or three weeks the back rooms, corridors and stairways of the Union building buzz with activity. Deals are done and campaigns hatched. Lunchtime crowds in the refectories are regaled with a series of running skirmishes called policy speeches. Secretaries struggle under a mounting tide of paper and hysteria.

There is usually one room in the Union building which can be relied upon to be relatively quiet, however, even in election week: the office of the External Students Committee — known as the 'XSC'. While the student elections succeed in exciting only a fraction of the large on-campus student population, they fail almost entirely to engage the interest of the external students. Nevertheless, the XSC was an important part of the Union structure, because of the external students' financial contribution through the compulsory Student Service Charge.

External students of the University of Queensland are dispersed all over Australia, and even beyond its shores. Many of them never visit the campus or meet any of their fellows, because attendance is not compulsory. Since they are usually at least ten years older than their full-time counterparts on campus, it is understandable that they do not feel much sense of affiliation to the Student Union, which provides a traditional youthful undergraduate political forum. In these circumstances the existence of a viable organization of external students, such as the XSC, within the Union framework would seem to be a fairly unlikely occurrence. That such an organization arose and survived for over a decade is something to celebrate.

This chapter describes the politicization of external students at the University of Queensland during the period 1975-1985. It is about the establishment of a student initiated political lobby and support system and its successful integration into both the Union and the University structures. It discusses an attempt at consciousness raising which was founded on the innovative vision, energy and commitment of the students who were involved.

The successful establishment of the XSC at Queensland University in 1976-1977 can be attributed to the coincidence of several circumstances. The University's commitment to external study was declining at a time when the number of mature age women undergraduates was increasing, as was the number of metropolitan residents gaining admission as external students. It is apparent that those who were involved in the moves to give external students an organized representation on the campus included people who perceived a threat to a new-found and highly valued educational opportunity; those who had the necessary motivational energy to do something about it; and those who had sufficient access to the campus for organized group activity. Most of them were women. To some extent this innovation should be seen as a phenomenon of its time.

In 1975 and 1976 cutbacks to the University's Department of External Studies reduced the staff establishment by about one-third. At that time the Department was both an academic department and an administrative operation. It had about forty academics from several disciplines whose teaching was devoted almost entirely to external students. There were about 3000 external students, approximately one-sixth of the total University enrolment.

During 1975 the student representatives on the Department of External Studies Consultative Council began to take coffee in the refectory after meetings, and discuss the issues raised. This was the germination of what later became the XSC. As a result of their participation in the Consultative Council meetings, the students shared an increasing awareness of the relationship between University politics and some aspects of their experience of external study. It was easy, for example, to relate staff cutbacks to their personal difficulties in planning a coherent course of study, as an increasing number of courses listed in the external studies handbook carried the annotation 'Not offered in 1976'.

The students also discovered that political issues were associated with prejudicial views. They were shocked to learn that in some quarters external study was regarded as a second-rate mode of study, and a degree gained in this mode as an inferior degree. This perception sat very strangely with their own attitudes, which included reverence for the University, and a high value placed on a degree for which they were prepared to invest many years of persistent effort in the face of considerable obstacles.

For some of the students who attended Consultative Council meetings their new-found knowledge about the impact of institutional politics on the quality of their educational experience crystallized into a burning indignation. They perceived external students as a disadvantaged minority who should be encouraged to fight for their rights. At the same time they were fiercely loyal to the Department of External Studies which they believed to be under threat.

It is not coincidental that most of the small group who shared this view and who were motivated to do something about the situation were women. Perhaps they felt so strongly because of the similarities between their experience as external students and their experience as women in a male-dominated society. They saw external students as marginalized, low-status members of the University community. This is not to say that they necessarily rationalized their actions in terms of feminist theory, neither was the organization comprised solely of women. The participation of men was actively sought, and some became involved. However, the influence of the women in the organization was dominant. It was mainly their energies which powered its development, and their concerns which were reflected in the way various issues were perceived and confronted.

The women's activism in student affairs was symptomatic of a more general challenge to the status quo which was expressed in both the public and private domains. One member was active in a political party, another was an activist on behalf of the aboriginal community, and some took part in the street march demonstrations which occurred in Brisbane in the late 1970s in the cause of civil liberties. Their attitudes to feminist thought varied, but they were all in one way or another challenging role stereotypes and negotiating gender issues in their personal lives. Some appreciation of personal histories is important for an understanding of the context in which this student organization emerged, because shared experience and values contributed to the development of group identity.

The two women who were most consistently active in the student organization in the beginning had a total of twelve children between them. Both had been divorced and remarried, and both had known periods of single parenthood. Another of the women was studying for a teaching qualification so that she could support her invalid husband and three children. A fourth had begun her external student career while helping her husband to run a roadhouse. She used to tell stories about how she kept her textbooks propped up beside the till, so that she could study in between pumping petrol and serving hamburgers.

I have mentioned that one factor in the politicization of the group was their experience as student representatives on the Consultative Council. Another factor was their awareness of the failure of the Student Union to recognize external students. A critical incident which helped to bring about this awareness happened during a Study School — a week-long residential school held annually in August during University vacation. A student from Darwin sought out the President of the Union to complain that there was no refectory open during the weekend of the school. She discovered that not only was the President unaware that the school was in progress; he had never heard of external students. He was about to be educated.

During a Study School some of the students on the Consultative Council canvassed the idea of forming an external student organization, and later, through a postal survey, sought all external students' views. By 1977 they had effected constitutional changes which established an External Students' Committee, or XSC, within the Union, with an allocation of funds and proportional representation on the Union Council. This gave external students elected representation on both the Department of External Studies Consultative Council and the Union Council. The two councils were quite separate, with elections conducted by the Department and the Union respectively. In addition to the Union Council representatives, other external students became members of the XSC through cooption. In practice the same students tended to appear on both bodies because the XSC always made sure that some of its members were nominated for the Consultative Council.

In the same year the committee made another coup when their first chairperson, Pam Jones, was nominated to be one of the Union's representatives on the Professorial Board. A local paper ran a story on Pam's selection with a picture of her at home, flanked by two of her daughters, and captioned: 'Pam gives them a say!' The publicity was deliberately sought by the XSC in an effort to raise the profile of external students both at the University and in the wider community. It was also part of what became a continuing campaign to raise the consciousness of external students as students and as members of the University community.

One of the first important innovations of the XSC was the

appointment of a paid organizer. Originally conceived as a secretarial position and advertized at ten hours per week, the organizer's role rapidly evolved into something much more. The External Students Liaison Officer (ESLO) was to coordinate outreach activities and to act as a trouble shooter or student advocate. The external students were apprised of the ESLO's appointment and invited to make contact if help were needed.

In their enthusiasm the XSC expected a super problem-solver, but overlooked the fact that they had only allocated time and salary for a part-time secretary. Perhaps their expectations of the ESLO reflected their own working conditions as housewives: high levels of commitment and achievement without pay. It is not surprising that the first ESLO resigned after a few months. The position was readvertized at twenty hours per week in 1978, and was progressively increased to become full-time in 1981. I worked as the ESLO from 1978 to 1985.

The emergence of the XSC was welcomed and encouraged by the Department of External Studies, as was the appointment of the ESLO, and the association between all parties continued to be close. The occasional conflict which was an inevitable feature of such a relationship was regarded as healthy and usually handled productively. The value of the ESLO's role was officially recognized with the publication of a report by the Deputy Vice-Chancellor on the future of external studies (Davies, 1979). In recommending the appointment of a counsellor to the Department, he cited the use made by students of the ESLO's position. Thus the student organization had demonstrated a deficiency in the University's services for external students.

The Department offered the ESLO a position on its Consultative Council. Participation in the work of the Consultative Council by the XSC included some useful work on its sub-committees, for example, ensuring that child-care was provided during the Study Schools.

The provision of child-care taught us a salutary lesson about the need for compulsory unionism. At that time, 1978, only the metropolitan external students had to pay the Student Service Charge, which for them was at the same rate as part-time students on campus. The Union was allowed to solicit membership from students outside the metropolitan area on the basis of a voluntary fee of $10 per year. Much of our energy in the first three years was invested in a membership drive, but we succeeded in attracting only about 5 per cent of the country students. Such was the altruistic idealism of the committee that the idea of limiting services to those students who paid the fee was rejected in the belief that the students would join when they realized how much the committee was doing for them. However, we discovered that most of the student parents who availed themselves of the child-care facility felt no obligation to join the Union, even when the situation was explained to them. After that we petitioned the University to make the $10 fee compulsory, which it eventually did in 1981.

One effect of this delay was that the XSC continued to work hard at communicating with the external students in order to promote the idea of organized group action. Two reasons for Union membership were identified: the need for political action and the need for alternative support structures. Political action was envisaged both at institutional level and nationally, through the Part-time and External Students' Organization (PESO), which was affiliated with the Australian Union of Students (AUS). Lobbying at the institutional level was mainly support for the Department of External Studies, and was referred to as the 'Save the DES campaign'. The external students were informed that the Department had been under review for some time and that it was not getting a fair share of financial resources. Strategies included representation on University committees, writing letters and submissions, and the promotion in the public media of the idea of external study, its value and benefits.

The high point of the XSC's campaign was probably the debate on the future of external studies at Professorial Board in 1979. It was known that the new Vice-Chancellor, who had announced his personal enthusiasm for distance education, would seek a commitment from the Board to certain future developments in external studies. On that occasion we organized a demonstration in the foyer outside the boardroom, something of an achievement considering that external students are by definition unable to attend the campus. The demonstration consisted of a few placard-carrying women, a pram, and several small children. Fortunately Pam's successor on the Board was present for the debate, and she bravely objected to the assertion made by one of the professors that external studies was a second-rate form of study. She argued that even if it were true, external students were not second-rate students and were entitled to a better deal.

The alternative support system established by the XSC was directed to breaking down the effects of isolation. Students were encouraged to make contact with the ESLO and each other, especially when they were in difficulties. It was thought that in the absence of other students to talk to people would interpret their difficulties as evidence of personal inadequacy and be inclined to give up the idea of getting a degree. My ESLO experience leads me to believe that women are more likely to think in this way than men, and that women are more active than men in contacting other students.

When I reflect on the ways in which the XSC members and I attempted to communicate these ideas, I am struck by our creativity and energy. We were active at Study Schools, making speeches and meeting the students. We produced a newsletter which was distributed up to eight times per year. In 1978 and 1979 I travelled extensively in Queensland in company with members of the Department of External Studies staff, or with the librarian in charge of the Thatcher Library, the University's specialist service for external students. We were also interviewed on radio, twice on the ABC's morning session, and also on regional stations.

The wish to publicize the availability of external studies was motivated not only by a genuine desire to spread the 'good news', especially to other women, but also because we recognized the importance of student numbers to the viability of the Department of External Studies. At that time University policy prevented the Department from advertizing its courses, so on one occasion the XSC decided to take the matter into its own hands. We placed an advertisement in local and national newspapers, inviting readers to contact the ESLO for further information about the availability of arts, law, commerce and economics by external study. We were overwhelmed by the response and had to hire special secretarial assistance to deal with the enquiries.

By 1980 our efforts to involve distant external students in the organization extended to the recruitment of 'Area Communicators'. These were students who volunteered to act as regional extensions of the XSC. This network was never as well organized or effective as we would have liked it to be, but nevertheless we did maintain a regional support system. The names and telephone numbers of the Area Communicators were advertized in the ESLO's newsletter and students were urged to use them as 'friends in need'.

We used some of our funds to pay the fares of Area Communicators to bring them to the campus for special occasions. One such event was a meeting with the new Vice-Chancellor. We managed to produce a delegation of external students from several distant country towns as well as the metropolitan area. I remember this meeting not so much for the discussion with the Vice-Chancellor, but for something which occurred afterwards which illustrates the kind of conflict which being a student created for some women. We went to the refectory for coffee to discuss the meeting and, as there was a lot to talk about, decided to stay and have lunch together. One of the group declined this suggestion, saying she had to rush home; her husband would expect her to prepare lunch. Of course the other women tried to persuade her that it was an important occasion for the XSC and that a grown man could fix his own lunch, but they did not press the point too strongly. They knew that often a woman's 'freedom' to study has to be 'bought'.

At the beginning of the 1980 academic year, and again in 1981, we brought several of the Area Communicators to Brisbane to meet the metropolitan XSC members over a weekend. We called these gatherings 'conferences', and invited staff of the Department of External Studies, some deans and administrators, including the Vice-Chancellor. In this way the students' needs and the University's problems could be aired in a fairly informal setting. On the second occasion our guests included the new Director of External Studies whose appointment followed the adoption of the Davies report. Lenore Coltheart, who was then a postgraduate student but had been one of the original instigators of the XSC, gave the following address or 'call to arms'.

External Students Must Help Themselves — or, Don't Kick the Postman Yet

We have been hearing a lot about the changes that are imminent in the Department of External Studies, and of course we need to be aware of, understand, consider and participate in these changes. Although we have become accustomed over the last few years to this atmosphere of 'imminence', to the sense that any moment now a new day for external students will be dawning at the St Lucia campus, we should not be dulled by the feeling of familiarity. I do not want what I have to say to be taken as recommending a quietist attitude in relation to the proposals for restructuring the University, to the proposed changes in the Department, or to the on-going problems that have triggered off these two different, but related, plans for the University of Queensland. You would adopt that attitude at your peril.

This afternoon I want to talk about what to do while we wait for the new DES — what you, as external students, can do in those long hours before your day dawns. I guess this was summed up by a statement one of you made this morning: 'You've got to be a real fighter to survive'. That's right. What follows are some thoughts on whom to fight — external students do not have much time or energy to spare and it is prudent to make best use of those scarce resources. Don't kick the postman if your assignment isn't returned — direct your anger to the right target.

I'm going to set out a few targets — one of which is likely to be the source of your problem and its solution. The biggest is the Federal Government and its Department of Education. There is a new Minister, and an economic climate in which education spending has a low priority. It's a good idea to complement your study with reading education policy bits in the paper and relating the facilities you have, and the quality of the service, to federal election decisions. For instance, diminished spending on tertiary education throughout the late 70s might have a direct relation to the delayed return of your assignment, in that most of the tutors in the Department of External Studies lost their jobs during this time and marking often now has to be sent out as a kind of modern academic version of piece-work.

So government at federal level can be the scene of decisions which will disadvantage you, as external students. Government at the state level can also operate in the same way. Since the federal Labour government abolished university fees, the universities are funded from the federal purse, but not surprisingly, state governments attempt to retain a measure of control. There is certainly, in Queensland, the potential for state government influence in universities. External students of Queensland, in fact, owe a debt to those state government members of 1911 who ensured that there would be provision for long-distance students when the University was established in that year. We shouldn't forget that, or let contemporary politicians forget.

The third 'target' is the University itself. Many decisions are made in the Senate, the formal governing body of the University, in the Vice-Chancellor's office, and in the Professorial Board meeting room. There are many committees at this level, and also within each faculty and department. Don't bother trying to probe this complex arrangement; it is easy to see why external students need a Liaison Officer to shepherd your requests and problems through such a maze. In order to understand why the University excised a disproportionate amount from the budget of the Department of External Studies in several years we need a team of accounts experts, but again, here is a link with late assignments. It is up to the University to distribute the money it receives from the federal allocations to tertiary institutions. There are no 'tied grants' to ensure any of the money is spent in a particular way.

Next, the Department of External Studies might itself be your target. The actual teaching of each subject is the province of the lecturer concerned and problems relating to content and conduct of a course should always be addressed to that person. If a difficulty is not resolved, then the Head of the Department and the ESLO will help. The reason for letting the ESLO know — a copy of your letter to the Head is sufficient — is so that if nothing seems to be happening, a phone call to her will put you in the picture, as she can find out what progress has been made. We are not supposing that the DES is incompetent, or insensitive to your needs and difficulties. It is more to the point that the system is skeletal and the place understaffed. But sometimes it is possible that a delayed return of assignment, or whatever problem you are encountering, is because someone somewhere isn't doing the job properly. You have the right to that information. It is a mistake for you to assume that people in this place are perfect, and that any imperfection is on your side.

At the regional level there are the officers-in-charge in the larger centres — some enthusiastic and invaluable, others appear to have been dragooned into service. As they receive minimal financial return for the time they must put in to fulfil their role properly, if they are not performing adequately there is not much you can do except tactfully initiate and perform services needed in your area yourself. If you don't do it, it won't be done, and this is one of the important aspects of serving as an area communicator. You might be able to work with the officer-in-charge to relieve his/her load and help the external students in your area. Remember, too, that you may know more about DES, the University, and external students than the O-I-C if he/she is comparatively new and you are a veteran.

We have now worked downwards and reached your communities. You may feel grateful to the University for the chance to study — though I'm not sure that too much of that is prudent at this time — but there is no doubt that your communities should feel grateful to you. No measurement, no cost benefit analysis, no accounting can reveal the value of your study to your community. Whether it is a mining township like Blackwater, or a provincial city, wherever you live, the people you come in contact with stand to benefit because you are an external student. Your families and friends, service clubs, local government organizations — all are enhanced by the broadening of understanding, your sharpened intellectual equipment and the simple matter of having direct contact through you with the largest University in Australia. You can, and should, expect to have this gratitude, and to have it expressed in some way that will help you.

Contacts with local Rotary, Apex and similar organizations could make the case for financial and other assistance, with purchase of books for a tutorial group, establishing a study centre, or even with a form of scholarship to enable someone to come to Study School who would not otherwise have been able to afford it. One would imagine that local graduate associations would perceive the fostering of undergraduate study to be an ideal activity. Don't fall into the trap of concealing the fact that you are studying — asking for the notes to be sent in a plain wrapper and so on! It is time for external students to come out of the closet, and bring your books with you. Your community needs you, and should acknowledge this.

Then we come to your fellow students. What actions are needed in relation to each other? Organizing your own tutorial groups, finding and supporting someone as area communicator, getting graduates, or people who have completed particular subjects to be discussion leaders for tutorial groups which have no tutor, publicizing the activities of DES so potential students know about it, being supportive to new students. Given the present situation, and while we wait for the new DES, these seem essential aspects of your role as external students. Taking notes and tapes back from Study School for those who couldn't come seems pretty obvious if you are already in touch with those people earlier in the year.

In a University as large as this one, with 18,000 undergraduate students, there is no cohesion in the student body, even that half, the full-time internal students, who are present on campus every day. As external students, although you are a varied group, and a geographically fragmented one, you have a potent bond. You are *external* students, people who must know how to help themselves if they are not to be treated as invisible and impotent. We have alumni to be proud of. There are politicians, teachers, professors, journalists, officers in the armed forces. There are people whose determination to continue and complete their degrees in spite of every imaginable obstacle just stuns you, until you realize that every external student shares that determination, even if we have to help each other search for it sometimes.

Finally, we need to look at ourselves. After all this action, directed to all these external targets, it is important to remember that sometimes we can be the source of our own difficulties. The external student syndrome, of course, comprises believing that one is inadequate, hopeless, unable to perform the simplest procedure the University requires, let alone complete an academic course. To have to wallow in these soggy thoughts might be comfortable but it is dull. I'm not advocating that generalized *ennui*. I do suggest that you examine your commitment to study, and rate it against the other commitments you have, which compete for your time. Each ten credit point subject is supposed to be given ten hours of study per week over one semester; about a hundred and thirty hours of study. If you cannot set aside this time regularly, should you be studying now?

Most people give family commitments their top priority, then maybe their job comes next, but make sure study does not get a place when there is no time left. You can't expect your family, employer, friends, to respect your role as student if you don't accord it importance yourself. For those study hours each week, remove yourself from other demands, even if it means locking yourself in the bathroom. Don't be dislodged or distracted for reasons short of disaster. It's amazing how quickly the world learns to find its own socks and sort out its own squabbles when the official sock and squabble sorter is absent. Have a mental sign which says 'external student' and switch it on when your allotted study time comes round. Because, of course, tertiary study isn't a breeze, it takes concentration, discipline and hard work. I don't think it is ever really the sort of thing you can do while you watch Mike Walsh, do your tax return and answer the telephone. It needs its own time.

This talk has been long and rather headmasterish. It is intended only to suggest the need for action, to show where action might be directed, and to urge you to think things through next time you feel the urge to kick the postman.

Subsequent Developments

With regard to the subsequent history of the XSC the expectation implicit in Lenore's address that external students would rush to the barricades did not eventuate. By 1980 most of the original members had graduated and moved on, and though others came to take their places, it was hard to maintain the momentum established by the original enthusiasts.

At various times in the following years only a small number of people were prepared to be actively involved. This was disheartening, but when we considered how difficult it was for external students to take part in such activity, we were satisfied that there continued to be enough people to maintain the XSC. The commitment of the few ensured a continuing external student presence on the campus through representation on various bodies such as the Board of External Studies. The ESLO position became an institution in the Union, and this in itself ensured that successive presidents and other office-bearers were alert to issues which affected external students.

Continuity of service was probably the most effective way of raising the awareness of the main body of external students of the existence of their organization and the issues it confronted. My communication with the students was through the newsletter and as recipient of their enquiries and problems. After eight years of acting as a trouble shooter for external students, I would have to agree that what Lenore described as the external students' syndrome does exist. Of course, this perception may be distorted, because only a small proportion of student enquiries came to my office. I was an alternative communications channel for the students; they directed most of their enquiries to the relevant University personnel. Perhaps a disproportionate percentage of all complaints came my way, and fewer of the routine enquiries. Nevertheless, on a number of occasions, when there was a problem with a particular course, for example, I discovered that the complaints I received were the tip of an iceberg. For every student who complained there were usually others who were suffering in silence.

Often people who called with a complaint about the conduct of a course were hesitant and apologetic, like the woman who said that she had been 'stewing over this for two weeks, wondering whether to contact the ESLO'. Typically they would put the case and then ask if I thought they were justified. 'Is there something wrong, or is it just me?' was a common question. Doubtless part of the hesitation was caused by anxiety that I might not handle the complaint with tact and sensitivity. Sometimes this was expressed overtly; the students would insist that they did not want to cause trouble for members of staff; they wanted simply to have the problem rectified.

When occasionally something went badly wrong with the conduct of a course, the people most ready to complain seemed to be those who were most confident of their academic ability, and who felt that their consistent high performance was prejudiced. Sometimes those who were most apologetic in presenting a complaint also described themselves as not very good students. Frequently the explanation of the study-related problem was mixed up with a description of other personal problems, and illness was often part of the picture. There seemed to be a pattern, particularly among women students, of being anxious about assessment requirements, taking personal responsibility for all difficulties, and getting sick.

It seemed to me that social isolation and ignorance of the institution exacerbated the students' predicament when things went wrong. Many had no way of checking their perceptions because there was nobody in their immediate social circle who had any real appreciation of what was involved in formal study at tertiary level, let alone external study. Some lived in a social context which was actually hostile to demonstrations of intellectual activity.

I presented my perception of 'the external student syndrome' to one of our weekend conferences for Area Communicators, and later printed the text of my address in the newsletter. The title, 'Is the University Awful?', was supposed to suggest, by the use of wordplay, an association between being in awe of the institution and having a bad time as a student. I said that isolation and ignorance breed awe of the institution, and that such awe is unwarranted. I recommended that when in difficulties students should ask, 'Who owns this problem, me or the University?'

I have to admit that not all students assumed personal inadequacy when things went wrong. Once I discovered that a student had attributed the non-arrival of his course materials to his wife's inefficiency. He accused her of forgetting to post his confirmation of enrolment form. She was very pleased when I explained that the cause of the delay was really an administrative failure at the University. Since none of the students enrolled in that course had received the materials, and only one had contacted me, I wondered what the rest were doing about the situation, and to what they attributed the delay.

Many of the enquiries I received demonstrate how difficult it can be to deal with a complex bureaucracy from a distance. Here is a classic:

> Yesterday I received the standard University form 'Confirmation of enrolment and statement of examination results', together with the standard 'External students examination entry' form, and 'Memorandum to students enrolled in courses in the Faculty of Commerce and Economics'. The statement of examination results indicates an 'incomplete result' in CO333, but I do not know what is meant by the term, or its significance. Neither of the forms I received yesterday, nor my External Studies Handbook, give any indication.

I presume that the incomplete result may be related to the fact that I submitted eight of eleven assignments. However, I wrote to the lecturer on 30 May concerning the outstanding assignments, and as I received no reply and sat for the examination, I thought I must have satisfied the course requirements.

Here is another letter which presents some typical problems for external students:

I am asking you to help me solve a problem. I am doing Education externally. I was originally taking first level subjects towards a B.Ed., but in March, the Uni advised me that because I was a three year trained teacher, I should be doing second level subjects if I wanted credit towards a degree. So I immediately made a switch over to ED200 (Comparative Ed) and ED220 (Philosophy of Ed).

My problem is that although all the lecture notes, etc., have arrived for Comparative Ed., I have received only lecture 4 and Assignment Guide 2 from the Philosophy Department. I am rather worried that I will not receive the others. I suppose that I should be writing to the lecturer directly, but honestly, every time I speak to or hear from the Administration, they seem to confuse me more than ever, and I just don't feel it is worth the effort and want to give up. I have been so messed about this year with my studies that I am beginning to lose all interest and at times just don't care, especially when teaching is very demanding and takes up a lot of time.

So I feel I would rather approach you and ask you to be my 'voice' in this matter. I would be so terribly grateful if you could arrange for the Philosophy Department to send me all notes and lectures prior to lecture 4 and especially assignment guide 1 and the list of textbooks I need. I'm glad you are available. It is a tremendous relief knowing that there is someone down there in that huge maze who is interested in and willing to help us out here.

The letter reflected a fairly alienated perception of the institution ('that huge maze') to which students are outsiders ('us out here'). It demonstrated a lack of information: the student refers to the 'Philosophy Department' when actually she was dealing with a lecturer in Philosophy of Education, located in the Department of External Studies. (How was she to know?) Her subjective state was characterized by confusion, doubt, failing motivation, timidity about approaching a member of staff, and a corresponding gratitude for friendly, personalized service.

General Lessons

What are the lessons for other contexts to be drawn from the experience of the external student organization at the University of Queensland? As far as the need for political activism is concerned, I have already pointed out critical features of the specific context in which this student organization emerged. External students were a minority group of a very large institution with a declining commitment to distance education. However, external students are effectively disenfranchised by their limited access to information and low sense of group identity and, therefore, there is a role for student organizations in distance education. Our experience demonstrates that it is inherently difficult, but not impossible, to create an effective external student lobby.

Whether this model is the most effective is difficult to say. My feeling is that the XSC evolved in response to particular circumstances and as an expression of individual personalities. Other situations may produce different responses. When external students congregate regularly on campus for residential schools, it is easier to create a sense of community and to organize politically. Having funds available to pay for travel expenses is another important condition for effective external student representation on campus. It can be argued that the appointment of a paid organizer operates to decrease the level of voluntary student involvement. On the other hand, there is no doubt that the presence of a permanent employee provides continuity, which is an essential ingredient for such an organization.

There are many similarities between the model evolved by the XSC and the Extra-mural Students' Association at Massey University, New Zealand, including the employment of a paid organizer and the establishment of a network of Area Communicators to provide support at the local level (Williams and Williams, 1987).

In relation to student support, it is easier to generalize from our experience. The University of Queensland is not presented here as a special case. Contrary to the implications of the correspondence examples, I am not blaming those directly responsible for services to the external students. I would say that the risk of alienation is inherent in the experience of external study, and in even the best systems the potential for error and conflict of interest is present. For these reasons there is always a place for an alternative support system such as the one we established. I would agree with Sewart (1982) that providing a variety of support mechanisms is the best way to meet the individual needs of a diverse body of people such as external students.

For me the experience of being ESLO was an interesting and enjoyable one. I'm glad to have been a part of something so visionary and yet so practical. I learned a lot about politics. It was rewarding to work with external students, and I made many friends. Like so many of them, I was continuing my education while negotiating major changes in my personal circumstances, and I benefited greatly from the sense of shared experience which the job gave me.

I am left with a residue of enduring interests and some unresolved questions, which is doubtless why I am writing about it. Among the enduring interests is a fascination with what I call the sociology of distance education. When trying to promote political activism, I was very conscious of the effects of the limited sense of community among the students. The production of the newsletter was an attempt to create such a sense. A relationship between integration into the social fabric of the institution and academic success is apparent, as others (Roberts, 1984; Keegan, 1986) have noted. My questions are about what it means to be an outsider in any given cultural context, and about how institutions can most successfully integrate their external students.

Events seem to have given some validation to the XSC's often-repeated contention that access to tertiary education through external studies at the University of Queensland was threatened. Ten years later, in spite of structural changes which converted the old Department of External Studies into a School of External Studies and Continuing Education, and in spite of the strenuous efforts of many staff, the future is still uncertain. In 1986 the Chairman of the Commonwealth Tertiary Education Commission publicly advocated the phasing out of external studies at the University of Queensland. The Director of the School and the present ESLO joined forces to alert the students to the situation. I understand that the subsequent deluge of letters from students all over the country made an impression on the Commission. It seems that the 'Save the DES' campaign continues.

Acknowledgment

I am grateful to Lenore Coltheart for permission to reproduce her transcript (pp. 62-6).

Chapter 6

Talking to New England:
Interactive Radio in Distance Education

Geoff Arger

The University of New England, located in Armidale in northern New South Wales, has over 6000 external students and is a major provider of distance education in Australia. The 'Talking to New England' interactive radio project commenced in 1986 and is one of the programmes being developed by the University to provide interaction between academic staff and their students. The project allows academics at the University (see Figure 6.1) to present material to external students through local FM radio stations in Sydney (550 kilometres away), Newcastle (400 kilometres away) and in Armidale itself. It also allows them to respond to questions 'on air'. Cassette tapes of the programmes

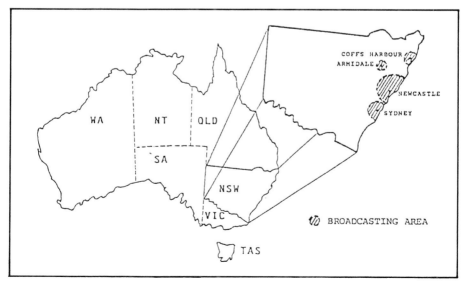

Figure 6.1   Broadcasting areas of the 'Talking to New England' project

are subsequently despatched by mail to students outside the broadcasting area. Another FM radio station in Coffs Harbour, 110 kilometres to the east of Armidale, broadcasts one of the hour programmes each week as a community education project. The overall result is a unique use of interactive radio in distance education, or as one local newspaper called it, 'educational talkback'.

The 'Talking to New England' project reflects Australia's long tradition of radio in distance education especially through institutions such as the School of the Air. It brings together the University's experience in distance education, the popularity of talkback radio, and the proliferation of FM community radio. With 45 per cent of the University's external undergraduate students in the Sydney area and another 6 per cent in the Hunter Valley area centred on the city of Newcastle, the project was addressing many of the University's external students.

Making a Programme

Academic staff members record programmes relating to their subjects in the audiovisual studio at the University of New England. Programme duration varies from eighteen to forty minutes, but is usually about thirty minutes. The style of presentation varies considerably among subject areas and among individual academics. Production features such as musical breaks and fade-outs are added at the time of recording. Tapes are sent to the radio station in Sydney at least a week before the evening broadcast date. The tapes are played with live voice introductions superimposed over the music breaks. After this prepared session the talkback line is open to the students, and to the public, who contribute up to 20 per cent of the calls.

The Sydney studio is linked by telephone landline to the academic staff member at the University. During this time the announcer joins in the discussion which is based partly on a list of questions provided and also on the announcer's own understanding of the subject. When there is a lull in calls, project staff from the Department of External Studies, some of whom monitor the programmes at home, call in with questions which have previously been solicited from students outside the broadcast area.

Technical Production

The broadcast programme originates from the studios of Sydney Educational Radio (2SER-FM) at the University of Technology. The station's transmitter is located on the roof of this institution, which provides good coverage for the wider Sydney metropolitan area. The station's talkback facilities are used, with a separate three-line switchboard to receive listeners' calls. The programme is broadcast in mono with the usual seven-second delay for talkback radio.

To enable the 'live' link with Armidale, a ten KHz line is used from the University of New England to the 2SER-FM studio. A second three KHz line is used to send the 'pre-delay' studio output signal back from 2SER to the University of New England studio. This line is also used for communication between 2SER-FM and University of New England technical producers. A further 10KHz line is used from 2SER-FM control room to Newcastle University Radio (2NUR-FM) in Newcastle. The Armidale relay is provided by a split from the return line to the radio station 2ARM-FM studio in Armidale. A tape of the total broadcast is despatched to Coffs Harbour Youth Radio station (2CHY-FM) for their weekly broadcast.

Listeners to 2NUR-FM and 2ARM-FM who wish to participate in the talkback are required to call 2SER-FM, where they are given priority 'to air' wherever practicable. Although this is more expensive than making a local call, it does not appear to discourage participation from the Newcastle and Armidale listeners.

The project is limited by its inability to broadcast live to all students. One of the strengths of the project — the use of cheap FM air time — is also one of its weaknesses because FM cannot cover a large area. Networking live broadcasts is difficult because it attracts high Telecom charges; nevertheless, the use of audio cassettes despatched to the students in non-broadcast areas, and the soliciting of questions which are asked live to air, have resulted in a very positive response from these students.

The partnership of a conservative university and a progressive radio station brings inevitable tensions. This is epitomized by the issue of whether the programme should appeal to the students, the public or both. The problems are mediated by the educational developers who work to improve teaching practices at the University. In this case the author, as Course Development Adviser, particularly in the project's first year, occasionally needed to emphasize to 2SER the conservative, élitist nature of universities and insist that the programmes be directed mainly at enrolled students.

Developing External Teaching at the University of New England

Before the development of the 'Talking to New England' project can be understood it is important to put the two partners into their historical institutional perspectives. By 1985 the University of New England had been in external studies for fifty years. As with many distance institutions, it was operating in the methodology and attitudes of its establishment days. Thus teaching material was seen as the responsibility of the academic. It was usually based on the dispatch of lecture notes either in print or audio form, supported by face-to-face sessions, usually residential schools on campus or weekend schools in Sydney. Until recently no professional advice or assistance was given to academic staff in preparing their material.

In 1985 the author was appointed as a Course Development Adviser in the Department of External Studies with a brief to develop the teaching material. The nature and direction of such development were not stated. One obvious area with a high profile was to make the teaching materials more interactive. This became one of the major aims of the Course Development Adviser.

The University of New England is not an institution where all teaching materials are processed by instructional designers and editors. Therefore, the strategy adopted to achieve interactivity in teaching material was three-fold: first, to change the organizational base in the Department of External Studies for wide-based improvements in teaching material; secondly, to initiate staff development experiences; thirdly, to establish exemplar models of teaching material.

The structural changes in the Department of External Studies included the removal of the hierarchical structure within the teaching material section; the introduction of a computer recording system to track the various production stages of teaching material; the in-service training of teaching material clerks about development objectives; the appointment of new professional staff in place of clerical/administration staff; and the overall movement towards a team approach to the development of teaching material.

The major thrust for staff development was through the evolution of an orientation kit for academic staff, which was based on the philosophy of mixing exemplar model and content advice — theory and practice. Thus the first part given to the academics on their first day was a kit with three components. The first component, set up as a distance education course, gives advice on how to 'Write Distance Education Teaching Material'. The second component, set up as an audio cassette with accompanying visual material, gives advice on 'How to Use Audiovision in Distance Education'. The third component, on a video, gives advice on 'How to Use Video in Distance Education'. The detailed administrative advice is sent as Part 2 when the new staff member's name appears in the University in-house news sheet. This is further reinforced by a series of ad hoc seminars on techniques in distance education covering topics such as unitization, game simulation, teleconferencing, computing and satellite communication.

Associated with this approach is the strategy to develop exemplar models. Contact with the course development staff may result in suggestions about which techniques should be used in developing teaching material and advice about the various ways to gain assistance such as the 'Academic Time Release' scheme, the 'Innovations Development Fund', participation in development projects, and assistance from the Course Development Adviser and Course Development Assistants. Exemplar models often flow from this assistance. One of the development projects mentioned above was to integrate study skills into first year teaching material, another was the use of interactive radio — the 'Talking to New England' project.

The other half of the partnership is Sydney Educational Radio (2SER). 2SER-FM is the radio station which operates the E (Educational) Class Medium Power Licence allocated to the Sydney Area. The station is owned by Sydney Educational Broadcasting Ltd, a company which is jointly owned by Macquarie University and the University of Technology. The company was awarded its licence in 1978 and first went to air in October 1979. The objective of the station was to broadcast educational programmes using the resources of the two institutions and the local community. Guidelines for its operations included that it should promote education in its broadest sense and that it should provide as much access to the community as it reasonably could.

It was planned that 2SER should build up a range of programming by encouraging academic staff, students and the local community to take an active part in production. The station now broadcasts 24 hours a day with a small full-time staff who work together with a large number of volunteers. These include university staff, students and members of the local community who take part in programme production, announcing and many other associated tasks.

In an historical sense it was inevitable that the University of New England and 2SER paths would cross; what was not inevitable was that the unlikely partnership would be successful. The people involved in the initial negotiations, although from very different backgrounds, found they had a common commitment to non-élitist education. Before the project could be initiated, however, it was necessary to develop an understanding of what interactive distance education broadcasting could achieve, and then endeavour to put this into practice.

Developing a Theory and Practice of Interactive Distance Education

The quest for innovative and effective specialist educational programming was the domain of 2SER. By 1985 it had undertaken many projects which linked specific audiences to educational institutions. In 1984 2SER was given a special brief by Macquarie University to help identify the problems which potential students in Sydney's western suburbs strike in trying to undertake study. 2SER responded with a six-month intensive project using live 'talkback' radio to elicit information. Although the Western Suburbs Talkback Project did not actually use formal course material, the possibility to do so became obvious. By 1985 2SER was ready to merge formal courses and live talkback in a unique programme initiative.

The University of New England has always been sensitive to the fact that many of its undergraduate students live in the Sydney area. In recognition of this the University has a Centre in Sydney and Weekend Schools are often held there. In early 1985 2SER and the Department of External Studies at the University of New England became involved in discussions regarding the possible use of radio programmes produced specially to complement the University's external teaching resources. It was decided that a pilot series would be produced and broadcast during October 1985. The pilot series would span three defined programming aims:

1 to introduce the University to potential external students in Sydney;
2 to develop a new and varied approach to distance learning using talkback radio;
3 to assist students with information and advice on all aspects of successful external studies.

A standard one-hour programme model was adopted for the pilot series involving a recorded session followed by live talkback. The approximate ratio of each component was 50/50 and allowed for live interaction between the programme host in Sydney who was linked by landline to the academic in Armidale.

Difficulty was experienced initially in involving academics in the series, largely because many could not conceptualize the project, and those that could were sceptical of whether it would work. The Course Development Adviser used persuasion and friendship with close colleagues to gain commitment for a three-programme pilot. Although the participants were mainly non-academics trialing a technique essentially for the delivery of academic content, it was felt that the pilot would be valid.

The pilot series was entitled 'Access to Armidale', and began with a programme entitled 'Tertiary Education Opportunities in Armidale'. As a general programme, it aimed at opening up communication with the University, and used staff of the Department of External Studies and Armidale College of Advanced Education. The second pilot programme was aimed at testing the feasibility of radio as a formal teaching tool. The topic chosen was 'The Role of Business Corporations in Politics', which was adapted from an external politics course. The third and final programme in the pilot series aimed to assist students in their forthcoming examinations, and was presented by the Course Development Adviser and the Student Counsellor.

Evaluation of the pilot project was positive: it worked technically and was clearly within the University's resources. Most importantly the Department of External Studies had an organizational structure which could cope with the necessary project planning. The Course Development Adviser is not élitist and remains a committed equalitarian and a strong believer in mass education. He was therefore able to become the vital link between technical, clerical, secretarial, professional and academic staff, and fostered a determination to succeed amongst all the project staff. In particular, academic staff involved thought it worthwhile, and several students called in, as did members of the public (five or six calls each programme). From the evaluation the basis of a set of aims and objectives and a programme format were established. It was very clear, however, that there were many issues to be resolved before the theory could become general practice.

Universities and radio stations do not have a large commonality. Thus it was felt important to establish at the outset a theoretical base for the practice. A set of aims and objectives was established before the commencement of the 'Talking to New England' project in 1986. These were developed through consultation between the University's coordinator and 2SER's coordinator.

The overall aim of effective distance educational broadcasting is sought jointly by the University of New England and 2SER; however, there are certain objectives that each partner holds as priorities. For instance, for 2SER 'Talking to New England's' development is pitched towards producing a well rounded radio programme which is formal in style, but not as rigid as broadcasting unadapted lectures on radio. The University of New England External Studies Department's main aim is to link as many students as possible with their lecturers in Armidale during weekly broadcasts. Each partner's particular set of sub-goals worked in a dynamic fashion to create an evolving theory of distance education radio programming. The desire to produce good radio, while at the same time retaining educational merit, put the series through a weekly test of checks and balances from the educationalists in Armidale and the radio producers in Sydney. The general objectives were:

> to link students in Sydney with their respective lecturers in Armidale using the radio medium;
>
> to develop a new and varied approach to distance learning using radio talkback;
>
> to create a strong feeling of identification and community amongst external students in Sydney;
>
> to allow lecturers the chance to develop innovative and alternative teaching strategies combined with opportunities to popularize and test their work on a mass communication medium;
>
> to develop talkback as a viable tool for teaching and in doing so extend the current boundaries of this popular form of mass communication;
>
> to spread awareness of the University of New England external studies course to potential students in Sydney;
>
> to present continuing education type programmes to the wider radio audience and encourage listeners to participate through the talkback component.

The successful pilot series in 1985 offered much regarding style and format to the 'Talking to New England' project. The one-hour standard programme unit was chosen where each unit would deal exclusively with one subject. The units themselves consisted of a 'lecture' — although these were often more than just a straight discourse pre-recorded at Armidale — and a live talkback session. The programme was linked by a producer/presenter and occasionally, depending on the peculiarities of the programme, music breaks were included.

It was decided to broadcast the pre-recorded lecture close to the beginning of the programme and for it to be from ten to twenty minutes in duration. To maintain the 'live' nature of the programme, however, a short music insert was programmed five to ten minutes in from the start of the tape to enable the producer/presenter to identify the programme and inform listeners of the talkback session to follow the recorded lecture.

At the conclusion of the lecture the producer/presenter used the outside broadcast line to Armidale to link up live with the guest lecturer. A short interchange followed, by which time callers would have occupied some of the available talkback lines ready for the talkback segment. An average of six to eight calls are taken during a standard programme unit. As part of the practice of educational talkback, the producer/presenter acted as a link between the caller and the academic and helped to develop the discussion.

Problems in Practice

From the establishment of a conceptual foundation for practice it was necessary to engage the University more generally. Whilst the rhetoric at the University is often in favour of projects which increase the interaction between teacher and learner and which have a wider appeal to the community, committing a budget and resources to such a project was another matter. The 'Talking to New England' project was no exception. Through the determination of the project team, with the Course Development Adviser in the vanguard, it was able to use the University system to effect change. The competence in action displayed by the project team established a broad-based support on campus, which was complemented by the arguments of the Course Development Adviser at the relevant University committees. Both were essential ingredients in the thrust for change.

Before the newly found ideas could be put into practice, many issues had to be resolved. It was not possible to put forward a grand plan to increase the interactiveness of distance teaching; incremental development had to be used.

Budgeting and Resources

The first problem to be resolved was money. Although the 2SER costs were reasonable in themselves, they were substantial for the Department of External Studies, which had no budgetary provision for development. One of the Course Development Adviser's duties, however, was to draw up the External Studies Teaching Material Budget, which included a small development fund for academic innovation in distance education. The Department's budget is approved by the Pro Vice-Chancellor and

Deans acting as the External Studies Sub-Committee. The potential demand for a project such as 'Talking to New England' was difficult to demonstrate and so it was decided to ask initially for a small amount for 1986 and finally A$3000 was approved. This amounted to less than 1 per cent of the total External Teaching Material Budget, which meant that strategically no department was noticeably worse off through the tiny amount being redirected to the project. However, the problem remained of whether the budget was sufficient to satisfy demand, and if not, where the extra was to come from. This had been tentatively allowed for by the Course Development Adviser who included a A$4000 contingency item in his budget, and he was also intending to use the A$4000 Initiatives fund if necessary. Demand was such that both these amounts were used.

The budget covered the direct financial cost, which was approximately A$500 per hour (made up of A$250 on production and air time for 2SER, A$110 air time for 2NUR, as well as A$25 air time for 2ARM, A$100 for telephone lines and A$20 for technician overtime). However, there were other large costs which remained 'hidden' in the work of project team members.

Because 'Talking to New England' was (and is) an important priority for 2SER-FM, two producers were given this work as a major part of their production duties. Both producers had been heavily involved in previous educational talkback projects on the station. 2SER's Technical Supervisor also spent part of his time in setting up the 'talkback' system in cooperation with his counterpart in Armidale.

In Armidale the Course Development Adviser and Assistants coordinated the lecturers and the production of their talks as well as targeting the specific student audience. Up to four other staff members of the Department of External Studies monitor and phone in with questions during the broadcast. Thus there were seven staff working on the series in addition to general assistance from the Department of External Studies in terms of dispatch, clerical assistance, word processing, etc. These staffing costs, plus the use of broadcast hardware resources, have been absorbed by the radio station and the University, perhaps without their knowledge.

Establishing a Production System

Another issue to be resolved was the need to establish a production system suitable for both the 'conservative' university and the 'radical' radio station. From a producer's point of view there were two main stages in the production of a 'Talking to New England' programme unit: the structured component coming from Armidale and the live radio component assembled in Sydney. All talks during the series were produced at the University under the supervision of the Audio Visual Sound Technical Officer. The taped talks, together with a written synopsis and a set of six or more follow-up questions, were sent by courier to the producers in Sydney.

Once in Sydney the tapes were checked by the producers, resulting in a script being developed from the taped subject matter. A further set of link questions was then created so that the producer/presenter could maintain the programme flow. The main priority for the producer was to become a successful facilitator on air, and the task of becoming familiar with two new academic areas per week was quite difficult. However, by carefully working through the material and developing tight scripts, the producers were never short of well conceived questions to use in exploring the programme area.

A standard programme introduction was produced together with special insert promotions which could be used at any point during the programme, especially between two distinct programme units. To ensure that things worked smoothly, production meetings were conducted over the telephone prior to each broadcast.

Selection of Programme Material

Another issue was the selection of appropriate course material. The choice of programmes was based on self-selection. A general invitation was circulated within the University and those who responded were accepted. A couple of academics with courses which had high student numbers were especially asked to participate, but no pressure was applied.

During the first semester of 1986 no advice on programme structure was given to academic staff. Hence the programmes ranged from lectures with very little opinion to informal discussions about problems in practical work. This lack of direction was deliberate, as the Course Development Adviser felt that the learning process for the academics was important. It meant that advice by 'experienced' academics could be given in second semester. If, however, it had been realized that the project was going to be so popular, maybe more direction in subject suitability would have been planned from the start. An obvious area would have been to concentrate on first year courses with student numbers in excess of 150 in Sydney.

Plugging in the Audience

Another issue was how to get the audience to listen. The success of the series depended on having the external students listening and participating. Incorporating the broadcasts as part of their course work was an important objective. All external students were sent a broadcast schedule at the beginning of the semester. Students in the subject were reminded by mail two weeks prior to the broadcast and were asked to listen if they were in the broadcast area, or send in questions if they were outside the area. Students were telephoned on the day of the broadcast and reminded to participate. Student representatives in the broadcasting area were given questions, which had been sent to the Department of External Studies prior to the programme, and were asked to pose them on air. Two assistants in Armidale monitored the programme and phoned in when necessary to keep the talkback session moving. This approach was successful and is still used.

To a lesser extent another objective was to attract an intelligent general audience who could interpret and explore the broadcast course material in diverse and perhaps refreshing ways. Planning for this audience included a script that accommodated the general listener. A typical script would read,

> . . . a warm welcome to you all, particularly students of . . . but also others interested in this subject, and we hope you will make the Armidale connection tonight . . . you are most welcome to take part in making some intelligent and stimulating talkback, even if you are not a student.

Attracting this general audience involved several publicity devices, most of which were implemented by 2SER because the University lacked the expertise and time. A promotional announcement lasting between 60 and 90 seconds was produced and programmed weekly in advance of each specific broadcast. The promotion highlighted the most interesting and accessible aspects of the forthcoming programme, and included tightly edited segments lifted from the pre-recorded presentations. The overall pitch of the promotions concerned the unique nature of the series and that it was a new listening experience as well as a totally new approach to talkback.

In addition to this 'on-air' publicity, articles and schedules were published in 2SER's programme guide/magazine, *Listening Post,* which reaches a strong core of station subscribers, as well as many other listeners in the general community.

As a major initiative in attracting general listeners, an article was published in the television and radio supplement of the *Sydney Morning Herald* on Monday 28 July 1986, which coincided with the beginning of the second semester series. Publicity for the project in Newcastle and Armidale centred on the local press, and in Armidale the local Australian Broadcasting Commission AM station was also used.

The Programme Schedule

The 'Talking to New England' schedule for 1986 included programmes on topics such as Hinduism, entrepreneurship, design, psychology, climatology, study and exam skills, music, poetry and 'Do we need a university in the western suburbs of Sydney?' The strength of this approach is that it is very varied; however, it does lack full integration with the teaching material. The academics tended to be enthusiasts rather than those with professional radio expertise. It became clear that whilst they were reasonably confident on air, their presentation style did not necessarily encourage the students, most of whom had never used talkback radio to call in. This was highlighted in the first two programmes; the first on cognitive psychology and the second on telephony. The first talk used educational jargon and resulted in one call; the other used a lighter approach and attracted six calls. Nevertheless, these initial programmes helped to establish a pool of experienced academics who were potential supporters of the project, and this constituted an important part of the project's incremental development.

An underlying issue was that the human resource assistance at the University was restricted to that already in place. The time expended on the project by the Course Development Adviser and his secretary created difficulties for work on other developments. Valuable assistance was provided by other members of the Department, but time was always at a premium. The academic experience and commitment of the Course Development Adviser to a fusion of theory and practice meant that the theoretical aspect was not pushed to counterproductive levels. Competency in action by the project team was emphasized; gentle use of rhetoric with the academics was seen as essential.

At the beginning of the project it was attempted to use the Radio University of New England (RUNE) linked to the University of Technology (and subsequently Newcastle), however, it proved to be more trouble than it was worth. The station was staffed predominantly with student volunteers who were not always reliable. On occasions the Course Development Adviser had to switch over to the 2SER landline link himself. Some listeners were upset at this educational use of the radio station and abused the station manager because the 'Wally Viscious Heavy Metal Show' had gone off the air! The quality of reception in the monitors' homes in Armidale was so poor that on occasions they had to phone in without having heard the programme.

A continuing problem was that a large number of external students did not receive broadcasts live, although the students themselves did not complain. Indeed, the responses from the students outside the broadcast area were every bit as positive as those within the broadcast area. The programmes did not become part of mainstream external teaching. Many students were unaware of the technique, and many academics were very unsure of its applicability to their subject.

Evaluation

From the beginning of the project student and academic evaluation was seen as important; on the basis of the evaluation findings several changes have been made to the current format of the project. At the end of 1986 academics were sent evaluation sheets about the year's broadcast schedule. In addition, students in the broadcast area were sent evaluation forms with memos reminding them of the broadcast, and those in the non-broadcast area were sent evaluation sheets with their cassettes. Also on-air questions and media coverage gave valuable information about the strengths and weaknesses of the 'Talking to New England' project. During 1986 2SER entered the 'Talking to New England' programme for a Pater Award for community broadcasting. This was successful and led to publicity in the local and national press. Such favourable press coverage was welcomed in the University and many congratulatory letters were received from within the university executive and council.

Academic Views on 'Talking to New England'

The evaluation responses from the academic staff at the University were very encouraging. Although they stated their preparation time as varying from one to thirty hours, all wanted to continue using radio in their teaching. It should be remembered, however, that these were academics who had initially volunteered their service. Typical academic staff comments were:

Surprisingly worthwhile and productive. (musicology lecturer)

We treated the Semester II programme as a means of aiding

students' 'revision' of material done in Semester I — it seems a useful way of doing that. (history lecturer)

Quite satisfying. Congratulate Sydney presenters — they did their homework. (history lecturer)

I found it enjoyable and stimulating and a valuable way of communicating with my students (as well as others). (education lecturer)

Finally, an unsolicited written comment by an English lecturer in mid-1987 stated:

Would you please convey my thanks to everyone involved. I gave a session last night . . . for English . . . students, and found that the whole operation worked smoothly and well. I was very much put at my ease by . . ., the announcer, who comperes the session and I was most impressed indeed by the amount of preparation.

Student Views on 'Talking to New England'

Each student in the broadcast areas was sent an evaluation form. They were asked to fill it in immediately after the programme and return it to the Department of External Studies. Students in the non-broadcasting area were sent a modified evaluation form with the cassette of the programme and were asked to return it with the cassette. Again the students were generally enthusiastic about the use of talkback radio. There were no significant differences in responses between subject areas, between semesters, or between broadcast/non-broadcast areas. Some typical comments were:

The talkback section gave a broader view of how the lecturer feels about his subject matter.

I feel this method of communicating greatly enhanced the course for external students and gives them a better feeling of participation.

Terribly unnerving talking on radio (but practice makes perfect so more talkback radio please).

Two related matters are worth emphasizing. First, the students outside the area consistently responded positively to receiving the cassettes. This can probably be explained by the advantage of being able to listen to them in their own time. The spontaneity of the broadcast cassette was also remarked upon. The fact that some of their questions were asked on-air further pleased them. In fact, the idea of soliciting questions from students in the non-broadcast area occurred as a result of previous suggestions made by students, as was the idea of networking the programme. Therefore, the Newcastle station, 2NUR, was brought into the project for a trial period in September 1986, and it remains an integral part of the project. 2ARM, an Armidale community radio station, is now used in Armidale, replacing the University radio station which proved unreliable.

Improvements in the rate of student calls also come from the use of suggestions made in the 1986 evaluation. More appropriate techniques to evoke talkback responses from students are now adopted by the academic, as is the judicious use of questions sent in by students outside the broadcast area.

The number of calls per programme varied from one to thirteen. The thirteen was for an ancient history programme on Sulla, where the question and answer session was very factual. Twelve calls were received for a programme on cancer cells, which seemed to generate calls associated with emotions. Five to six seems to allow optimum discussion between student and academic. The number of questions received from outside the broadcast area has varied from nil to eight with the average being three and a half.

The calls vary considerably, but the following give an idea of their tone.

(Poetry programme) *Student:* ' . . . Hello Professor . . . you gave a very explicit talk — I'm in my first year and was wondering if I have to use all the literary terms that you used? . . .'
Academic: 'No . . . but you'll pick them up gradually — this talk is available on tape and you can listen to it later in the year and you can stop the talk at your own ease and look up the unfamiliar terms in the library.'
(Business programme) *Student:* 'Hello Professor . . . in a recent Residential School we talked about the concept of self-help with respect to small business . . . and I just wondered whether you have come across any examples from overseas of this aspect of small business — the ideas of small businessmen getting together to form lobby groups, extend political pressure to affect policies . . . do you know of any examples of that sort of thing happening?'
Academic: 'I suppose the biggest example would be in the USA where the National Federation of Independent Business had

500-600 thousand members . . . and Canada and Japan both have large, small business lobby groups . . . however as I mentioned in my talk — Europe is different, exhibiting a strong linkage between small enterprise, large enterprise and government.'

(Hinduism programme) *Student:* 'Yes, hello Dr . . ., in your course I'm doing the essay on Hindu art and spiritualism and I find that I keep coming up against the problem that we've got as Europeans — that we describe other non-Europeans' types of art as grotesque, coarse or very fine. I wonder how much you can apply European aesthetics to Hindu aesthetics. . . . Could you define what you mean by art in that essay question . . .?

Academic: 'Well you've certainly given me quite a difficult problem there [combined laughter]. Let me try to tackle them one by one . . .'

(Telephony programme) *Academic:* 'This idea with children competing with telephones is something I hadn't thought about — and I should have done — it's a very good point — and I'd like to turn the thing around to you and ask if you have a howling child and a ringing telephone which one would you answer first . . .'

Student: 'I think probably . . . I would pick up the howling child and try to cope with both of them — the howling child first and then the telephone — and try to cope with both.'

Academic: 'That's a nice compromise — but your basic point is totally legitimate — one of my problems is I don't have a telephone at home and I have never thought of the phone competing with children for the mother's attention — and that's something I'm very grateful to you for bringing it to my attention . . . extremely grateful.'

(Design programme) *Student:* 'Hello, my name's Anne . . . I was listening last week and was interested to hear you talking about the planning process . . . I've just discovered a lot of frustration — you spoke about leaving your work for a while, and then coming back to it with renewed confidence . . . I've done that but I certainly haven't felt that little warm feeling inside . . .'

Academic: I'm sorry Anne, if I gave the wrong impression — it takes a while to cultivate this approach — in one semester, we can't open up that magic door to the world of design . . . but you should get a surprise by the time you get to the end of the course. Particularly when we start to work in field groups in a few weeks time. As I have made the point to many students — more than

50% pass at credit level or better . . .'

Student: 'Yes, I just feel that not having done any courses like this before — and I've never had any drawing experience — so I've been thrown in the deep end . . .'

Academic: 'It's a good place to start . . . yes it's harder for external students because design is traditionally taught in a studio where students bounce ideas off each other — so the internals have a somewhat easier time.'

Student: 'Yes, the isolation does cause a problem — you can't talk to anyone about what you're doing . . .'

Academic: 'Yes, well hopefully when we get the class together at the weekend school — that a lot of these problems will become less difficult.'

Radio Presenter: 'Yes, on that feeling of isolation we're doing our little bit with the radio programme to beat that problem . . .'

Academic: 'I'm very much interested in this programme for that reason — it's another way in which we can get in touch with the students . . .'

(Another) *Student:* 'Hello Chris . . . towards the end of the talk you spoke about leaving room for individual expression, I was wondering whether you could elaborate on that idea a bit more and especially maybe give examples of city sub-divisions where that has happened. . . .'

Academic: 'Yes Bill, next week my talk will feature that very question . . . but I'll give a basic outline of that. . . .'

Concluding Comments

The 1986 'Talking to New England' project's success was due in the first place to the joint commitment of the initial project personnel to non-élitist interactive distance education and their ability to take advantage of the fact that the historical environment was ready for such a development. The momentum for success was given a major fillip by the subsequent enthusiasm of the academics and students for the project. It continued because of the remarkable amount of support given by 2SER staff and up to six staff in the Department of External Studies who worked in a non-hierarchical organization and gave up their own time on Monday evenings. The University has thanked them but not rewarded them in any other way.

The project was repeated in 1987 with some improvements. The networking permanently included the 2NUR and 2ARM community radio stations in Newcastle and Armidale. Dealing with a professional body, as opposed to a student body, has organizational advantages — radio is no exception. The change from the University of New England's student radio station to 2ARM provided not only professional broadcasting techniques but also better quality FM reception. This meant that all internal students in Armidale could tune in, as well as the Department of External Studies staff monitoring the programme. Programme link-up through Telecom was the responsibility of 2SER in Sydney who were closer geographically and personally to the key link in the project: the Telecom Sydney Operations Centre. By 1987 the style of the announcers was even more finely attuned to the academics.

Some individual academics or academic departments broadcast a series of programmes with marked advantages in the subsequent student/teacher relationship. A wider range of academic disciplines became involved, and their positive support was an important factor in the University eventually making a continuing commitment to the project. Some academics were beginning to develop their on-air techniques in ways which encouraged talkback. The following responses in the 1987 academic evaluation illustrate this:

> There is no doubt in my mind that the talkback segment is the main attraction. Therefore the pre-recorded lecture should be limited to 20 minutes and the topic should appeal to as wide an audience as possible. I suggest the pre-recorded segment would be less stilted if it were in the form of dialogue — not scripted dialogue because that could only be carried off by professional actors. In fact, the sort of dialogue that is carried on between lecturer and anchor person in Sydney is often more educative than the 'lecture'.

> I think that presenters ought always be sensitive to the specific advantages of the medium and not merely use it as just a 'lecture' forum.

In general, the project helped increase the profile of external students in the University. Broadcast delivery of teaching material was dealt with for the first time. Subsequently, another project using one-way video with two-way audio was supported by the academic administrative hierarchy (Deans and Pro-Vice Chancellor) as well as by individual academics and departments. It has also helped raise the profile of community extension work. The following comments from the 1987 academic evaluation illustrate this:

These broadcasts, besides being an excellent teaching medium, are extremely valuable in their own right as extensions of the university role in the community.

[They] provide an opportunity to publicize the sorts of things we do to the broader community [sic].

On one occasion a call made by the Mayor of Newcastle on his car phone, to a programme about city planning (or lack of it) epitomized this sort of community response mentioned by the academic above.

The University subsequently agreed that interactive broadcasting be a line item in the 1988 External Teaching Material Budget, which enabled an early commitment to fifty hours of air-time for 1988. This attracted a reduced broadcasting rate and perhaps more importantly enabled the University to negotiate a more favourable broadcast time (8-10 pm, rather than 9-11 pm). This commitment allowed earlier programming and publicity to the potential audiences, including Newcastle and Sydney, and the on-campus students in Armidale, as well as specific interest groups (such as teachers and Bush Fire Brigades), depending on the programme.

This earlier commitment of resources by the University encourages notification of the programmes, if not the programme content itself, to be integrated into the teaching material. By second semester 1987, the fourth semester of broadcasting, some of the programmes were being integrated into the material. An ancient history course audio cassette to introduce the teaching staff was dispatched to all students with a promotion for the radio programme. Another ancient history course and an education course referred in their print materials to the content of their forthcoming radio programmes.

Some interesting side benefits have emerged from the 'Talking to New England' project. For example, many of the lecturers who took part in the broadcasts gained insights into their own teaching and communication methods. The relationship with their students was put on public show and added a dimension to their own self-assessment; a good performance added to self-esteem. The same could be said concerning students' self-expression skills. The added pressure of being on talkback radio could be seen as inhibiting, yet students asked a host of interesting and creative questions. No student 'clammed up' on air. Many became entertaining and anecdotal about their course work, through which much 'healthy' conversation followed with their academics. However, it would be interesting to know more about those students who did not directly participate because they felt nervous or inadequate about the experience. For the ones who did participate live talkback was a positive influence on the way they communicated about their work.

Nowadays at the University interactive radio has been accepted as a legitimate delivery technique for course content. Academics and students alike find it an appropriate and enjoyable delivery mechanism and even the University establishment supports it. The 'Talking to New England' project is an example of how innovation can be successfully introduced into a conservative institution.

Exactly why it succeeded when it succeeded is not difficult to identify in hindsight. There is no doubt that the time was right at both 2SER and the University for such a development. Equally important was the non-hierarchical organizational structure of both arms of the project team, which encouraged the team members to give a commitment above and beyond what could have been reasonably expected in both institutions. The philosophical commitment to non-élitist education demonstrated by the team's actions and the project leader's rhetoric gave it a sound ideological underpinning.

The wider message for distance education development work is that if the complex interaction of the historical environment, organizational structure and ideological commitment, which allowed the 'Talk to New England' project to succeed, occurs in other development projects, the possibility of success will be greatly increased.

Chapter 7

Teaching Distance Education

Bruce King

There were expressions of interest in a professional qualification for distance educators at the Fourth Biennial Forum of the Australian and South Pacific External Studies Association (ASPESA) in Perth in 1979. The South Australian College of Advanced Education (SACAE) made the first move and proposed a Graduate Diploma in Distance Education which the Forum endorsed. This was subsequently developed by the College and submitted to its local accrediting authority in April 1981. The course enrolled its first students in February 1983. This chapter considers the development and delivery of that programme.

It is probably helpful to put the cart before the horse for a moment. The focus here is on the development process, but some introduction to the product will provide a point of reference in the following discussion.

Description of the Graduate Diploma

The course is the equivalent of one year of full-time study. It is only available externally and is normally taken part-time over three years. This is acknowledged in the course structure which consists of three year-long units, comprising between them some eight discrete modules. The modules were initially conceived and taught as separate units and were combined into their present form to accommodate changes to the College's academic calendar. The annual units and their modular components are:

Development and Design in Distance Education, incorporating
    Introduction to Distance Education
    Programme Development in Distance Education
    Instructional Design in Distance Education

Technology and Student Support in Distance Education, incorporating
    Communication Technology in Distance Education
    Administration of Distance Education
    Student Support in Distance Education

Evaluation and Project in Distance Education, incorporating
    Evaluation in Distance Education
    Distance Education Project

The final modular component is double-weighted, in that expectations of students are twice those which apply in each other module and it is normally taken over two-thirds of the final year of the course. Each of these modules will be discussed separately, as they were designed and developed, but first some attention will be given to more general issues concerning the steps taken in developing the programme which, from an unsteady beginning, has enjoyed considerable success. Part of the purpose here is to chart that unsteady beginning. This is in keeping with the strongly held view of the small group who were responsible for the Graduate Diploma that the experience of distance educators should be documented and shared.

The Core Team

The term 'core team' had no status within SACAE and was a matter of self-designation. Although many others were involved in preparation of the Graduate Diploma course, it was always the case that a small group took responsibility for managing the process, determining not only what would happen but how their purposes would be met, and arguing for their standards with others they persuaded to work with them. Despite a change in membership and the absence of one member on leave for several months, the core maintained their control over the course development process throughout. The members of this group were initially Gary Willmott, Rosemary Luke, Ian Mitchell and the present author. Anne Forster subsequently joined the team.

Willmott and the author had enjoyed a close professional relationship since 1975 as the two lecturers in curriculum studies at the City Campus of the College. Their educational perspectives were very similar, to the point where either worked easily with course materials developed by the other. They joined the distance education group, having been responsible for a Graduate Diploma in Curriculum

Development which was largely taught by working with teachers *in situ* as they undertook various practical projects. Both lecturers had considerable experience in producing external teaching materials with a strong applied focus, and drew heavily on adult learning theories, (e.g., Brundage and Mackeracher, 1980) and contemporary British approaches to curriculum theory, (e.g., Stenhouse, 1975; MacDonald and Walker, 1976) in their work. Willmott was the first Coordinator of the distance education programme and assumed major responsibility for it, both academically and administratively. He left the College in mid-1984 to take up a senior administrative position within another institution; the present author was appointed Head: External Studies within SACAE in August of the same year, but continued to work in the team until the course materials were completed early in 1985.

Rosemary Luke entered the programme on a short-term research contract, having previously lectured in English and librarianship. Her early responsibilities included the compilation and authorship of an annotated bibliography on distance education. Although intended to assist course planning, this was eventually distributed to students as part of the first set of course materials. Luke quickly acquired a comprehensive knowledge of current and available sources on distance education and assumed the role of editor within the group. Her incisiveness and authority on matters of presentation and style were accepted, and she was given final editorial authority over all written contributions to the course. Over her own objections, Luke was pressed into both writing course materials and teaching in the programme and was appointed to a lectureship in distance education in 1984. At the end of 1985 she left the College to become a teacher librarian.

Most of the team were newcomers to the distance education fraternity in Australia. Ian Mitchell provided the link with the personalities and practices of those we came to see as our colleagues. As Head of External Studies in one of the colleges subsequently amalgamated as SACAE, he had initiated the proposal for a distance education course and participated in the planning process since 1979. His knowledge of the field was drawn both from an extensive range of personal contacts and several years as the foundation and executive editor of *Distance Education.* Although involved in the writing process, Mitchell moved quickly into organizing the teaching of the course and worked closely with tutors drawn from outside the core team. He is now the Course Coordinator of the programme.

During early 1984 Rosemary Luke was on leave, and Anne Forster was appointed as the first Lecturer in Distance Education within the College. Her background included research at the Institute of Educational Technology at the Open University of the United Kingdom and involvement in external programmes in the New South Wales Department of Technical and Further Education, and at the Royal Melbourne Institute of Technology. Following Willmott's departure, Forster exercised a shaping influence in the philosophy of the course team, drawing both on her formal studies in evaluation and on a passionate commitment to the liberating power of external study for students. In late 1984 she became Course Coordinator, holding the position until the end of 1985 when she moved to Canada.

The Course Team Process

In the planning which preceded accreditation it was agreed that the Graduate Diploma would be produced using a course team approach. Two things need to be said about this decision: first, it marked a significant shift in practice for SACAE, in that hitherto most external materials were prepared by individual academics, working alone; second, the group was initially conceived of as being quite large, involving all who would make a contribution to a given unit, including personnel from outside the College.

The group process prevailed, but it tended to be dominated by the personalities and commitment of the core team. Planning for the first unit began with a larger group which fragmented after the first one or two meetings. The core team quickly came to reject the notion of drawing on a wide range of expertise across and outside the College and preferred to make their own way, consulting with others over quite specific contributions which were then incorporated into the materials by members of the core.

There was a number of reasons for this. First, the core argued that all those in the course team should accept a collective responsibility for the course. Some who had expressed initial interest did not share the commitment or academic orientation of those who became the core and were not prepared to assume the responsibility being offered.

Second, both Willmott and the present author rejected conventional approaches to instructional design and asserted their views from the earliest meetings. This may well have caused those with different views to lose interest in the proposed course. The particular arguments will be discussed later.

Third, Willmott had a very firm view of the quality of course content he wished to achieve and was determined that the course materials should be both attractive and accessible to students. Those who became members of the core shared Willmott's perspective and were prepared to ensure that his view of the quality of the proposed course prevailed.

Fourth, dissatisfaction with the first contributions to the materials produced under contract reinforced the growing view of core members that quality would come from exercising much greater group control over the drafting of course materials than contracting allowed. Perhaps too much had been expected of contract authors working in isolation. This further constrained participation in the group working on the award.

Fifth, the actual drafting process adopted under the notion of group responsibility was intimidating, particularly as participants had little or no experience of the elements of peer appraisal it involved. This may have simply been too threatening for some. While the core team came to value and even enjoy the group review process, it was stressful for those who made early contributions. Despite attempts to handle the review of materials in a sensitive manner, it was simply the case that the core were using a process they had adjusted to over time and which, for others, was more direct and critical than they may have expected. Further, through their shared experience core team members had reinforced personal friendships and the normative commitments they had to the programme. Critical exchanges were less likely to threaten them as individuals.

The stress for newcomers to the review process was exacerbated by the speed at which the core team worked. Consciousness of limited time was ever present, and with experience the group became skilled at collective editing under pressure, often working and making shared decisions at a rate which others, new to the group, could not match and found disconcerting. In part, of course, the core team had developed shared understandings and communication short-cuts which made their work both more efficient and less accessible to an outsider. In retrospect, this seems a critical component of the kind of creative process under study.

The notion of collective responsibility involved an understanding that decisions about the programme would be group-based. Further, the team would all be designers, authors, editors, transformers, teachers and administrators of the course. Two comments are necessary here. First, within this collective model some members had special responsibilities, for example, Luke acted as a team member and then subsequently undertook final editing responsibility. Similarly, the course coordinator was officially responsible within the College structure for administration of the course and often had to take decisions with minimal consultation, although these were rarely contested because of the shared perspective of the group. The Coordinator also chaired meetings and was expected to exercise some leadership within the team. Second, the roles fused over time. Members became adept at incorporating design and transformation considerations into their own writing and in the group review of draft material.

The writing and review process involved the following steps:

1   a team would be gathered to prepare an individual unit;
2   one member would assume responsibility for managing the meetings, for example, convening the group, arranging photocopying, etc.;
3   there would be an attempt to take decisions on the structure and general approach of the unit;
4   individuals would nominate for (or be pressured into) writing tasks;
5   at subsequent meetings the group would review and comment on drafted materials (and this was frequently done at first sighting);
6   the writer would rewrite the materials in the light of comments made, or another team member would take over the redrafting;
7   the materials as improved would be subjected to a further review, although sometimes at this point they were rejected;
8   there would be a further tight edit undertaken outside the group and, depending on available time, the manuscript would be either brought back to the group for a final review or sent straight for typesetting.

From what has been said above, and because of its nature, the process generated a degree of conflict, although less than might have been expected because of the cohesiveness in the core team. The judgment of those involved was that the approach adopted was successful on at least two other counts: the course materials produced were very well received and the process was a most powerful professional development exercise.

There were drawbacks, however. Conflict and the difficulties associated with new members have been mentioned. Perhaps the most persistent was fatigue, the product of too much to do, too little time to do it, and the knowledge that with the completion of every unit it had to be taught as the next cycle of development began. On two occasions, when preparing the *Administration* and *Student Support* units, core members were almost too tired to function properly, yet were driven by timelines which could not be exceeded. Considerable time was wasted in each instance as the team sought, without success, for a fresh approach to structuring the new unit.

Part of the trouble was that staff were overcommitted. At SACAE staff workloads are based on students taught, and no allowance is made for the development of teaching materials. Such overload may be inevitable in periods of limited resources, particularly if one accepts that people with the necessary energy or enthusiasm for development projects are likely not to be underemployed when new ventures are proposed.

The fatigue problem was most evident when the core team faced the last major undertaking, preparation of the unit *Student Techniques in Distance Education*. There was no real agreement on what we should attempt to cover and a total lack of ideas for some conceptual framework. The group faced a real tension between our theoretical perspective and confidence in our students and the weariness and sense that we just could not do it all again. The resolution of this dilemma is discussed later.

The relationship between the course team process and the membership of the core group was very close. Because of this, change was to be expected when its membership altered. Comment has already been made on the difficulties facing new members of the course team. The hegemony of the core group was such that newcomers tended to adapt to the existing process or be bypassed by it. On one occasion at least 'outsiders' joined together in a de facto sub-group in an attempt to maintain a degree of control over their intellectual product, and so manage their contribution to the course development process.

Furthermore, there was a discernible shift in emphasis when Anne Forster replaced Gary Willmott in 1984. Forster brought a new perspective to the award and was a significant influence on the rest of the group. Her specific contributions included the advocacy of a much stronger and more applied focus on evaluation within the course, both as content and process, and a deep personal commitment to supporting students towards the personal liberation and goal realization distance education affords. The team would have contended that these were both major emphases in the award from the beginning, but this would have reckoned without Forster's commitment and advocacy. She moved the team from an intellectual commitment to distance education and a preoccupation with developing a course which would be favourably received towards better, practical and interactive distance teaching. That she did so, and maintained the close ties of friendship in the group, further underscores her considerable personal and professional strengths.

If one may be permitted a generalization which both oversimplifies individual contributions and reveals a major truth about the course team process, Willmott and King provided the focus and determination which were necessary to get the Graduate Diploma up and running, while Forster and Luke modelled how we should work with our students.

Ian Mitchell's role was rather different. He was the one member of the group who had any standing or was even known in the distance education community when the course was mooted, and we relied on his knowledge and extensive personal connections. It was very much in keeping with his personality and commitment to the field that he both accepted and supported others shaping the course; indeed, his commitment to delivery of the prepared units made the continuing development process possible. Mitchell understood that the rest of the team did not know as much about distance education as might have been expected of them, given the task they were undertaking. By gently seeking to extend the boundaries of what was being addressed, in particular in relation to the academic and research expectations we had of students, and avoiding obtrusive reference to mistakes being made, he both influenced and gave licence to others who helped in bringing his initial conception to reality.

Finally, there was a serious commitment on the part of the core group to involving students in the course development process. This was never realized to the level of our aspirations, but steps were taken in the right direction. First, the course planning process involved serious consideration of feedback from students on a unit-by-unit basis. It was possible in some instances to address a specific point of concern, such as assignment work, in the subsequent unit. This process was largely reactive, although the team actively sought student comment. For example, a telephone conference was run in the third unit and staff met with almost half of the first cohort of students at the ASPESA Forum at Toowoomba in 1983. Second, contributions to content were sought from students who were experienced practitioners, for instance, one student was interviewed as part of a group of expert practising instructional designers in Unit 3. Third, there were student representatives on the Planning Committee of the award throughout, who acted as sounding boards for course development suggestions. Fourth, a comprehensive unit monitoring instrument was incorporated into the materials for the *Evaluation* unit, which afforded very specific feedback thereon.

These steps notwithstanding, the core team wished to share the development process in some more substantial manner. Considerable scope given to students to pursue their own professional interests through applied assignment work and a high degree of interactive sharing of experience were created in the *Student Support* unit by using part of the course development process as content, and by allowing students to determine their own purposes for the unit and achieve this through one-to-one dialogue with their tutors. This is described in more detail below.

Design Decisions

Both prior to accreditation and in the early weeks of planning the *Introduction to Distance Education* unit, decisions were taken which affected the whole award. In retrospect it is difficult to explain some of them. Often quite pragmatic arguments prevailed, yet the decisions were consistent with the educational stance of the course team members. This may be explained in part by the sometimes unspoken but nonetheless shared understandings we had about what the group was trying to achieve.

The three most important determinants of the decisions taken were: the political judgment that an in-service rather than pre-service course would receive widest support in the field; a view of our likely clientele, informed by a perspective on adult learners; and a commitment to producing course materials which were of very high quality. The last of these was very much a product of the group's desire for legitimacy; we shared the view that a potentially critical professional community would determine the success of the award very much on the basis of the quality of the first set of teaching materials produced. Our collective fear was the judgment that the College had taken upon itself the task of providing in-service for the field and then failed to match the quality of course materials emanating from other institutions.

There is a tension between these three shaping elements and the group was very conscious of this at the time, for instance, the potential conflict between our preoccupation with the course materials and the commitment to students shaping their own study goals through the programme. The tension was not resolved. Our stance was that curriculum development necessarily involves an accommodation of the ideal to the practical, that the quest for perfect solutions to developmental problems is misconceived, and that our approach should be as defensible as possible.

Equally there were positive relationships between the three areas. For example, in considering potential students, it appeared likely that enrollees would bring very different levels of sophistication as distance educators to the programme. This was consonant with our view of an in-service course providing opportunities for students to meet a range of professional needs of their own determination. Further, it related to design decisions about the course materials, including the need to provide alternative study pathways and responsiveness to students' proposals to vary aspects of their programme. Thus the major determinants of design decisions existed in a dynamic tension, reflecting the need to marry practical and educational considerations without conceding some overall coherence and defensibility.

Some of the decisions taken were:

1 in relation to the quality of materials
   a materials would be print-based, typeset, and packaged in a coordinated set of purpose designed loose-leaf binders;
   b each modular unit would be structured differently, to demonstrate a range of presentational, methodological and assessment techniques;
   c the course materials would be conceived as a set of professional resources, to be retained by the student, and embodying exercises and models which could be applied in a variety of distance education settings;
   d the print materials would be complemented with a range of non-print media; and
   e materials would be visually attractive, accessible to readers, and provide a production standard within the field;

2 in relation to perceptions of students
   a students would be distance education practitioners with a diversity of special interests, in fields like teaching, administration, graphic art, instructional design;
   b students would reflect the range of distance education applications, e.g., schools of the air, primary and secondary correspondence education, universities and colleges, technical and further education;
   c students would have very different levels of understanding and skills in distance education;
   d students as experienced practitioners would wish to be valued, have their expertise acknowledged, and be trusted to exercise autonomy and professional responsibility in relation to their own study programmes;
   e traditional power relations between staff and students should be broken down as much as possible;
   f each student should be expected to develop professionally through the programme and, while no status or exemption would be granted, could negotiate study outside that provided in the course materials, or pursue different paths within them;
   g students would be encouraged to contribute to the course materials; and
   h attempts would be made to engage with students beyond the conventional tutor-student relationship, for example, in

organizing conference participation, assisting with publications, and encouraging open dialogue with students as professional equals;

3　in relation to the in-service nature of the course
   a　the course materials should provide both flexibility and support such that students could pursue interests at levels commensurate with their professional experience;
   b　the experience of practitioners at all educational levels should be valued and acknowledged within the course;
   c　the course would be available only to practitioners;
   d　all practitioners would be exposed to the experience of being an external student through the course;
   e　students would be encouraged to undertake applied assignments within their own professional contexts;
   f　students would not be required to attend on-campus at any point in the programme or in any other way cut across their vocational and personal commitments beyond the necessary allocation of time and energy demanded by their chosen study programme;
   g　assessment requirements would be varied to meet the needs, interests and previous experience of individual students; and
   h　the course would provide opportunities for students to clarify their personal learning goals and reflect on their progress towards achieving them.

Development of the Modules

Introduction to Distance Education

There were three notable features of the development of this unit: first, the course team was conscious that many of the decisions they were taking related not only to the unit, but to the whole programme; second, the process of course team activity for the programme was established through the development of the first unit; and third, the notion of contracting authors to prepare unit materials, which had been strongly argued for during accreditation, broke down in practice.

Much of the course team work for the first unit was also about planning for the Graduate Diploma as a whole. A number of the design decisions discussed above were tested immediately. For instance, having determined that the course would be prepared for people currently employed as distance education practitioners, our conception of the range of professional activities which might be covered in the course was challenged. Would we, for example, accept public radio broadcasters or tutors based on remote cattle stations as students? Conversely, additional commitments were entered into which locked the course team into particular approaches for the rest of the programme. For example, the decision to package course materials in a series of four specially designed ring-binders involved graphic art, structural and purchasing considerations to cover a three-year period.

The need to be conscious of the entire process of development was a source of chronic stress. Despite the range of decisions already made, members had considerable uncertainty about the approach and likely content of most of the proposed modules. It is not going too far to say that the team commenced the development process for almost every unit with no clear notion of what they intended to produce. This was offset by a confidence, at least on the part of Willmott and King, that it was all manageable. This may have been unduly arrogant, but their stance was essentially that the Graduate Diploma was no more than another curriculum development exercise, and if specialist expertise were required, it could and would be found. What was not foreseen was how quickly the contracting and brokering processes for obtaining course content foreshadowed during accreditation would break down.

The group development process was established at this point. The personnel, the ways of working, the roles individuals played within the group, were all being sorted through with the knowledge that we would be doing these things for some time together. What should be noted is that there was a political as well as an educational dimension to the decision to proceed using a course team. The educational argument was centrally concerned with staff development and the coherence which could be attained through collective endeavour. The political dimension, and 'political' is used here in a very broad sense, reflected a concern by the dominant group to protect their own view of the standards and course orientation necessary within the award. The collectivity allowed the core group to vet all contributions and propose amendments to, or even reject, material from individual authors about which they had reservations. The group's legitimacy came from educational arguments and notions of participatory democracy; in fact, it was an oligarchy which drew upon others only on its own terms. The members of the core were prepared to be judged on the quality of their product and to triumph or be damned.

As indicated earlier, there was some reinforcement for the

concentration of control in the hands of the core team by the early breakdown of the proposed contracting system for producing materials. The most serious criticism was that the material presented was heavily didactic and did not fit at all well with the commitments made to respecting the experience and expertise of students. Our view was that the students should be able to locate themselves personally and professionally within the course through the first unit, and be assisted to develop their own strategies for using the Graduate Diploma to meet their own legitimate needs. As a result, a new section was planned, the 'Autobiography of a Distance Learner', which came to comprise the first third of the module. This provided a series of structured activities to assist students to reflect on their personal and professional circumstances, reasons for taking the course, learning styles, vocational goals and strategies they intended to adopt for achieving success — however they defined it — throughout the programme.

The course team quickly realized that the time available for the development of each unit module did not allow for such reworking of proposed content. Further, there were some aspects of the proposed course on which they had a considerable agreement and about which they would rather take on additional workload than compromise. An important dimension of this understanding was the recognition that agreement on process, on the approach to be taken in the module, was more important than being clear about the content.

Programme Development in Distance Education

Willmott and King undertook the drafting of the module, as other course team members turned their attention to teaching *Introduction to Distance Education*. The result was their attempt to apply the work they had been doing in curriculum studies to distance education, and in some ways it is the most conventional section of the Graduate Diploma programme. This is particularly so in relation to its structure and presentation.

The content was more interesting and constituted something of an assault on the field. It drew on a series of five propositions which have been discussed elsewhere (see Willmott and King, 1983) and can be restated in the following manner:

1   There is no coherent general theory or broad paradigm of programme development in distance education. The field needs to develop conceptual schemes for drawing together its

fragmented literature and guiding research and practice.

2   The literature on programme development in distance education draws upon the limiting traditions of instructional design and educational technology. The field would be better served in this regard by a curriculum theory which embraces a wider range of concerns and treats them as problematic.

3   Programme development in distance education is characterized by a series of myths and untested assumptions which most

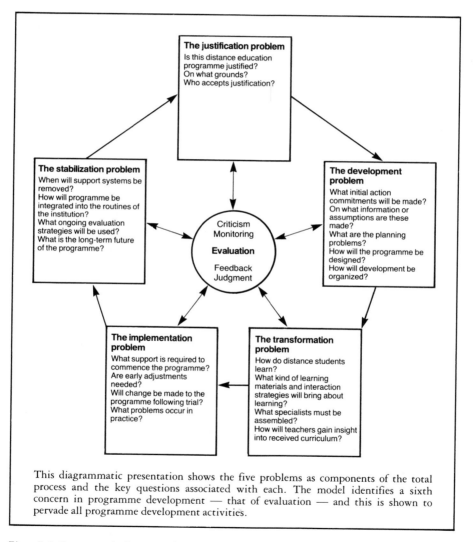

This diagrammatic presentation shows the five problems as components of the total process and the key questions associated with each. The model identifies a sixth concern in programme development — that of evaluation — and this is shown to pervade all programme development activities.

Figure 7.1 Programme development in distance education

analysis fails to acknowledge and examine. There are important questions about the legitimation and justification of distance education which should be of concern to programme developers.

4   Existing analyses of programme development in distance education fail to acknowledge the significance of post-implementation procedures characteristic of successful innovation.

5   To a large degree the literature on course design in distance education is either unknown or ignored by practitioners, probably because it fails to recognize the realities they face.

Using the propositions as points of departure, the authors proposed a conceptual framework (see Figure 7.1) as one possible way of making explicit the critical tasks, problems and relationships which exist in programme development in distance education. Its rationale will not be rehearsed here (see Willmott and King, 1983).

The conceptual framework provided the structural basis for the module. In retrospect the diagrammatic representation suggested a simplicity and linearity of approach which might better have been avoided, although the text stressed the complexity of issues, their diverse interrelationships, and the problematic nature of course development decisions.

Two comments should be made about the application of this model to development of the Graduate Diploma. First, it was very much a reflection of the kind of deliberations involved in preparing the first module. This continued to be true for the remainder of the course development process. Secondly, the consideration of problems and generation of strategies for dealing with them at no stage conformed to the sequential scenario offered in the model. Rather, decisions were taken in the light of a range of concerns which frequently cut across a number of the identified problem areas.

Instructional Design in Distance Education

Because of the theoretical stance outlined above, the course team did not want a unit on instructional design. It was included in the award at the insistence of the Accreditation Committee. Initially nobody wanted to draft the materials. In the attempt to find solutions to our own discomfort, some quite bold design decisions were taken. These also addressed other issues.

For the first time we were confronted with the certain knowledge that some part of our clientele would have considerable expertise in the substantive area of the module and it would be necessary to accommodate hugely different levels of sophistication between students. Further, the team were strongly of the view that any approach to designing distance education which did not have a focus on the preparation of print materials ignored the realities of the field. This took us well outside conventional instructional design approaches but was in strong accord with the transformational principles of MacDonald-Ross and Waller which had assumed considerable influence in our thinking about the course.

The design strategy adopted involved the preparation of three discrete sections. The first was intended for students who sought a good, standard introduction to instructional design or those with some experience of the field who wished to pursue an interest in the area. The section had two distinct strands to meet these different needs. The first strand was a twenty-page guide to an introductory text. The second comprised a series of resource papers and readings designed to extend students' analyses of key debates and alternative viewpoints about aspects of instructional design. The second section looked at the way instructional design was undertaken and considered by five distance education practitioners. It consisted of audio-taped interviews with the five, questions on each, tape transcripts and a general commentary on the interviews. 'Practising Instructional Design in Print' was the third section and covered planning, writing, transformation, review and editing, binding, packaging and assembly of print materials. It was print-based, with a tape-slide presentation and a display of sample print-based materials prepared by individual practitioners which demonstrated a range of cheap, non-technical strategies requiring little professional expertise.

Students were given the option of doing specified assignments from any two of the sections or negotiating a single assessment on any matter of interest to them generally relevant to the area. Within the specified assignments there were both opportunity for directly applied study and considerable difference in the level of sophistication required, although all assignments were equally weighted.

The materials responded to the diverse experience of students by providing quite separate study pathways through the module; thus individuals could complete the requirements by studying quite different things, and by rewarding accomplishment at the student's own self-nominated level of expertise. These were significant departures from existing external teaching practices at SACAE.

This module also marked the end of attempts to contract authors from outside the College. The problems encountered might have been predicted: failure to meet time-lines, incompatibility of what was provided with the orientation of the in-College course team members, and obstacles to participation by the external author created by his own institution (which saw itself as a potential competitor). The decision not to use the contracted materials created a substantial problem for the team, all of whom found themselves unexpectedly pressed into designing and drafting sections of the course. Major assistance came from Ted Nunan, who developed the notion of different study paths, and the External Studies Unit, with both the senior academics, Graeme Speedy and Deane Hutton, taking responsibility for sections of the materials. Rosemary Luke added course writing to her editorial responsibilities.

In part the burden was one of the team's own creation. The decision to contract authors had been taken before the core team had emerged and asserted their control over the programme. It was very much a matter of unwillingness to compromise with their own standards. The delays in submission also enabled the core to consider strategies for dealing with the diversity of student experience in the area. The failure of the contracting process had two consequences: first, the core was left to develop the rest of the programme, and second, it could no longer avoid more conscious planning of the modules before drafting commenced.

Communication Technology in Distance Education

This module is remarkable for the fact that the course team agreed to present the instructional content on video-tape, which may have been the worst design decision taken. It has been subject to the greatest modification following its initial offering and is in the process of major revision.

The decision to base the module on a three-hour video tape was in keeping with a determination to model a range of delivery techniques, a desire to be innovative, and the availability of a staff member with considerable professional expertise in video production. The core team was very inexperienced with the medium, however, and unaware of the constraints involved. There were communication problems, arising both from the difficulties of the inexperienced trying to control the technically expert and the obstacles to close contact between staff working on different campuses. Further, the core were unaware of the limited opportunities for editorial revision of a complex video production and the time involved in post-production and tape duplication. In short, the core lost control over the teaching materials. Our difficulties were compounded by the nature of the content (for example, a section on computers rapidly became embarrassingly out-of-date) and overestimating the accessibility of the materials to students (for instance, nearly all students had indicated they had access to a video-recorder, but the team failed to recognize that this did not mean regular or convenient access).

The module was the least satisfactory overall. Core members were reinforced in the belief that if their view of necessary standards were to prevail, control of the process could not be allowed to move outside the group again. One does not need the wisdom of hindsight to be aware of the objections which could be raised to such assertions of the need for control. The stance of the core team was very much that of the need to maintain control to avoid prescription of content and inflexibilities for students. We saw a necessary disjunction between ends and means.

Administration of Distance Education

This module was largely written before the course team could find an intellectual framework within which to structure the teaching materials. The final product reflects the course team as its most pragmatic, attempting to make virtue out of necessity. The course team was expanded to include other College staff with expertise in educational administration, and various members had views on desirable content. What was missing was any sense of the overall structure or intellectual framework for the module. There is some irony in this, given the determination of the core to exercise greater control over the direction and substance of course components, although the frustration members felt over the development and late delivery of *Communication Technology*, together with a general weariness, was clearly affecting their efficiency. The strategy belatedly adopted was born of desperation. Those wishing to contribute were asked to draft material without considering how their sections might relate to the module overall. This reflected a concern that, as time was running out, we should have something on paper, if only to provide an impetus in some other direction.

The components prepared covered: an introduction to administrative theory, the impact of governmental enquiries on distance education, financial management and planning, staff development, the administration of policy development and change, and staff and job management. The orientation of these discrete sections was very different. The problem for the course team was how these might be brought together and appropriate study paths created for students with different expertise and interests.

This did not afford an easy solution and, after time, the group opted for the non-solution of passing the problem on to students. The decision was taken to make no attempt to bring the six components into some coherent whole, but to emphasize their separate concerns. Students were invited to select any two areas and to undertake an applied exercise in each. Despite their different emphases, levels of sophistication and demands made on readers, the six sections were treated as equal. This decision was not taken as casually as it might seem. Members recognized that the areas had equal potential to allow students to pursue matters of interest and professional relevance to themselves.

Subsequent evaluation supports the design decisions taken. Students were not bothered by our lack of conceptual clarity. Without wishing to diminish the force of that support, it is worth emphasizing that at best the design of this module was the result of a search for a way to capitalize on educational difficulties.

Evaluation in Distance Education

This module drew heavily on the expertise of other College staff who had not previously worked in the Graduate Diploma programme, but was shaped and tightly controlled by the core team. It is more coherent than the sections which precede it, and models the view of the *Programme Development* module that evaluation is central to planning and teaching.

A particular strength is the assessment activity, which is embedded in the substance of the module and establishes an unambiguous connection between content and process. Students' reactions to the module are more rigorously sought through an inbuilt monitoring instrument. The centrality of evaluation in course planning is highlighted by a recapitulation of activities undertaken by students in each earlier module which were evaluative in nature. In essence, there is a movement from the stance of the course thus far, which might be characterized as opening up issues and providing opportunities for students to engage with them both reflectively and in application, to obliging students to identify and come to terms with issues as they arise from their own practice. The difference is one of degree but it is there.

There were excellent contributions from staff outside the core who entered into the course team process wholeheartedly. However, the review process became too daunting and two of the outsiders formed a sub-group, preferring to work on one aspect of the module on their own. Another felt unable to make deletions from an analysis of theories of evaluation which the core felt unbalanced the module through its length. The section was reduced by about one third by the present author, but the original contributor was clearly dismayed by this aspect of the group process.

The assessment activity guides students through the planning of an evaluation exercise in their own field, and is possibly the best example of teaching by involving students in a process offered in the course.

Student Support in Distance Education

This may well be the most satisfactory module in the course. Yet the core team was so overstressed at the point where its development was scheduled that it was decided to produce the *Evaluation* unit first, out of sequence, using the expertise of other staff.

The support module is notable for the following: considerable time was again expended in attempting to find a structure for the materials; the orientation of some of the course team changed markedly during the development process; working on the materials became so engrossing that we had consciously to avoid recommitting the contents of earlier modules; it was during the development process that many of our own ideas and practices were clarified; and finally, the module is so different from where the programme started that it would be better located at the beginning of the Graduate Diploma.

If we had experienced problems in finding a coherent framework for earlier modules, they were as nothing to the difficulties which now confronted the group. The team met for hours over several days in an attempt to find a structural framework and orientation for the module. There were quite different perspectives on what we should be doing. Unfortunately, the view which ultimately prevailed was not clearly understood in the early weeks and for some time members talked at cross purposes.

In introducing the module to the first group of students, we outlined some of the matters which had been important during our discussions:

1   we wanted to reflect adult learning theory in our own teaching to the greatest possible degree;
2   we had a commitment to modelling quite different approaches to written materials with each module;
3   we had been very conscious of the different interests of our students, some of whom worked with children and others with adults, and our concern was to maximize flexibility;
4   we wanted an approach to the materials which allowed us to

raise issues without having to treat them in an equally thorough manner; and

5   we wished to avoid the suggestion that the area lent itself easily to some comprehensive theoretical overview.

This suggests a greater clarity than initially existed. At first we had sought an overview and wanted to provide students with a comprehensive and up-to-date perspective on student support. It was also the case that while team members were not complacent about the degree to which the Graduate Diploma had been responsive to meeting students' perceptions of their own professional needs, most were proud of what had been achieved in the programme and believed its general orientation was sound. Anne Forster challenged us to take a more radical stance. Her view was that members had not yet grappled with their own conceptions of distance education and that this was evident in the way students were regarded. Further, if there was to be any change, this module provided the last opportunity.

The difficulties in finding some direction became so acute that, as Course Coordinator, I attempted an assumption clarification exercise which was referred to above under the heading 'The Course Team Process'. While this made some of our attitudes to the programme more explicit, it did not resolve the block members were experiencing.

Progress was first achieved with a decision on the nature of assessment within the module. The team had been impressed by the work of Barbara Comber, from the College's Graduate Diploma in Reading and Language, who had experimented with assessment based on correspondence with individual students (Comber, 1983). We agreed students would be asked to establish areas of interest for themselves and to write their tutors four letters during the teaching period about what they were learning and any other related matters. The tutors would write individual responses, and participation in this correspondence would be the sole basis for determining assessment, which would be in the form of a non-graded pass.

Secondly, and soon afterwards, the group began to understand Forster's criticisms. In module 2, *Programme Development,* we had argued against adopting deficit approaches to distance education, for example, by assuming that the course materials were the sole determinants of the learning experience and had therefore to be as near perfect as possible. This was very close to the stance we were taking with the present module. We decided to require students to become more self-directed than earlier modules had encouraged or allowed. Further, we wanted to alter the staff-student relationship to make it more collaborative and exploratory than before. These decisions have been discussed elsewhere (Forster and King, 1985).

There was still the problem of how to present the various resources we believed students should receive. We adopted the approach taken in relation to assessment for the rest of the module. All the content would be in the form of letters to the general student group from individual staff. There would be no attempt to present comprehensive treatments of various issues, or to relate the letters one to another. In some instances this would happen, but only because the author concerned chose to do so. Contributions would vary in length, focus and approach, depending on the interest of the lecturer concerned.

This was a new stance for the group. Previously all materials had been presented as products of the course team. Members would this time be exposing themselves as individuals. The group review process was still retained, however, although the attention given previously to consistency of style and approach no longer applied. The approach liberated members of the course team. There was no attempt to produce the definitive contribution; rather, as individuals we took chances and tried to communicate our interests and enthusiasms to students. Often the substance of a letter from another member of the team would stimulate each of us to write something else. There is little doubt that the team found the module easier to write for than had previously been the case, once this stance was adopted.

Two things happened as a result. First, some of us began to realize the satisfactions of a new approach to distance education. Despite long-standing involvement with external students, the genuinely interactive approach had both intellectual and social rewards which some had not previously found in their distance teaching. Second, without initially realizing the implications of our stance, and as a result of Forster's gentle insistence, the group was reconceiving distance education as support for students who faced a particular set of problems in achieving their personal study goals.

Another aspect of this approach was that it contributed to the breaking down of barriers between staff and students. By writing as individuals rather than a group, a personal dimension was added to the course materials. This brought the core team closer to the collaboration with students as equals it desired and espoused, but had found difficult to achieve. Further, it was a much more honest communication. The covert message of much distance course writing is: 'As your tutor, I have a thorough grasp of the field, which I am presenting here in a form you will be able to manage, and with exercises and assignments at points which will reveal to me how well you are mastering and applying the material I am opening up for you.' The message of the materials in this module was closer to: 'I think this item is relevant to the general topic of the module. What do you think? Do you want to pursue it any further?' This may overstate each position, but the team felt they were closer to the second stance.

We tried to be honest about our own uncertainties and described the difficulties we had been having in our attempt to establish a conceptual framework, including the reasons for ultimately rejecting it as a legitimate undertaking. The assumption clarification exercise had not solved our problem, but it did make clear a number of attitudes team members had to our students and as such seemed potentially useful. It was described in one of the letters, and students were invited to reflect on its possible application in their own situation.

Distance Education Project

This double-weighted module had been the subject of longest planning in the award, having been the subject of considerable discussion during the accreditation process. The course materials are briefer than for any other section yet they represent the culmination of the educational intentions of the programme.

It had been agreed from the very early stages of course planning that a substantial part of students' work in the Graduate Diploma would be in the form of an applied project in an area of professional interest of their own nomination. The Assessment Committee during accreditation had been concerned about the degree of supervision possible in the distance mode, and the group had agreed to adopt a process of regular reporting to meet such concerns, although at the time the module was prepared our emphasis was more on negotiation and collaboration than supervision.

Three factors in particular shaped the approach taken. First, the evaluation module provided a successful model of structured and supportive guidance through project planning activities. Second, one student had already completed the project under special arrangement, having taken an overload in other modules to complete the course ahead of schedule. In determining the approach to be taken with him, the team had already considered the emphasis to be given to research method-ology, the range of approaches which might be acceptable, likely areas for investigation and the methods of assessment. Finally, the very positive response of students to the high degree of interaction with tutors in the *Student Support* module gave staff good reason to think that communication and negotiation would be a strength rather than a difficulty in this final course component.

The purposes of the module firmly establish it in relation to the rest of the course, in that it aims to provide an experientially-based component which enables students to:

> reflect on their total experience of the course, while interpreting issues relevant to their professional role in distance education,
>
> select and frame a distance education project which will contribute to their professional growth in the field,
>
> develop and apply a set of skills in project planning, systematic application to project goals and project completion, and
>
> to pursue, with supervision and through negotiation, a specific project in the field of distance education, and to submit the results of the project for assessment.

Each student's proposal was vetted by an approvals group, comprising members of the core team, who then assigned a supervisor competent to support the individual in the nominated field. In some instances, where the intended project required specialist expertise outside the scope of members of the course team, an additional external supervisor was nominated. The final project reports were assessed by the supervisor and an external assessor, who reported to the approvals group. Reports were then forwarded to the students concerned.

Reflection on the Development Process

In retrospect the rationale for course development in the Graduate Diploma in Distance Education appears to have been based on:

> a concern to improve practice, both through modelling a range of strategies in the delivery of the course and providing opportunities for students to reflect on their practice and attempt modifications of it;
>
> a rejection of the familiar, rule-based instructional design approach to course development;
>
> adoption of a curriculum model which identified a broad range of areas which would impact upon course development decisions;
>
> an acknowledgment that the broader range of issues which thus became a concern in course development should be treated as problematic;
>
> a determination to apply precepts from adult learning theories in the design and delivery of the course, particularly in the

acknowledgment of the expertise of our students; and
a commitment to taking decisions which, in the language of Stenhouse (1975), were intelligent, thus making best use of the information available to us at the time.

Course team members were aware of each of these elements during the development process and saw their stance as differing from much of the practice and precept of the field. What was missing, I suspect, was an acknowledgment that one teacher-dominated model had been replaced by another, albeit one which was more liberal and open to student concerns. In this there was a disjunction between the aspirations of the group and the practical consequences of the approach adopted, and members were not initially aware of this. We were unintentionally taking decisions on the basis of a too limited perspective.

The course development strategy altered about two-thirds of the way through the process. Course team members may not have fully appreciated how they were changing the 'curriculum' model they had initially adopted. The change in strategy began during the drafting of the *Evaluation* module, but had a significant impact on the group's practice when, during its delivery to students, tutor-student interaction became more genuinely interactive. This coincided with the development phase for *Student Support,* during which the team came to terms with the altered directions in which they were moving. The difficulties experienced at that time within the team may have resulted from a basic misunderstanding of what was happening. Those who had been with the award longest regarded the changes being proposed as extensions of the stance they had already taken, that is, more 'freedom' would be extended to students. But this was not what was being suggested, and it took some of us several weeks to understand that what was sought was a new basis for legitimating the course development decisions we were taking.

Thus far the decisions were legitimated not by recourse to rules of procedure, as in the instructional design approach, but by a view of what constituted appropriate behaviour for tertiary teaching staff, which affords a more comprehensive, subtle and sophisticated basis for judgment. Nonetheless, whatever its refinement, the curriculum approach still establishes what will count as valuable knowledge and appropriate ways of acquiring it within the constraints of the expertise of the academic staff involved.

What Anne Forster was asking us to contemplate, and what the rest of us gradually came to understand and value, was that if you believe that the knowledge of the field rests with the experienced practitioners, then determining what is important to study cannot be dissociated from practitioners and the context in which practice is displayed. This becomes a real problem when designing a course for practitioners in diverse fields and with a range of professional interests. Practice is difficult to talk about without contextual knowledge and 'thick' description. Understanding comes from the meanings found in the practice of mature and experienced professionals when comprehensively described and subjected to informed reflection. It does not easily lend itself to the establishment of commonalities and prescriptions which are inter-contextual.

The test of a course like the Graduate Diploma must be the extent to which it endorses this approach to understanding through its own practice, while continuing to serve the other purposes for which it is also established, for example, certification of achievement. As such, decisions which address different ends must not become simple compromise. Our stance changed. The course team relinquished a considerable part of its control of what and how students should learn. The team determined to use its expertise to negotiate with and support students as they sought to find meaning in their own professional actions or in the institutional practice with which they were familiar. In the *Student Support* and *Distance Education Project* modules this new goal was achieved to a significant degree.

In summary, the rationale for the development of the Graduate Diploma in Distance Education was transformed through the course development process, although at such a point that only one-third of the present programme reflects the altered orientation of the course team. The determined move from an 'instructional design' to a broader 'curriculum' perspective both empowered the course team in the first stages of course development and later restricted what it attempted. The energy required to break with the conventional wisdom of course development in distance education and the sense of saying something different provided both a bond and an impetus within the group, which enabled them to mount and deliver the early modules of the programme which broke new ground. The belated recognition that the cost of the position the members had taken was to restrict both their own and their students' discovery of the field came at a critical point in the course development process. In responding to the challenge to adopt a more student-responsive stance, the team was able to move beyond difficulties it was having in the design of each new module. What we had not understood, and may not have fully appreciated even when the change had been implemented, was that the lack of energy and uncertainty about conceptual structure experienced at the beginning of each new module was a product of the paradigm within which we had been working as much as the constraints of time and our limited knowledge of the field. A major cause of our difficulties was the sense that for the course to be academically respectable the team had to 'get it right'. Recognition that this degree of staff determination of what counted for knowledge and how it was to be accessed was 'getting it wrong' was liberating both for our students and the team. The challenge before the remaining team members is to recommit the programme and redesign its earlier sections within this new paradigm.

Chapter 8

Using Journals to Encourage Critical Thinking at a Distance

Helen Modra

The work described in this chapter took place between 1980 and 1987, during which time I was teaching distance education students in librarianship in an Australian College of Advanced Education. The particular commitments which were expressed in my teaching practice had been developing over a longer period and owe much to engagement with a number of movements, social and educational, with which I had been involved from the late 1960s.[1] Important influences on me in this period came from a number of writers, notably Paulo Freire, Carl Rogers, Charles Hampden-Turner, Fritz Perls, Matthew Miles, Erich Fromm, Jonathon Kozol and Tom Lovett.[2]

By the time I took up my first full-time teaching job I had developed some fairly clear ideas about education. Chief among these are that: (1) the librarian is first and foremost an educator; (2) education is not and never will be neutral; (3) adults are people who can and do change and to this end their education is something over which they should have as much control as possible; and (4) it is the job of education to help usher in a more just and humane society. A corollary of this last position is the belief that it is our unique role and right as human beings to critically engage our society in order to transform it. All of these ideas are, of course, interrelated.

In the context of librarianship, which was my field for many years, perhaps the most problematical of the above ideas was the second, namely my rejection of the claim that education is or should be neutral. Librarianship has always had an educational mission which has been pursued in the context of an ideology of neutrality and objective professionalism. This has been articulated in many ways but perhaps most tellingly by the British librarian, D.J. Foskett, who declared that the librarian must have 'no politics, no religion and no morals'.[3]

Neutrality claims are equally powerful in the library profession in North America; and in my own recent research into the fate of social activists in the library profession in Australia in the 1970s I found ample evidence of the continuing dominance of the neutralist ideology within librarianship here.

My interest in fostering in librarians a critical rather than a detached perspective, such as that supported by claims to neutrality, was very much enhanced by interaction with professional colleagues and trainees over a number of years. In my work as a library adviser in a state library agency during the 1970s I had ample opportunity to talk with librarians about their work, to read widely in the literature of the field and so to develop an awareness of the power of the neutralist ideology in librarians' discourse. Following an idea developed by Kozol,[4] I now name what I discovered then as the language of unconnectedness. It seemed that librarians saw 'no connections' between their own lives, what was going on in the world of politics and what happened in their library service.[5] They seemed to have no language or framework to enable them to see connections between, for example, their position (for many) as women, their relations with authority figures outside the profession, for example, employers and policy-makers, and the policies which circumscribed their practices. On those occasions where some relationship was seen, the usual response was one of powerlessness, which the following comment from a middle manager in a public library system typifies: 'The whole outlook as to what you are up against and what results effort might have is fairly depressing. What point motivation? I feel more comfortable with illusions.'[6]

Another reason for the lack of critical attention by librarians to libraries' political and social contexts is that debate about means in librarianship has, particularly in recent years as librarians have leaped upon the bandwagon of new information technology, overshadowed interest in ends. Increasingly the discourse of librarianship has been shaped by that technical rationality which Schon calls 'the positivist epistemology of practice'.[7] Elsewhere I have discussed the relationship in librarianship between the profession's neutralist ideology, its domination by technicist thinking and librarians' general lack of awareness of the political ramifications of their practice.[8] Suffice it here to say that by the time I got into the teaching of librarianship and was assigned to teach a subject called 'Libraries in Society', I knew that I wanted to design an approach to learning which would involve students in making connections between their private sphere, their work and the larger society, and in critically reflecting upon those connections. In retrospect it is not surprising that I was to discover, when I was only a few years down the track, that such modest aspirations would be regarded as an unacceptable 'politicization' of teaching. In keeping with its neutralist claims the library profession was, and still is, wedded to what the sociologist A.R. Welch has called 'the liberal ideology of non-ideology'.[9] In the pages which follow I shall describe how I framed my concerns into a pedagogy and with what results.

Formulation of a Pedagogy

Having gone to work in a College of Advanced Education which was greatly involved in distance education, I had to find out about distance education in a hurry. I had neither direct nor vicarious knowledge of it, and my first experience of attending a conference of workers in distance education suggested that it was seen by perhaps most of its practitioners as being about delivery systems rather than about adults learning and changing.[10] It seemed that technicist thinking was not confined to the library profession. However, in the first year or so the sheer novelty of preparing materials in different ways and meeting production schedules was very distracting, and in the period before I took charge of my own group of distant students I derived my satisfactions as a teacher from my contact with the small group of on-campus undergraduates whom I saw for about three hours a week. But I did do some marking of other lecturers' external students' work, and began to feel more and more uneasy about what looked like a production line approach to education. This concern increased when I began to coordinate and teach subjects in my own right and to experience the interactions with students, with other faculty and with the system which are part of a coordinator's role. Determined as I was to discover the possibilities for 'connected' and critical approaches in my new setting, I decided to try to reframe the things that frustrated me about distance education and turn them into opportunities to put my developing philosophy into practice. Some of the frustrations that I was coming up against were that:

1 I never saw 'my' students, as the subjects I taught did not have their own Residential School. If I saw them at all, it was usually only accidentally, at someone else's Residential School;

2 The students in my subjects did not meet as students of that subject but only in the context of excursions or residential segments of the course, unrelated to the work they did with me. Even teleconferencing opportunities were not available when I first started teaching;

3   The long lists of readings which I started out suggesting were really only available to students in the capital cities, but a lot of the students were in extremely isolated locations (for example, on a ranger station in Kakadu National Park in the Northern Territory) and tended to rely heavily on the books of readings supplied by the college which were only ever intended to supplement other sources;[11] and

4   the student population was extraordinarily heterogeneous insofar as class, status and educational experience were concerned, so there was not a great deal I could reasonably assume that they would have in common.

How did I deal with these 'problems'? As I thought about them, the ideas that I had been developing from adult learning theory and the work of Paulo Freire seemed more and more relevant. The biggest issue was that the problem of distance — from major libraries and their resources, from other students and from me — meant that either I was going to have to supply all the course content for students, or that each student was going to have to learn to use her or his own environment as a resource for learning. The fact that for my rather eclectic subject 'Libraries in Society', which looked at the social and political context of libraries and the library profession, none of the standard (British and American) textbooks satisfied me, exacerbated the problem. Even if I had wanted to prescribe completely the agenda for learning, this would not have been possible. As I thought about that, I began to see that what had started out looking like problems were in fact becoming means for me to put into practice some of the things I believed in — to try to take student autonomy seriously and to avoid the trap of what Paulo Freire has called 'banking education'. He uses this term to describe something which has become standard practice in many educational settings. In this process students are regarded as empty beings who are filled by 'deposits' of knowledge from the all-knowing teacher. This has ontological implications, as Freire points out:

> It is not surprising that the banking concept of education regards men [sic] as adaptable, manageable beings. The more students work at storing the deposits entrusted to them, the less they develop the critical consciousness which would result from their intervention in the world as transformers of that world. The more completely they accept the passive role imposed upon them, the more they tend simply to adapt to the world as it is and to the fragmented view of reality deposited in them.[12]

Geography, then, was a factor mediating pedagogy in such a way as to render transparently inappropriate any notion of a 'banking' education, even if I had wanted to teach in that way.

A corollary of this related to students' autonomy: along with banking education the idea of the teacher as expert could also go, and this pleased me. The banking notion is based upon the commodification of expertise. Whilst Freire does not deny the existence of different levels of awareness and competence in teachers on the one hand and students on the other, his work suggests that what is more important is how the teacher chooses to act in any situation. Misgeld points out that for Freire expertise must be made accessible to the total group and experts must be accountable to the group:

> Expertise is special knowledge of some field of activity that can be entered into the common knowledge of a cultural group under two conditions: the appropriate vehicles of translation and interpretation must be available . . . and those possessing special knowledge must be accountable to the cultural group with which they work. [13]

Freire uses the term 'dialogue' to suggest that students are teachers of the teacher at the same time as the teacher is a student of the students. In a pedagogical context in which mutual trust and self-suspension are crucial, the parties come together as equally knowing subjects to engage in dialogue:

> There is no 'expert' who knows the answers and whose job it is to transmit those answers. Individuals come together with equally valid, but different, perspectives, sharing problems which have yet to be defined, seeking answers which have yet to be formulated. [14]

To me, as a beginning teacher, there seemed to be many points at which the work of Freire resonated with some of the concerns of adult learning theory, T-group theory and the theory of experiential learning, namely, the valuing of participants' own backgrounds, the encouragement given to reflection and the norm that members of laboratory groups are autonomous beings, trainers and participants alike. One implication was that issues addressed in learning should be of immediate relevance to the learner, and I saw this as related to the unavailability (to many students) of the standard resources for the subject I taught.

As I tried to see the creative opportunities inherent in what had started out as problems, I noticed that most of the concerns I had were about process but that content was not insignificant. The necessity for process and content to be congruent was part of my approach to teaching.[15] In Freirean terms an essential prerequisite for dialogue is the educator's understanding of the 'situatedness' of learners' discourse and of the capacity of teacher and learner to analyze and critique their daily reality in order to discover and exercise their capacity to transform it.

As I saw it, then, seven or eight years ago, my challenge was to create a vehicle for the study of my subject which would (1) free students from over-reliance on libraries and textbooks, (2) enable them to start 'where they were at', (3) enable me to let go the role of expert and instead encourage and (4) reward students for discovering the resources for learning that their own situation already contained. I also knew that I had to try to build some element of critique — of librarianship, of society and of libraries-in-society and society-in-libraries — into the process, that is, to tackle what Freire calls *conscientizaçao* — the development of critical consciousness. For various reasons it was a few years before this element of critique became a strong focus in my work.

What I chose eventually to do was to have students prepare a structured *journal* instead of the more conventional forms of assessment.[16] After some years I experimented with a different style of work, the *reading log*. I used these formats for about six years, varying my approaches from year to year. Several hundred students, both under-graduate and postgraduate, studying via the distance education mode, tackled these exercises in that time, with results which to me are very intriguing.

The Journal: Processes and Problems

The *journal* was to be a structured assemblage of comment and criticism on subject-related readings, events, media items, thoughts, conversations and the like, which would require the student to investigate political, social and cultural events and trends — local, national and international — and think and write about how these did, or could, affect libraries and librarianship. The subject guide gave several pages of guidelines for journal work, and set out the criteria by which it would be assessed. As a completely prescriptive journal process would only have amounted to a form of banking education, I had to tread a careful line between being too directive and too vague in my instructions. Finding the right balance was a constant source of tension. I tried to suggest ways in which students might think about the issues they explored, and by providing one or more sample entries endeavoured to model the process. Journal criteria emphasized the need for the student to reflect on material encountered and to make links from it to subject-related concerns.

In addition to including a few sample entries in the subject guide I sent out an audio-cassette in which I explained my approach to the whole subject and to teaching in general and endeavoured to create a sense of excitement about the work. The teaching package also included 'Notes' on the topics covered and a book of readings. In one-semester subjects there was usually one such package, and three packages for year-long subjects. Rather than tackle the entire contents of the subject, students could select one theme, which they were asked to link to a particular aspect of the philosophy of the profession; for example, a student might elect to focus on multiculturalism and libraries, as a manifestation of the social responsibility of librarianship.

The format suggested was a large scrapbook of the kind readily available in chainstores, however, I made it clear that I would be happy to receive work in another format, for example, a video.[17] The journal could include a reasonable number of clippings and so forth, provided that their relevance to the theme was made clear and they were commented upon in a reflective manner rather than merely assumed to speak for themselves. I also pointed out that I did not see the journal as a private diary and I had no expectation that students should go beyond a level of self-disclosure which was comfortable to them.

A recurrent issue for my attention was the awarding of grades for journals. Over the years I varied the proportional value of the journal in relation to the total grade for the subject, from as low as 20 per cent the first year in a year-long undergraduate subject when I was extremely tentative about the process, to 100 per cent in 1985 in a one-semester subject in the Graduate Diploma course. I was never satisfied with my approach to grading: to award grades at all in such a process was surely an anomaly, yet institutional pressures were considerable. In fact, the ways in which an institution's climate and administration act to constrain pedagogy were somewhat of a surprise to me, ideas about academic freedom notwithstanding.

By the end of 1982 I had had two years experience of using the journal with undergraduates, and decided to extend it to graduates. I was becoming aware that undergraduates found the journal process rather anxiety producing, largely because they were accustomed to work to a strategy of figuring out what the lecturer wanted, whereas journal required them to do what they wanted within general guidelines. Their phone calls and letters for help were invariably requests for me to tell them precisely what to do. This reveals a form of rationality that is culturally widespread, and serves to support Freire's assertions about 'banking education'. In planning for 1983 I amplified the explanatory material about the journal process and rewrote it for a postgraduate audience. I also made the very curious decision, after taking advice from the college's experienced external studies people, to award the subject's grade on this occasion on the basis of two conventional essays and to require a journal as well, as a qualificatory exercise in which a pass had to be obtained if an overall pass in the subject were to be achieved. It seems strange now, but I really believed that by providing even more explicit criteria for journal work than I had given earlier students, I would be simplifying and demystifying the process and making it easier for students to focus more on doing the journal and less on worrying about it. What I achieved, of course, was an escalation of student anxiety. After all, if two good essays could be negated by an 'inadequate' journal, then the journal was indeed something to worry about. Despite this, only three out of eighty-six students who finished the semester (from an initial enrolment of 132) failed the subject because the journal was unacceptable, and in none of those cases was the journal work other than glaringly inadequate in terms of the stated criteria.

In each subject guide I suggested to students that in their journal they might find it useful to reflect on the actual experience of doing a journal, and there were always some students who took up this idea. In 1983 most students who commented on the process were reacting to the horizon-expanding agenda of both subject content and subject process, which they appeared to have enjoyed. The following comments were typical:

> I enjoyed reading about computers in the world and I discovered issues in computing that were new and at times scary. I thank you sincerely for opening my eyes to issues in the 'real' world that I had never before encountered.

> The end has come. This is my last entry. I have found making the Journal a useful exercise as it has made me more aware of how issues in the social, political and economic environment affect the librarian, the library, and services offered. It has made me try and think of ways to cope and solutions to problems that arise.

> I would like to say that despite the misgivings I had when I first started on this project, I have thoroughly enjoyed doing the work and I think I have learned a great deal about the problems facing libraries today. These were things I never even considered . . . . My mind, after four years of comparative stagnation, has finally experienced some stimulation and this I appreciate.

For some students the journal was a useful substitute for the challenges on-campus students obtain more readily:

> Keeping a Journal was, for me, a substitute for being able to discuss with fellow students. As an external student, one often feels the need to talk about issues. Often, when I wrote a comment about an article that I had read, it was like verbalizing my thoughts and discussing it with a second person.

> It may not always appear so, but it has acted as a stimulant to my understanding of the subject, and allowed me often to instigate a thought process or clarify in my head problems I have had with my essay and with other subjects. In fact I wish it might have been employed in other subjects.

> It has helped me to clarify my responses to much of the readings, to think more clearly and precisely, and to express these thoughts in writing. This last aspect I have found particularly useful, not having written seriously for some years. I have approached the writing of assignments with considerable trepidation but the keeping of this Journal has enabled me to build up the habit of writing; it is a practice that may well be useful in other subjects particularly in an external course where communication is necessarily so limited.

Those students who were most bothered by the journal either expressed concern about how to handle the relative amount of freedom they had in its compilation, for example, '. . . problems of knowing what to put in, what is relevant and how to phrase it', or castigated me for requiring them to do something they regarded as highly inappropriate. The following comments came from students who were experienced school teachers.

> As, one assumes, mature adults, it is humiliating to be treated like children in school. 'Now that you have done the activity you must write about it to show me that you have done it properly.' . . . The Journal takes no account of the person for whom scrapbooks have never been a source of interest, the one who does not need them.

> I estimate that I have spent sixty hours on what I consider to be a pointless activity . . . . In most cases comments were superfluous, in some cases unprintable.

In relation to these two cases I hypothesized that the more one is steeped in the banking mode of education, the less one will be able to engage processes of critique and reflection.

The potential of the journal exercise to encourage students to change the way they work and the way they view the world was encapsulated in the following comments which I quote in full:

> My say on the Subject. This Subject has been the most work, required the most time and caused me the most anxiety. It has also been the most interesting, evocative and thought-provoking. I have often felt that it would be nice to hear the other students' view on matters raised as I feel many are open-ended and invite discussion. I would prefer that the residential school was for this subject than any other. I have found the Journal exercise more behaviour modifying than random breath-testing. From a *Women's Weekly*-reading housewife I have become an avid reader of the better example of Australian journalism and take an interest in so many issues that I previously just ignored. The journal has forced me to make the effort and in doing so I feel a greater self-esteem.

In 1985 in response to student feedback about journal work, I decided to make the journal the sole assessment item for my postgraduate subject in the first semester. My main reason for doing this was that I had come to see that journals were producing far more interesting and wide-ranging responses by students to subject contents than seemed to be the case with essays, so it was time to focus my attention and that of my students on this one effort.

I thought about introducing learning contracts as well, because I was becoming more and more uneasy about the position I was placing myself in by being the one who determined grades. Whilst my aim was to give up being 'the expert' this would be impossible while I remained in sole charge of grades. But I continued to be constrained by the norms of the institution I was working in: results in all subjects were expected to be normally distributed and student-centred teaching and assessment were almost unheard of. Nobody else was using learning contracts. The expectation was that staff were, in fact, 'experts' and were to behave as such. The dominant views of teaching and learning were technicist ones, and in my particular department these views were buttressed by years of unquestioning adherence to notions of detached and objective professionalism and to the 'legitimacy' of scientific and instrumental models of research and education.

A significant change in my approach to the journal in 1985 was that I specifically introduced consideration of the notion of praxis — the dialectical relationship of reflection and action or theory and practice. I wanted to encourage students to think through the possibilities for action to which their reflection led them.[18] This was done through the posing of what I called 'Focusing Questions':

1 What is it that is actually being reported? or, What's really going on here? (in the situation).
2 Why are things this way? What are the causes and where lies the responsibility for this situation?
3 What can and should be done? Specifically, what can you do/will you do?

This was the first specifically Freire-inspired change in the journal agenda. The ideas came out of Freirean work done in Ecuador by Alschuler, Smith and others from the Center for International Education at the University of Massachusetts at Amherst. The cyclical stages through which critical consciousness develops can be referred to as naming, reflecting and acting, and each of these suggests questions to be posed, questions which I have outlined above. Students' responses to these questions reflect their particular way of thinking and world-view, for example, people with low awareness of the structural constraints upon their professional practice, or of the mechanisms whereby power is exercised, may see professional problems as due to causes quite beyond their capacity to influence, in much the same way as a peasant, not knowing the economics and politics of the fertilizer industry, may attribute crop failure consistently to God or Fate.[19]

Whilst I asked students to attend to these focusing questions in their journal work, I made it clear that this task was only one of a number of elements to be considered in the assessment of the journal. Other criteria included: evidence of wide reading; conceptual sophistication; evidence of linkages perceived between issues studied and events in the wider world; and evidence of critical reflection and personal insight.

On the whole students did not engage the focusing questions. My feeling now is that such questions may have been too much to ask in a situation in which students had to be quite dedicated enough to handle the novelty of both the subject's contents and the journal as the assessment medium. If I had had the chance to work closely with each new intake of students over two or even three subjects and not just for one semester, I would have had a better chance of helping them develop their reflective and critical capacities.

In addition to the focusing questions I provided in the 1985 subject material a new, longer sample entry (about the effects of religious fundamentalism on the state education system in Queensland), and instigated a process whereby students would negotiate with me early in the semester over theme selection as well as send in their own sample journal entries for comment. As these came in I copied one or two that I thought were good, made them anonymous and sent them out as additional feedback to some students who were clearly having trouble doing the journal.

One hundred and twelve students began the semester and sixty-three were still registered at the end of semester. Twenty students did not receive a pass, but in only ten cases was this because their work did not meet the stated criteria: the other ten simply did not submit a journal at all. Almost all the latter group had shown in their early sample entries that they had considerable difficulty with the whole process, and despite my sending them prompt feedback and guidance after the first stages they did not send in further work as I requested, but dropped out.

Student response to the journal was expressed in comments similar to those I had received in previous years. Initial anxiety about the process was replaced in most cases by a sense of accomplishment and often enjoyment once the exercise was fully engaged. The lack of opportunity to discuss subject contents with other students was seen as a problem by some; others reported that they felt the way of thinking stimulated by journal work would be difficult to 'switch off' (itself an interesting comment on their approach to the total course). Whilst the focusing questions received very little attention, some students made an effort to reflect on practical and policy implications of the issues examined, as was evident in these comments:

> I studied the role of the public library about which I knew very little. I now see the public library as an essential community service and realize that it has great potential for meeting social needs in a number of areas, a potential which is not being realized in many public libraries.

> I think librarians should become more involved in issues but have worked out that most librarians are employed by the various state, local and federal governments and must toe the line. That's where the Library Association of Australia should do collectively what librarians can't do singly — lobby and express opinions wisely.

Student reaction against the journal being the sole assessment item was much less than I had expected. A couple of students said they preferred doing essays because it is easier to schedule work. Also, once an essay is done, they said, they feel they have 'cleared the decks' ready for the next task, but as the journal required regular and continuing work to these students it felt like a constant burden.

Some students started on their journal feeling that it was not a fit task for postgraduate students: 'I thought that completing a Journal would be a real bludge', was one comment. All but one of those who reacted in this way had changed their mind by the end of semester, discovering that journal work was far more demanding than they had anticipated. The number of students who also found the work absorbing and exciting was gratifying to me, though I was not sure what to make of the comment that 'this course "Libraries in Society" has been like a dose of salts'!!

The things I had learned about journal work in early 1985 would undoubtedly have led to very substantial changes in the way I approached this particular subject, had not officialdom intervened in the middle of the year while I was on study leave. It is not my intention in this chapter to describe or analyze what took place in the following couple of years: that story, when published, should prove an instructive case study in the politics of curriculum innovation. I just want to point out that if we have more than a merely instrumental approach to teaching and want to explore the relations between education and social change, we should expect to encounter many difficulties as we struggle to find what Freire has called 'free space' within our institutions. We may find some space, but it never comes 'free'.

In 1986 I completely dropped the journal and set three traditional essays in my postgraduate subject. I did my own evaluation that semester, largely to provide some student-based arguments for the retention of the subject (or at least its major content) within the programme: a curriculum review was imminent and my field was in danger of being edged aside to make way for a compulsory unit in accounting or computing or algebra which were deemed essential to the 'training' of 'information professionals'. By and large students in 1986 found the subject both stimulating and demanding, and some observed that its contents needed more than one semester of work if they were to be tackled effectively.

During 1985 a colleague in another tertiary institution had told me about a somewhat different style of work which he thought might serve at least some of the purposes of the journal. This was the *reading log,* and it was being used by Ann Zubrick, Head of the Department of Speech and Hearing at the WA Institute of Technology (now Curtin University). I visited Dr Zubrick who generously shared her ideas and materials with me. I introduced the reading log in the second semester of 1986 in a new undergraduate subject, 'Issues in Public Libraries', and in

1987 I extended it to postgraduate students in 'Libraries in Society'. The log was only one assignment: two formal essays preceded it and it was worth 40 per cent of the total grade. Students were expected to work on their log throughout the semester, sending in sample entries for comments part-way through the semester. Log entries were to be reflective and critical responses to reading that students chose to do in preparation for their formal essays.

I provided students with a statement about the place of a log in their studies and a couple of pages of guidelines and sample entries. The criteria for log assessment would pay attention to the amount, relevance and breadth of material read, the clarity of comments, and to the level of critical thought demonstrated. I emphasized that the log was a flexible tool that would give students the opportunity to respond to their subject reading in a style quite different from that of formal essays. I again set out a statement of my approach to teaching and learning, emphasizing student autonomy, the idea of teacher as learner and learner as teacher, and my belief in the importance of developing critical awareness.

Graduate students in 1987 took to the reading log rather more readily than earlier students had taken to the journal, probably because the scope of logs was more narrowly defined and the perceived burden of endless choice removed. The work submitted was of a much more even and high standard overall than journal work, and I suspect that this was because the log required somewhat less skill in conceptualizing, and also because students were relieved of the necessity to become avid media watchers and were free to focus in more detail on material that was to them more obviously subject-related. It was possible for students to do an adequate log using only their book of readings and some selections from the lists of recommended supplementary reading. They could, however, range as widely as they chose and no items were 'prescribed' reading.

Zubrick uses the log with on-campus students and sees it chiefly as an instrument for developing students' writing.[20] This outcome of log work turned out to be very important with my students also. Using a reading log can certainly assist the teacher wanting to encourage the capacities that Ira Shor refers to when he observes: 'Reading closely, writing clearly, thinking critically, conceptualizing and verbalizing are some means to penetrate the maze of reality. These are foundations of becoming a conscious re-maker of social life.'[21]

I conducted an evaluation of students' response to the log in 1987. Most of those who replied to the questionnaire — some 40 per cent — were, not surprisingly, very much in favour of the use of logs and claimed to have benefitted from this work. Many students also pointed out that they found the log had been very hard work, more so than they expected, and in some cases the contrast between the styles of log and essay work was seen as hard to handle. One respondent said that external students 'simply don't have time to read widely and put their reflections into writing'. As with journal work, students reported being glad that they had been required to read more than they might otherwise have done, and some commented that the discipline of log work meant that the material they read had more meaning than usual. For example:

> Great benefit from it. Articles etc., tended to stay in my mind longer and were more readily applied to professional situations.

> Usually, I write assignments and mostly forget about them as soon as they are done. The whole formal writing process makes me lose any initial interest I had and get bored. With this Log my entries were shorter and more informal and my interest did not wane. It was of help because the reading I did I ENJOYED and I REMEMBERED. [Student's emphasis]

For a couple of students the log had been frustrating since they liked to tackle things in greater depth than they felt was appropriate in their log. As one said:

> I enjoyed the exercise however I felt I wasn't necessarily broadened or overly extended by the exercise as I was responding to a variety of issues without approaching any of them with great depth. However it did raise issues for me. I felt I became a bit glib as time went on.

For some the open-ended nature of the log — as with the journal though to a lesser extent — was anxiety-inducing: they would have preferred to be told exactly what to do.

> Thought readings and suggested readings should be more guided — there were too many potentially interesting paths to pursue.

> I found it hard to know if I was on the right track . . . .

This contrasted with the experience of students who had a sense of being in control:

> I like the element of freedom that the Log allowed me.

> Not only did it [the log] mean I did a lot more reading than perhaps I would have if I'd had to read them but it also gave great scope for individuality — I could comment on issues I found interesting rather than those my lecturer chose.

For one student the log served as journals served others before her, as a substitute for tutorials: 'It was valuable on a personal level. I suppose it functioned in the same way as a tutorial — providing an opportunity to discuss which I miss as a correspondence student.'

Whilst no one said specifically that doing the log had changed her or his world in a major way, which I did not expect anyway, it was clear from the following comment that by requiring some disciplined reflection on subject contents a teacher may very well set in motion a process which will have major implication in the lives of students:

> My perceptions and understanding of library work were extended more by this exercise than any other subject in the course. Unlike the other subjects I learned something and I was given the opportunity to think and make choices in my learning. Isn't this what tertiary post-grad work is about? I thoroughly enjoyed your subject. Unfortunately it was in stark contrast to the others [which offered] no time to think . . . I have become quite disillusioned about library work and have deferred study . . . your course clarified some of those issues for me . . . .

Such are the unanticipated consequences of teaching!

By about the middle of 1987 I was feeling that I had exhausted the possibilities for innovation that my job had offered. I was pleased that the opportunity of a major change of direction came up not long after this. Towards the end of 1987 I left the College and at the same time concluded twenty-five years formal involvement with the library profession.

To conclude this chapter I offer some critical reflections on my work, both to assist my own developing practice as a teacher in a different field and in the hope that such reflection will be useful to others who may wish to work in ways similar to those I have described.

Looking Back and Looking Forward

As I look back on the way my teaching practice developed over the last eight years, the aspect that seems most significant is that it was a continuous experiment which I was at no stage fully able to critique and reshape by means of one coherent framework. It was an enterprise in which I oscillated between two desires: on the one hand, to increase students' engagement with the political ramifications of the pedagogy, and on the other hand, to attend to students' intra-personal development more fully. The first concern came out of engagement with the work of

Freire, the second from my background in experiential learning in human relations training. I do not see these concerns as mutually exclusive, but I feel that this tension kept my practice too far from what I would regard as an authentically Freirean praxis to warrant the label. A crucial difference between the Freirean and the various humanistic/experiential approaches to learning is that the former contains an explicitly social agenda which is not necessarily shared by the latter. As Freire says,

> It is sufficient to know that conscientization [the development of critical consciousness] does not take place in abstract beings in the air but in real men and women and in social structures, to understand that it cannot remain on the level of the individual.[22]

I think my work would have required a far more overtly emancipatory agenda and be much more deliberately and carefully embedded in the material and social conditions of students and myself to be truly Freirean.[23]

The biggest problem I faced, which I recognized very early in my work but never managed to overcome, was that distance education was and is — with almost no exception — an individualistic, asocial process. And so — though for a long time it did not occur to me — was the work done for both journals and logs.

However, as Freire's own work demonstrates, education for critical consciousness is a thoroughly social process requiring far more than the limited, one-on-one communication that still, according to Evans and Nation, characterizes distance education.[24] Not only was I, as a teacher, frustrated by lack of contact with students: it is clear from student comment reported above that students also were frustrated by lack of contact with each other. It has to be remembered that at the time I was doing this work the institution where I taught was only just beginning to experiment with teleconferencing, and electronic mail was only available to students in a few courses a year or so before I left. From what I saw of the use of such facilities — as technical means to serve unexamined ends — I derived no strong feeling that they would enhance the kind of pedagogy I was developing. I may be wrong. Anyway, the numbers of students who said to me over the years that my subject needed its own Residential School because the issues it raised — intellectual freedom, for example — required group discussion, indicated that possibly the 'horizon-expanding' that was quite evidently prompted by journal and log work may have served to exacerbate students' sense of isolation. I now wonder whether distance education is not, almost by definition, anti-dialogical. What shall we do about this?

One of the reasons why Freire's educational work in Latin American contexts was so effective was that an enormous amount of 'cultural spade work' was done in advance with the participation of intending students and their communities. This work involved the painstaking examination of the everyday world of these communities and the codification of aspects of this reality into generative themes and words which could serve as vehicles to transform learners' perceptions of themselves and their world at the same time as they were being used as tools for the teaching of literacy.[25] The exhaustive preparation done by Freire and his teams enabled them to be effective in the chosen setting. I wonder, in relation to this, what is the 'setting' of distance education, when subjects such as those I taught have enrolments of over 100 students, very different people, scattered all over Australia? What 'cultural spade work' can educators do in such situations? What can students do? What might we not be able to accomplish together?

To attempt to ground one's pedagogy in the students' own experience is certainly necessary. Another aspect of that experience that warrants our attention is that they bring to our courses a whole host of expectations about learning, that is, their experience of a good many years of banking education. This certainly explains, for example, why some students would ring me with queries as to whether they should write on both sides of the page in their journal scrapbook.

The students I taught had to confront three demanding situations at once, because of the sequencing of 'Libraries in Society' as a first-year, first-semester subject in the Graduate Diploma course. These were (1) returning to study, (2) dealing with the 'internal' novelty of the assessment process in my subject, and (3) handling the more convention-al requirements of other subjects and their own mixed feelings about the conflicting requirements and expectations of different subjects in the one course. A redesigned approach to journal work — and log work to some extent — would require more careful attention to these matters.

Another important issue concerns what Ira Shor calls 'interferences to critical thought'.[26] He sees that the chief source of such interferences is the very culture in which we are all immersed, which alienates us from each other and from our 'own conceptual habits of mind'.[27] Shor says that

> The mass denial of reason is achieved through a network of cultural instruments . . . . The variety of anti-critical forces in American life include vocational culture in school and on the job, several forms of false consciousness . . . the absence of democratic experience, the demands of private life and the aesthetics and social relations of school in general and the community colleges

in particular . . . . In some instances, a single cultural interference serves several thought-denying functions. The electronic mass media . . . not only convey carefully managed information about reality, but they are also a form of speeded and debased communication which inhibits the mass practice of careful scrutiny.[28]

Despite my intentions, my approaches did not engage these problems in sufficient depth. Whilst the work I received from students showed that they paid a lot of attention to the media and that they found much that was relevant to the concerns of the subject, this seemed to be such a novel experience for most that their treatment of the materials they found remained descriptive rather than analytical. It was as if their energies were exhausted in making the effort to discover that relevant material was all around them, as C.W. Mills noted years ago.[29] A reconstructed pedagogy would demand a great effort in enabling students to deconstruct the media and their messages — including, of course, the media used in distance education.

Early in this chapter I referred to my discovery that librarians' discourse demonstrated a lack of any strong sense of connection between libraries and the social structures with which they are in tension. A very early comment from an undergraduate I taught provided a telling example of this:

I felt ignorant when I started this subject. I did not see what libraries had to do with the rest of society and how they were affected by, for example, political or economic changes. I thought, and still do to a large extent, that libraries were in a world of their own — something stationary in an ever-changing society.

The nostalgia inherent in such a position is inseparable from the singular lack of political clout of the library profession and one pertinent reason why teaching for such a profession urgently needs a new, critical agenda.[30]

Whilst it is quite evident that working with journals and logs made students a great deal more aware of the social world and challenged them to think — often for the first time, it seems — about libraries in relation to social, economic, political and cultural change, I have the feeling that for a good many students the process of reflection did not do much more than raise their consciousness. Whilst the results of students' new awareness were exciting to see and read — some journals, for example, displayed a humour and sophistication that were quite stunning — I have often asked myself, in a slight paraphrase of a question that Ira Shor asks, 'Am I merely drawn to liveliness or is that dynamism as transformative as it feels?'[31]

While the journal or log can be a most successful consciousness raising tool, there is a world of difference between consciousness raising and the development of critical consciousness. Though many would claim that it has been of powerful and lasting value to them, consciousness raising is very often devoid of political content: one may develop a heightened awareness of pain and contradiction but still feel powerless to resolve problem situations. Awareness that 'the personal is political' — a catch-phrase of some recent consciousness raising movements — does not automatically produce appropriate programmes for action. In other words, consciousness raising can so easily become the reflection without action which Freire calls wishful thinking. On the other hand, critical consciousness facilitates analysis of the context of problem situations for the purpose of enabling people together to transform their reality rather than merely understand it or adapt to it with less discomfort. If such transforming action is the goal of pedagogy, this suggests the need for serious attention to the atomization and alienation of students which distance education at present seems both to presuppose and to reproduce.

Alienation and isolation in distance education are just as much problems for the teacher as for the students, particularly if one as a teacher is working to introduce a pedagogy which is tending in a very different direction from the accepted practice in one's institution.

'The Pedagogy Is the Struggle and the Struggle Is the Pedagogy'[32]

Whilst the choices one makes in distance education, as in any form of education, have political content and the educator must, as Freire says, be very clear as to the model of society towards which he or she is working, the sheer size and complexity of the tasks confronting those of us who wish to explore new and critical ways of working are such that we may see no way to begin. I certainly felt like this for a while. However, my experience confirms that of Shor, who found, as he struggled in the extraordinary environment of Open Admissions in the City University of New York in the 1970s, that we may need to start with the cognitive underdevelopment of students, at the same time that we are dealing with the reality of other aspects of students' lives and experiences. I found that whilst I often underestimated students' ability to develop insights into the influence of society on libraries, I invariably overestimated the level of skills that they would be able to bring to articulating their reflections.

I had made a deliberate decision not to write comments all over journals, though I do this with ordinary assignments. Journals were such personal things that I felt my busy green pen had to keep out, so I restricted myself to writing comments on the official cover-sheets. I therefore gave up one means I had to comment very directly on students' cognitive skills. I had plenty of opportunity with on-campus students to develop their skills in listening, speaking, paraphrasing, criticizing, synthesizing and so forth, and was perennially frustrated not to be able to do this with distant students.

This is not to imply that underneath it all the critical teacher is just an old-style grammarian, or that the difficult work of dialogue can be conveniently suspended while one 'fixes up' students' language problems in true banking fashion! On the contrary, the critical teaching enterprise is multidimensional. Because one is aware that the language of pub and party is insufficient to enable students to overcome the disabling effect of immersion in mass culture and penetrate the reality of that culture, one has to be prepared to share with students the exhausting work of achieving new, critical levels of literacy at the same time that one is exploring with them the more immediately apparent agenda of a subject. To do this in the distance mode is a huge challenge. No two classes or intakes of students will ever be the same, there are no rules, and one cannot just follow a syllabus. The teaching process is a continuous learning process, an exploration of possibility.

Shor's comments on this issue, though arising out of on-campus teaching, are applicable to our concerns in distance education.

> For all their processing through the many layers of public schooling, college freshmen and freshwomen arrive with weak literacy, low bases of information, and unevolved conceptual skills. The liberatory class will have to deal not only with many bad feelings about school, but it will also have to present critical problems at the same time that it develops the cognitive faculties needed to handle critical inquiry. Nothing can be taken for granted here. The liberatory enterprise is pulled in many directions at once, as it evolves in a social field full of obstacles. The critical teacher who begins the study and teaching of mass reality starts without knowing what the students know and don't know. The encouraging news is that despite all the interferences, critical thinking happens regularly, in classes where students display a startling richness of intelligence and humanity.[33]

Conclusion

My seven- to eight-year struggle to create a critical approach to distance education in librarianship resulted in a pedagogy which was quite successful in raising student awareness of the library-in-society and society-in-the-library. Much like the character in Moliere's *The Bourgeois Gentleman,* who made the discovery that he had been speaking prose all his life, I found out when I was in the middle of all my experimenting that what I was attempting was what others elsewhere were already engaged in and were calling 'critical pedagogy' or 'critical teaching'. In this regard my encounter with the work of Shor has proved crucial.

If I had only wanted to have students become more aware of social issues, I might have felt, when I left that particular teaching job, reasonably satisfied with what I did. But it was not nearly enough: the development of awareness is only a small, albeit necessary, part of the creation of a praxis which might contribute to the transformation of life and work in a professional milieu. To facilitate this in distance education, new and solidly dialogical approaches are called for, and I conclude this chapter, as Shor concluded his first book, in the knowledge that we have to go much further than the experiments reported here.

Notes

1 These included the social responsibility movement in the professions, the human potential movement and the adult literacy movement. I have discussed these things in greater detail in Modra (1979, 1984a, 1986).

2 Freire (1972a), Rogers (1961), Hampden-Turner (1970), Perls *et al.* (1973), Miles (1959), Fromm (1960), Kozol (1977), Lovett (1975) were all significant, though other works by the same authors were, and remain, important. I cannot help but notice, now, that there is no female voice in this list.

3 Foskett (1962), p.4.

4 Kozol (1977), Ch.4.

5 See Modra (1986) for treatment of this and related issues.

6 This comment was made during a series of workshops I ran in 1978 which are written up in Modra (1979). A number of similar reactions was observed.

7 Schon (1983), p.31.

8 Modra (1984b).

9 Welch (1980), p.78.

10 What I discovered was that distance education was dominated by what Evans and Nation call 'instructional industrialization'. I found, as they did, that 'distance education has remained isolated from the historical, philosophical, political and sociological critiques of education'. See Evans and Nation (1987).

11 After a few years I began suggesting to students that they cultivate the art of finding alternative sources to the ones suggested. Part of my reason for doing this was that it is a useful skill for a librarian to develop: when one is helping a client, inevitably the most useful item is already out on loan and one has to find relevant material elsewhere.

12 Freire (1972b), p.47

13 Misgeld (1985), p.107.

14 Smith (1976), p.4.

15 In other words, one does not learn to be democratic through being submerged in an undemocratic classroom; and it is not possible to foster dialogue by delivering a monologue. That this chapter is essentially a monologue is, however, inescapable!

16 I first began to have students prepare journals in 1981, when I introduced this exercise to undergraduates. In subsequent years I extended it to postgraduate students. I guess it is in the nature of such experiments that one does not undertake them with an eye on posterity: particular to the semester are the problems of that semester, especially when one is solely responsible for subjects having enrolments of over 100 students. In commenting on the first draft of this chapter, a colleague said it was a nice irony that I had not kept a journal about the experience of doing journal work with students: in fact, I did begin to do so in two different years but did not maintain my momentum. I know how students must have felt! In the absence of adequate information or personal reflection on each year's work, I have had to draw heavily on data I had kept concerning journal work undertaken by postgraduates in 1983 and 1985, and reading logs done by postgraduates in 1987.

17 I always got scrapbooks.

18 One year a couple of students working in the libraries of different schools in a particular region reported their decision to get together informally to try to address problems of censorship in schools. This was a direct result of their work in 'Libraries in Society', but I have no data on the experiment.

19 Smith (1976), p.43.

20 Zubrick (1985).

21 Shor (1980), p.37.

22 Freire (1976a), pp.146-7.

23 I have some concerns about the sort of work often announced as Freirean (e.g., some simple experience-based approaches to literacy tuition) but which does not engage the inescapable ontological and political ramifications of Freire's work. Kidd and Kumar (1981) provide a critique of the 'cooptation' of Freire using examples with somewhat more disturbing implications than the one above. It is interesting to note that Kidd and Kumar criticize, inter alia, the University of Massachusetts. I am not sure I agree with them on that. Of course, the opposite sort of orientation to Freire — an uncritical 'romance' with his ideas — is probably just as shortsighted as cooptation. Some articles in Robert Mackie's excellent book on Freire (Mackie, 1980) are an antidote. A very different critical analysis of Freire's ideas by Facundo (1984) is also recommended. Both books demand that the reader be familiar with Freire's output.

24 Evans and Nation, *op.cit.*

25 Most books on Freire explain something of this process. Barbara Bee's article, 'The Politics of Literacy', in the Mackie collection (Mackie, 1980), provides a very clear and accessible account of Freire's teaching process and its social and culture bases.

26 Shor (1980), p.46.

27 *Ibid.,* p.47.

28 *Ibid.,* p.49.

29 Mills (1970), p.232. 'You do not really have to study a topic . . . once you are into it, it is everywhere.'

30 Background for this claim can be found in Modra (1984a, 1984b, 1986). It is clear to me that the library profession is paying the price of professional education which is becoming more and more drastically decontextualized. The field is in thrall to unexamined notions about 'the information society', adequate preparation for which is assumed to consist in the acquisition of technical and managerial skills quite divorced from any solidly-based social critique.

31 Shor (1980), p.xxvi.

32 Petrik (1987), p.133.

33 *Ibid.,* p.81.

Chapter 9

A Distance Education Curriculum for Curriculum Theory

Lindsay Fitzclarence and Stephen Kemmis

This chapter represents the results of our reflection on a specific innovation in distance education: the Deakin University Master of Education course 'ECS 802 Curriculum Theory'. As the reader will soon discover, the course was informed by a particular view of education and curriculum, but (in the way it always does) practice turned out to be something other than our theory envisaged, giving us the opportunity to improve the theory and our practice. In the following pages we give a brief outline of the structure of the course and offer an interpretation of some of the issues it has raised for those working on it over its five-year history. The chapter is organized in two major sections with a brief conclusion. The first section is a descriptive account, giving the background, rationale and brief history of the course from 1983 to 1987. The second provides an analysis of several issues which emerge out of the self-understanding of the course — a perspective which attempts to place the work and ideas of the course in a general curriculum context. In the conclusion we return to some of the central concerns which have structured, and continue to structure, the nature of the course as an examination of 'the curriculum problem'.

The 'Curriculum Theory' course is one of about eighteen courses available within the Deakin University Master of Education and Master of Educational Administration degree programmes. It is a whole-year course, valued at two semester units (eight are required for Deakin's MEd or MEdAdmin degrees). The handbook outline for the course reads as follows:

> This course distinguishes theories of curriculum from theories of curriculum development, and introduces students to an approach to curriculum theory. Students read monographs introducing some 'conceptual furniture' for thinking about curriculum.

> The course is modeled on a professional association: the main work of the course is expressed through professional reading in curriculum (guided by a course bibliography), writing for other students in a course journal, and carrying out a project.
>
> Through this collaboration, the course community develops a critical perspective on contemporary curriculum theorizing and the conceptual furniture proposed in the monographs. (Deakin University, 1987, p.38)

This outline introduces several points about the course: its particular view about curriculum as dynamic, the idea of students learning as part of a community of scholars, and the idea that students should develop a critical perspective. These were initial aspirations about the course and after five years they provide a basis for a critical review. To use the words of Ulf Lundgren, one of the original course writers (in the title for a 1983 monograph he wrote for the course), we have come to recognize that there is a large gap 'between hope and happening' in the course, just as there is in any curriculum. This chapter will attempt to explain something of both the hope and the happening. In order to do this, it will be necessary at times to reflect on issues in a wider frame of social change, away from the specifics of curriculum and the course itself.

General Background: 'The Hope . . .'

To make sense of the idea of a Masters level course taught in the distance education mode, it is first necessary to know something of Deakin University and its charter as a provider of distance education. Of the four distinguishing features of the University noted in the 1988 *Handbook,* the following is given the most emphasis: 'but perhaps the most singular distinction is that it provides the option of either on-campus or off-campus study, being considered a leader in the field of distance education' (p.vi). Established in 1977, Deakin University was invested with a charter for providing courses in a distance education mode; a model that had already been developed in the Open University in Britain. Deakin University started at a time of dramatic expansion of the tertiary education sector in Australia; thus its formative years were in a period of relative luxury for tertiary education.

In the late 1970s and early 1980s the School of Education at Deakin University became involved in the development of postgraduate courses that were innovative in two senses: first, they were to be offered solely in the distance education mode; and second, they involved offering a range of fresh interpretations of the areas of curriculum, classroom processes and educational administration. The course 'Curriculum Theory' aimed to be innovative in both these senses. In its development phase it was conceptualized as a key unit in a sequence of courses in curriculum in the Masters programme — one that would not only introduce students to curriculum as a field of study, but which would also help students explore recent developments in thinking about curriculum issues — the forms of theorizing and of reasoning which the literature increasingly regarded as appropriate to the content, problems and issues of the field.

The initial ideas about the 'Curriculum Theory' course were inspired by an increasing concern to explore the general patterns of thinking in the field of curriculum. Yet course team members found themselves caught in a unique dilemma:[1] the course they offered was not only *about* curriculum, at the same time it *was* a curriculum. To avoid contradiction, the course would have to be quite explicit in exemplifying any curriculum ideas and principles it chose to advocate. Course team members realized that they could not offer just a guided tour of the literature of curriculum — a reading course which left questions of the 'lived curriculum' of the course to chance. It had to model a set of curriculum principles in its practice. The issue of theory and practice in curriculum (from which Ulf Lundgren had fashioned the phrase 'hope and happening') was thus a real and compelling one for the makers of the 'Curriculum Theory' curriculum. Their own curriculum and curriculum development practice should provide a model of the practice of curriculum theorizing, and the course should construct a set of tasks for students in such a way that they, too, could encounter and engage issues of the relationships between theory and practice in their own curriculum work (in their work roles as teachers, curriculum developers, or school administrators, for example).

But the problem was not only one of exemplifying an agreed or accepted theory of curriculum in practice. As the recent literature of curriculum had shown, new views of curriculum theory were emerging in the field. The idea of 'theory' also needed to be made problematic. It was recognized that students might well find this unfamiliar and difficult; it could not be assumed that many, let alone most, had previously encountered the idea that, to construct a theory, one actually needs a theory of what 'theory' is — a *meta-theory*. In curriculum this means having a (meta)theory about the nature of curriculum theory. It means being able to distinguish different kinds of curriculum theories in terms of their theories of curriculum. In identifying the need for a discussion of meta-theory, the course team was acknowledging that presumptions about the nature of curriculum theory and theorizing are potentially invidious, carrying sometimes unrecognized and unexamined assumptions about the nature of curriculum itself. Particularly at the time when the course was first mooted, the course team was aware that the terms of curriculum theory were changing — that the field was entering a new phase. These changes could be understood in terms of meta-theory (theories of theory and practice), so the course team regarded it as important to focus on meta-theory in order to offer an interpretation of the quite concrete, changing patterns of assumptions that characterized contemporary trends in the field.

A first aspect of the change in curriculum theory and theorizing could be discerned in its view of the central role of teachers in curriculum theorizing — in addition to their role in curriculum planning, curriculum change and curriculum realization. The emergence of a strong professional consciousness in the teaching service had been given structure by the trend towards school-based curriculum development and away from the central control of the curriculum processes by state education departments. In Australia this trend was the product of a struggle by Victorian teacher unions for greater influence in curriculum matters as a 'terms and conditions' issue through the late 1960s and early 1970s. They saw curriculum issues as of similar importance to other industrial issues, since curriculum matters so directly affected the nature and conditions of teachers' work. Outside Australia the trend had been fostered by British arguments for the centrality of teachers in curriculum research and development, for example, in the work of Lawrence Stenhouse (1975),[2] and in the United States by arguments for curriculum deliberation by teachers as a mode of curriculum theorizing, for example, by Joseph Schwab (1969) and Decker Walker (1970). An awareness of these theoretical arguments and political struggles had led various Deakin researchers to work on the development of 'action research' as a modus operandi for those people at the front line of curriculum actualization — an approach which recognized the exigencies of specific social sites and the importance of the active participants in the work at those sites having control in the planning processes.[3]

A second set of changes in the understanding of curriculum in the literature was the emergence of 'critical' theorizing about curriculum. At the time the 'Curriculum Theory' course was being planned, course team members were grappling with some of the implications of this view of curriculum theorizing in their own work. One source of this new 'critical' view drew on the insights of the 'new sociology of education' (Young, 1971) and the Marxian/structuralist work of people such as Bowles and Gintis (1976) in North America. Another source was more local: Deakin theorists of curriculum were beginning to explore the ramifications of the

Frankfurt School of critical theory which had produced a critique of 'scientistic' reasoning in contemporary social life (including social science research, educational research, and social and educational policy);[4] they had begun to make new connections between action research and ideology-critique in a conception of a critical educational science. These developing theoretical perspectives on curriculum, based on work at Deakin and elsewhere, when combined with the awareness of the impact of the school-based curriculum development trend, provided some foundational ideas for a course about curriculum.

In 1981-1982 the course team began serious work in preparation for teaching 'Curriculum Theory' for the first time in 1983. They were assisted in their work by consultants appointed to bring particular expertise to the development of the course. These consultants were the late Professor Lawrence Stenhouse and Dr Jean Rudduck,[5] at that time members of the Centre for Applied Research of the University of East Anglia in England, and Professor Ulf Lundgren from the Department of Educational Research of the Stockholm Institute of Education in Sweden. Stenhouse and Rudduck brought with them a great deal of experience and insight into the matters related to thinking about the roles of teachers in curriculum research and development; Lundgren brought with him ideas emerging from the Marxian inspired theories of social reproduction. These three people provided perspectives which, when combined, picked up on two of the major trends in thinking about the curriculum of the time.

In deliberations with the course team Stenhouse and Rudduck explored ideas related to students thinking about curriculum within the context of their particular forms of teaching practice.[6] This notion developed from the attempt to hold the theory/practice relationship together and to avoid the separation of these elements which characterizes many postgraduate courses. From the outset the course aspired to develop approaches which helped teachers and others to articulate and elaborate ideas and issues based on actual teaching situations. Stenhouse and Rudduck thus provoked a subtle but significant shift in the self-understanding of the course — a shift from 'theory' to *'theorizing'*. On the basis of Stenhouse's previous work developing the notion of the teacher as an 'extended professional', the course team began to explore ways in which the course could support the development of extended professionalism in its students. The trilogy of elements that constituted extended professionalism, in Stenhouse's view, included:

1   the commitment to systematic questioning of one's own teaching as a basis for development;

2   the commitment and the skills to study one's own teaching; and

3   the concern to question and to test theory in practice by the use of those skills. (1975, p. 144)

This action-based approach to studying one's own work context provided a fundamental statement of principle and a practical basis for the development of the pedagogy of the course. One of the ways this orientation to action came to be enacted in the course design was in the notion that students would conduct *projects* in which they explored their own work and working situations. It was also to be enacted by making the theorizing required by these projects public. This idea echoed Stenhouse's definition of research: 'I see academia as a social system for the collaborative production of knowledge through research. Research is systematic enquiry made public. It is made public for criticism and utilization within a particular research tradition . . .' (1979, p. 7). In keeping with this definition Stenhouse and Rudduck advocated the development of an information exchange forum within the course and, given the nature of the distance education situation, in which students would not have direct contact with either their peers or tutors, the idea turned out to be extremely important for the pedagogy of the course. It took concrete form with the development of the idea of a *Course Journal*.

The idea of the 'Curriculum Theory' *Course Journal* was regarded as significant not only because it could provide a medium for students to exchange ideas. It also offered the possibility of enacting Stenhouse's notion of 'academia as a social system for the production and utilization of knowledge through research'. A journal offered the prospect of collaborative exchange in which course team members teaching the course could enter the forum on a more equal basis with students.[7] For this reason there was some spirited discussion in the course team about whether and how it should operate as an 'editorial board' for the journal. Would it accept all student submissions? Would only those submissions be published which seemed particularly meritorious? In the end it was agreed that all student work should be published, but that all work should be checked against explicitly stated criteria of acceptability (for example, that they be relevant to central concerns and theoretical ideas introduced in the course, written in an acceptable academic style, presented in acceptable camera-ready copy, and the like). Work which did not meet these requirements would be returned to students for resubmission. On this model of the journal, with the course team operating as this particular kind of editorial board, it was thought that the journal could become a medium for declaration and dialogue between students and course team members. On this basis, perhaps, staff and students could exchange ideas as a *community of enquirers*. Moreover, the idea of a journal readily addressed the problems posed by distance education as the print medium formed the basis of most of the Deakin courses, even though it was likely to put students in an unfamiliar role, where their work was written not only for tutors but for one another — indeed, where all the writing for the course was to be 'public' rather than a 'private' exchange between individual students and their tutors.[8]

Working from this image of the course as a community of enquirers, the course team began to consider the course on the model of a professional association, in which members contributed to and received a journal, but also participated in an *annual conference* at which they read and discussed papers face-to-face. The ideas of the journal and the annual course conference thus became central to the pedagogical design of the course.

Ulf Lundgren's contribution occurred after that of Stenhouse and Rudduck. As noted previously, he brought with him an interest in understanding the curriculum in terms of the relationship between schooling and society. Lundgren's work had led him into a way of thinking about the structure of the curriculum in terms of its relationship to the economic mode of production in a society. In this sense his was a classic Marxian approach — one that formulated a way of thinking about social institutions in terms of their relative positions in the base/superstructure framework of Marxian thinking. His analysis was fresh and powerful. It built on an emerging tradition of a critical or conflict approach to thinking about the structure of the curriculum.[9] While Rudduck and Stenhouse had greatly influenced the course team's ideas about the pedagogy of the course, Lundgren's contribution was especially important in giving focus to the content of the course. It was agreed that he would write a monograph for the course as a statement of his theoretical ideas about curriculum which could, on the one hand, problematize the field and the notion of 'curriculum' for students, and, on the other, provide a common point of reference for students and the course team in their own projects, reflection and writing.

In the 'Foreword' to the Lundgren monograph Stephen Kemmis provides an analysis of the text through a comment on its title: *Between Hope and Happening: Text and Context in Curriculum,* noting that

> Curriculum is to be understood as part of the social and historical process by which the social relationships necessary for production are reproduced.

On the other hand, the phrase 'text and context in curriculum' captures the dynamic of processes of social formation, some of whose traces can be read in curriculum, both as an historical artefact and as an historical force — shaped by and shaping history. (p.5)

Lundgren suggested that the problem of curriculum could be thought about in terms of the social necessity of sustaining a society's basis of production through reproducing — passing on to rising generations — the knowledge, skills, practices and social relationships needed for production. He argued that curricula are one of the ways in which the gap between production and reproduction is bridged. People wanting to ensure the future of existing means and modes of production must select and decontextualize the knowledges, skills, practices and social relationships required for production from the context of production, then recontextualize these knowledges, skills, practices and social relationships in forms suitable to the needs, traditions and patterns of work of the settings in which reproduction occurs (for example, in forms suitable to support teaching and learning in schools and other educational institutions). The results of this process of selection, decontextualization and recontextualization are curricula. Curricula thus embody ideas about how production and reproduction can be related, and about how rising generations can be inducted to the forms of life generations that have gone before. As such, curricula are important historical documents, providing evidence about the ways in which societies understand themselves — evidence about what aspects of production a society regards as so important that reproducing them cannot be left to chance (for example, left to socialization in the workplace, or upbringing in the family).

According to Lundgren, the development of curricula is a continuing struggle to develop 'texts' which adequately represent the knowledge, skills, practices and social relationships needed for production in the context of reproduction (schools, colleges, etc.), thus bridging the gap between material production and social reproduction. On this view, the central problem for *curriculum* is thus *'the representation problem'* — the problem of adequately representing the knowledge, skills, practices and social relationships needed for production in forms which can be taught and learned. When a group or a society resolves this problem for itself by developing a curriculum, it reveals something significant about itself — it reveals the way it understands the relationship between production and reproduction, and the relationship of rising generations to previous ones. When people studying curriculum reveal these understandings, they begin to unravel a society's underlying theories about itself, its economy and its culture, about the nature of education and schooling, and about the relationships between them.

From this analysis, Lundgren argues, it follows that the central problem for *curriculum theory* is the problem of finding the theoretical means to interpret different curricula in different cultures and societies in different epochs — by interpreting them as texts which, in their own ways, for their own times and settings, reveal specific ideas and theories about how the specific needs and contexts of production (for example, in the economy) are thought to be related to the specific needs and contexts of reproduction (for example, in schooling). If every curriculum reveals a specific theory of the relationship between production and reproduction, then the task of curriculum theory is to develop general theories capable of understanding and explaining the specific theories which inform specific curricula. In this sense Lundgren regards the study of curriculum theory as meta-theoretical.

Lundgren's ideas, when placed beside those of Stenhouse and Rudduck, helped provide a general conceptual framework for the course. Stenhouse and Rudduck had provided the basis for the primary pedagogical considerations of the course, while Lundgren had provided the primary theoretical questions. At the same time the course could also understand itself in the terms of Lundgren's theoretical framework as aiming to produce — or reproduce — a different kind of teaching force in Australia: one committed to what Stenhouse described as 'extended professionalism'. The course team understood itself to be selecting (from the context of educational production in schools and education systems) the critical curriculum theorizing and practice of some teachers and teachers' organizations, and preparing a pedagogy capable of reproducing this extended professionalism among its students as a rising generation of curriculum theorist-practitioners. The way these two dimensions came together can be seen in an image provided by a short comment in the *Study Guide* produced for the first offering of the course in 1983. The statement read: 'The long term aim of the course is to help you change the way you do things in the light of what you know (and change the way you think in the light of how things work out in practice)' (p.7). This major aspiration of the course was given a structure by the ideas and suggestions of Rudduck, Stenhouse and Lundgren, but it is equally important to recall that the perspectives of these people were set against a stream of research and theorizing by Deakin researchers over the preceding years. That is, the ideas built up in the planning phase of the course were set down on a foundation of several years of work that related to different aspects of the problem of the curriculum.[10] This point is clearly demonstrated in the following extract from the 1983 *Study Guide*:

In terms of historical and political processes which produced the *Curriculum Theory* course, it is a product of a continuous line of development in the work of Deakin staff interested in curriculum — a development which has taken place over the last few years. It has involved research on teacher action research (a form of self-reflective research by teachers for teachers), theoretical work on modern critical theory (a theory of social science whose aim is to facilitate the development of a more just and rational society through critical analysis of our present social and educational institutions and practices), long-term in-service work with teachers helping them to develop a critical perspective on their own practices, and a great deal of critical reflection on our own teaching practices. (p. 8)

At a more concrete level the work of the course team, in the planning phase, can be characterized in terms of the agreement reached on the key ideas or propositions of the course and the actual structural components of the pedagogy of the course. These were described in the first *Study Guide* which presented students with four key propositions and one supporting theme, a composite list which provided the surface text of the theoretical aspirations of the course:

1   Any curriculum (text *for* pedagogy) or any curriculum theory (text *about* pedagogy) is a unique product of the *historical and political circumstances* and processes which produced it.
2   Any curriculum or curriculum theory expresses particular values and value systems; implicitly or explicitly, it expresses a social and moral philosophy. By examining these value commitments and the social relationships which support them, we may identify the *ideological* aspect of the curriculum or theory.
3   Any curriculum or curriculum theory likewise takes an implicit or explicit stand on the nature of knowledge. By examining its perspective on subject-matter (of learning or of curriculum theory) we may identify the *epistemological* aspects of curriculum theory.
4   Any curriculum or curriculum theory expresses, implicitly or explicitly, a view about the organization of teaching and learning. A curriculum theory therefore, is also a theory about *pedagogical* action. (p. 10)

A fifth point, which emerges out of these four, was that a dialectical conception of theory and practice could assist students to develop a platform for *critique* in which action and understanding could be seen as mutually constitutive, constantly and critically informing one another.

The pedagogical structure of the course was designed to permit students to explore these five points critically and self-critically in their own day-to-day practice as well as in the work of the course. It included:

1   the production of a *course journal* based on contributions from all course participants (students and course team) in several distinct 'departments' *(theoretical articles* addressing the 'conceptual furniture' of the Lundgren monograph, *activity reports* through which students reported on their explorations of the key propositions of the course in their own practice, contributed *abstracts* of reading done for the course, and *correspondence* with other course members about their contributions);[11]

2   the holding of an *annual course conference* at which papers would be presented and discussed;

3   *project work* by course participants which would permit actual curriculum theorizing undertaken in participants' own curriculum settings, with a major project to be conducted throughout the year and reported on in a project report, and smaller-scale investigative activities (perhaps contributing to the major project) to be carried out along the way and reported in the *Course Journal* and at the conference; and

4   engagement in a wide range of *reading and reflection* on curriculum as a basis for reflection both on one's own practical activities and on theoretical ideas being discussed in the *Journal* (in one's own and others' contributions).

Being constructed on these pedagogical principles, the 'Curriculum Theory' course set itself against the view that it is the task of teachers to present a 'correct' view of the subject matter of a course, or a variety of competing but more-or-less adequate views. In this way it challenged a conventional liberal view, widely held in universities since the Enlightenment, that a variety of competing, more or less adequate, views of a subject should be presented so that students can choose among them. This Enlightenment view may seem to be important in any course which aims to be 'critical'. In practice, however, the presentation of alternative views in many higher education courses is frequently no more than a manifestation of the 'marketplace' notion of debate criticized by MacIntyre (1981). On the 'marketplace' notion staff frequently present views without sufficiently engaging the arguments between them (and sometimes distort their presentations so that their theoretical preferences are clearly implied even though insufficiently justified by argument).

Similarly students are not compelled to argue the strengths and weaknesses of competing theories; a choice between them is regarded as a matter of private conviction, not public justification. In such cases the substance of points of view is regarded as separate from the substance of arguments for and against them; by this means the process of debate itself, through which the compulsion to support or reject views is secured, is made secondary, and 'holding' views is treated as more significant than sustaining them through argument. For such reasons the 'Curriculum Theory' course constructed itself as a 'community of enquirers', creating a journal and a conference, and requiring correspondence between students. For such reasons also it prescribed the Lundgren monograph as a focus for debate — as a proto-theory to be tested against students' views and the views of the literature of curriculum. The course was thus to be constructed through critical and self-critical debate in which students would be required to argue about the strengths and limitations of Lundgren's views, the views of the course team and each other's views. Their commitment to the debate would be secured by making their own practice a source for and an object of their enquiries.

The description of 'Curriculum Theory' so far has given some background to the development of the course for its first offering in 1983, illustrating some of its major assumptions and its strong sense that it should be explicit about its own pedagogy as a curriculum about curriculum. It describes features of the course that were themselves to undergo change in the light of experience of the course in practice, when its 'hopes' became — or did not become — 'happenings'.

A Description of Five Years of ECS 802: 'The Happening . . .'

The first number of the *Course Journal* was prepared by the course team and some other people, such as David Hamilton from Glasgow, who might be described as an 'outer circle' of 'associate members' of the course. It was a primer, one to be set up as a starting point for the sort of contributions which were anticipated from all course members. The protocol for student publication involved submission of articles to a tutor who would determine if the pieces satisfied explicitly stated course requirements (laid out in the *Study Guide*) for journal submissions. If there was any doubt about the standard of the work submitted, it was to be second-checked by another tutor and returned to the student with recommendations for rectifying the particular problems. In this sense the course team was to function as an editorial board. The difficulty in entering into the sort of public exchange anticipated by the *Journal* structure is captured in the words of one of the first contributions in Volume 1, Number 2 (the first 'real' *Course Journal,* containing student work). The statement commenced with the following remark:

> I hate getting started, I'm nervous. Like an old-style bush kid confronted for the first time by the sea. (I hope its okay to collaboratively share some panic and feelings of inadequacy along with the engagement in pedagogical discourse!) I'm just wanting (hoping?) to get started, to get the toe in. Nothing flash. (Poynter, 1983)

It is not clear if this statement represented the view and emotions of other course participants. People wrote articles about theoretical issues, about their attempts to interpret the curriculum activities they were engaged in, about the books and papers they were reading *and* about their reactions to other people's ideas (as reported in previous *Journals*). The *Journals* came out on a regular basis and information started to filter across the various departments (theoretical articles, activity reports, abstracts, correspondence). People wrote about Lundgren's monograph and started to move around the various pieces of his 'conceptual furniture'. Lundgren's proto-theory provided the common reference point for placing curriculum issues in a wider context. In August 1983 a course conference was conducted in which people who had known each other only abstractly, through their journal writing, met each other and talked in person. Fifteen people attended, including some invited speakers. Those people unable to attend submitted 'display papers'. The forum provided a significant extension to the theme of the course, giving it a moment of life and vitality that is important in all forms of education.

Looking back at the entries in the *Journal* in 1983, one can detect a sense of the long-term patterns of concerns which were to emerge time and again in subsequent years. The following comments lifted from Volume 1, Number 4 (the final issue of the first year of the course) are indicative of trends and concerns which were to become consolidated in subsequent years. For example, with regard to the Lundgren monograph: 'The more I am working through this course the more restricted I am beginning to feel having to use Lundgren's furniture. I feel the meanings of some of the terms he uses are too narrow, or fluctuate' (Gossage, 1983). A different type of comment, but one that clearly related to the philosophical underpinnings of the course, noted the following concern:

> to my mind the real reason for the reactionism emanating from the course developers is their inability to appreciate that although

this course is based in materialism (which they acknowledge) they have been prepared to accept material from participants who do not utilize materialism's philosophical underpinnings. This does not mean that course participants must believe in materialism, rather I am expressing the view that argument put forward in course material must be based in support or attack of that philosophy. However, what has been obvious from the first articles in the Journals is writing based in Platonic idealism but lacking a perspective critical of the Marxist materialist view. (Green, 1983, p.153)

Comments like these raise questions about the epistemological framework of the course and its pedagogy, especially its notion of the course as a 'professional association'.

At a different level other comments point to a different type of reaction, one that aligned more closely with the *hope* of the course team and, in particular, to the ideals espoused by Stenhouse and Rudduck. This point relates to the opportunity afforded by the course structure to take apart and reassemble one's particular context of work. This point is well explained in the following comment:

I have found the course has pushed me to describe and analyse my actions and viewpoints as a curriculum practitioner and more importantly clarified these points of view and, I consider, led to informed considered action: praxis . . . .
What has appealed to me is the valuing and recognition of my everyday knowledge about curriculum by the course team and other course participants. This affirmation via the journal, curriculum conference and tutor's comments has encouraged me to lay out more of my practice for scrutiny and in so doing has given me greater control over it. (Cleary, 1983, p.183)

Not all students had such a positive reaction to 'Curriculum Theory', of course, and course team members were not uniformly satisfied with the quality of students' work.

In the latter part of 1985 a review of the course was conducted by Terry Evans from the Deakin University Distance Education Unit (Evans, 1985b). This evaluation provided insights into both the theoretical scope and the pedagogy of the course. Evans discovered a high degree of confusion and apprehension amongst the students he interviewed. In his words, '. . . the most important single point about the students was that they were not expecting the sort of course that they received' (p.2). The largest cause of this confusion, in his opinion, was students' lack of familiarity with the neo-Marxist perspective and/or the history of educational thought. This particular concern was most manifest in having to work with the Lundgren monograph. Evans noted that 'the monograph represents the central component of the course and is also the location of most of the problems for the students' (p. 5).

Staff were running into difficulties too. In the area of the course pedagogy there were many concerns associated with the trials and tribulations of turning course material around in sufficient detail and time to be meaningful. The process required that tutors read and check submissions against course requirements, decide whether they could be published as they stood or whether resubmission should be required (a judgment to be checked with a second tutor), hand over material to be published to a course assistant who would collate, paginate and index the material, send it off to the University's Printery for reproduction, and ensure that it was sent out promptly to students. The process, while administratively routine, was easily disrupted. Tutors might be away at the time material was received, arranging the first check of material against course requirements might take longer than the few days allowed in planning the process, second checking adds time to the process, compiling the material might be held up by late student submissions, and occasionally delays could occur when the University's Printery or mail-out facilities were unable to process the material speedily. Alongside this production process, tutors were expected to respond to students' work individually, offering suggestions, advice and evaluative comment. This assessment process was also demanding, since students' work varied greatly with their individual interests and work settings, so no marking could be considered 'routine'. Through the year students were submitting as many as fifteen pieces of work, varying from one-paragraph abstracts of *Journal* articles to substantial project reports. The assessment load was thus substantial in quantity and demanding because of the rather relentless course schedule.

One of Evans' concluding comments provides a summary for the first few years of operation:

> The task of constructing a critical community at a distance is no mean challenge. From the evidence of the present group of students it has not been achieved, but there has been some progress. For example, almost all the students said that they did not feel that they were members of a *Curriculum Theory* critical community — one said that the feeling was of a 'sense of loneliness on the course' — but several students did feel that they were more involved with each other than in other distance education courses at Deakin or elsewhere. (p. 8)

These points are worthy of some elaboration, for they pull into sharp relief the different elements of this course. The substance of Evans' analysis will be developed further through the ideas and observations of one of the students of the course who, in the pages of the *Course Journal*, provided some telling insights into the life of 'Curriculum Theory' as a course for students.

In 1986 one of the students, Rigmor George, conducted a continuing critique of both the course in general and the Lundgren monograph in particular. Her comments neatly encapsulated concerns expressed by some students and the course team:

> Critical Meta-Theories
> . . . Now it is in this context that ECS 802 is presented. Not only is it dealing with meta-theories of education, it is itself (of course) a product of one of them. Not only is it alerting us to the ideological implications of curricula, it carries with it (of course) its own ideological message. (1986b, p.85)

George notes that a 'critical theory approach to curriculum' is one that '. . . maintains the issues are political and related to the much wider and more pervasive social theory which is capitalistic' (p.83). Her comment exposes a major point of contention about the way the theory and pedagogy of the course are interrelated. Her concern was that the critical meta-theory, as represented by Lundgren, failed to say enough about the complexity and richness of human experience. She opens up this concern with the question, 'What is this proto-theory (and meta-theory) saying about human beings?' (1986a, p.75). She expressed the more substantive point thus:

> The most fundamental question — What is the nature of our 'humanness'? — will determine the direction our education 'system' will take. It is at this level that I see a basic problem with the theory. Society's views on humanity and the means used to assist the growth and development of that quality are so divergent that it is not possible to provide educational curricula which can openly and honestly accommodate the different world views which generate them. (1986a, p.75)

The full implication of this concern goes back to the point made earlier about the expression of humanness. The critical meta-theoretical position calls forth a communitarian ideal — the idea that the course can be in some concrete sense a living community. But such an ideal usually rests on the notion that members of the community can interact face-to-face. Distance education challenges this basic assumption. The attenuation, intangibility and transience of relationships in the distance education mode make the communitarian ideal highly problematic. The following assertion concerns the central problem of distance education:

> We need to learn a new role of relating to each other as colleagues. Relationships of any sort are delicate, complex affairs . . . . Let's build on the relationships. Perhaps personal individual relationships would work better — phone calls, in person conversations, and letters between students might be a good idea. (George, 1986b, p.92)[12]

The idea expressed here has been the concern of a number of students other than Rigmor George; and their concerns are legitimate. What comes into question is the very frame we use to think about this issue. Using ideas lifted from the times and places when education was always intimate and face-to-face does not help in our understandings of the form of social relationships which are increasingly separated and distant. This is the substantive curriculum question of 'Curriculum Theory' and other distance education courses. Among the course team, at least initially, there was a tendency to see the issue as a problem of a 'theory/practice gap'; one in which theorizing is done in one context and practice in another. Some may see this as a technical issue in which the challenge is to find a technical and bureaucratic solution to the delivery of educational ideas. This approach accepts as fundamental a distinction between theory and practice. Others, however, regard a distinction between theory and practice as committing one to a false dichotomy. Such people attempt to demonstrate in the design of courses (as elsewhere) that theory and practice are mutually constitutive. On this latter view the so-called 'gap' is treated as a matter of logical inconsistency. Many of the arguments associated with 'Curriculum Theory' have been set within the limits of one or other of these positions, embracing different dimensions of arguments that have held sway in earlier times. Lundgren's insight into the 'representation problem' is one way of characterizing the parameters of the theory/practice issue, at least to the extent that Lundgren's view of meta-theory puts the theory/ practice issue on the agenda of curriculum debates. The debates in the pages of the *Course Journal* have generally utilized a limited range of perspectives for thinking about the substantive problem of the curriculum, but in doing so they have remained wedded to the ideas of a bygone era. They have accepted as fundamental the distinction between theory and practice in ways characteristic of the curriculum theorizing that developed and took root in an earlier period of curriculum theory. What is required now is a fresh perspective on the curriculum issue. In words reminiscent of Geothe's views of 150 years before,[13] the contemporary Australian curriculum theorist Doug White (1987b) wrote: 'Thought and action, intellectual and material production are inextricably linked in the modern world . . . . The issue before us is not whether intellect and action are combined, but on what terms' (p.68). The final part of this section will highlight the attempts within the course to move towards such an understanding.

In 1986, partly as a result of the survey conducted by Terry Evans, we decided to introduce a second monograph into the course to supplement the Lundgren monograph, *Between Hope and Happening.* This second monograph (Kemmis with Fitzclarence, 1986) developed an argument about the changing meta-theoretical commitments of several key curriculum theorists of the last forty years, to illustrate how and why the 'critical' position of some contemporary curriculum theorists had emerged. The importance of this new position, it was argued, is that it has not only put new issues on the curriculum agenda, but it has also required new social relations and forms of organization among curriculum workers (including academic specialists in the field, teachers, specialist curriculum developers, students and others) for these issues to be addressed. These social relations of curriculum theorizing recover theory as an equally central concern for curriculum practitioners in schools and classrooms as for curriculum policy-makers and designers outside classrooms. This focus on the social relations of curriculum production was, of course, simply another reflection of the trend which had set the scene for the emergence of the 'Curriculum Theory' course. At one and the same time the course acknowledged the contested nature of the curriculum and asserted the legitimacy of the teacher's role in these contests. The pedagogy of the course was one which set out to draw this conflict and debate into the open, making it public through the *Course Journal.* The course thus put itself at odds with the conservative view of curriculum which assumed or asserted that curricula could and should reflect a social equilibrium, and it did so by making debate (and conflict) a material feature of the life of the course.

While the course was constructing this form of life for itself, however, there were important shifts taking place in the culture more generally, and the course was far from immune to them. The course had arisen from a context in which there had been a long struggle among Victorian teachers (as well as teachers elsewhere) for a greater say in curriculum matters, and it aimed to extend that struggle into the domain of curriculum theorizing (a domain in which curriculum ideas had been justified and legitimated largely by groups which teachers saw as 'external' to the working profession — people in tertiary institutions and state education departments). By the late 1980s, however, the course found itself operating in a very different climate, in which the achievements of teachers in their struggle towards greater control over their own curriculum practice were being eroded. There were increasing signs that the state was once again exerting a more active control over the construction and legitimation of curricula — for example, in the reconstruction of curricula to meet the demands of a changing economy.

In the view of the course team, the 'Curriculum Theory' course could not be regarded as immune from these more general shifts; in higher education, as much as in schooling, the state and the economy were imposing new demands on the curriculum. The 'Curriculum Theory' course, with its particular theoretical bias and pedagogical emphasis, could be a forum in which this shift could be addressed and interpreted. The confusions over the theoretical perspective adopted in the course and its relationship to the course pedagogy noted in Terry Evans' course evaluation can be understood quite concretely in addressing this confusion. The course aimed to take on board contemporary social issues, and to see itself as part of a broader set of curriculum relationships in society. The course team was committed to modelling critical and self-critical curriculum debate through the practice of the course. Unlike other courses whose curriculum is more 'closed', the 'Curriculum Theory' course aimed to remain 'open', to allow students to debate and explore issues. Perhaps for this reason some students found the course confusing. In coming to grips with such issues in its own pedagogy and its own curriculum, members of the course, both staff and students, attempted to explore formative ideas and value positions in a rapidly changing social context. In the next section we will return to explore this issue in more depth.

To summarize: in the volumes of the *Course Journal* over the five years from 1983 to 1987 there are numerous examples of work where people have managed to analyze and interpret a wide range of curriculum issues relating to different educational spheres. In this sense the course has staked a genuine claim in the territory of curriculum theory and as a component of the idea of distance education. A brief elaboration of the different perspectives developed, highlighting an emerging thread which has held the practice of the course together, would confirm this point. Yet to do so risks remaining on the surface of the activities of the course and taking different participants' views of the course at face value; beneath this surface, between rather than on the lines of its text, however, an unfolding logic can be discerned. This unfolding logic shaped, and continues to shape, the cultural foundations on which the ideas of the course are constructed. In the words of the Kemmis/ Fitzclarence monograph: '. . . the central problem of curriculum theory is to be understood as a double problem of the relationship between theory and practice, on the one hand, and of the relationship between education and society on the other' (p. 22). As we have attempted to show, the course strove to make students aware and active in their roles as curriculum workers, not simply as cogs in the machine of social reproduction, but as the producers of curriculum, and through curriculum as producers of a future society. As we have also attempted to show, the course was only partially successful in achieving this aim. The 'hope' was yet unrealized in the 'happening'.

Nevertheless, the course team retained the 'hope' of enacting (and criticizing) the view of curriculum workers as the producers of history in a communitarian curriculum practice. Evidence of this hope is to be found in the 1986 Kemmis/Fitzclarence monograph:

> The challenge for curriculum theory is to create new forms of studying and transforming curriculum through the kind of critical curriculum theorizing outlined in this monograph. A study of contemporary curriculum concerns will suggest to curriculum workers some starting points for concrete, local analysis; more importantly, they may suggest areas in which they can use the research process as a step to action, and in this way become involved in the struggle to transform school curriculum, schooling and the operations of the state in education — a struggle to emancipate students, teachers, parents and society generally from the irrationalities, injustices and deprivations which currently disfigure both the lives of individuals and the social structures of our society. (pp. 139-40)

This is no easy task. Changing social relationships to allow curriculum workers to enact this emancipatory ideal requires not only changes in the social relations of schooling but also new kinds of interpretation of curriculum work and the social condition. These changes must occur not only in schooling but also in the construction of courses about curriculum (like 'Curriculum Theory'). Reflecting on our emancipatory aspirations in the light of our analysis of the 'Curriculum Theory' course, we have come to an understanding of a new dilemma confronting the course: the dilemma of creating a *communitarian* practice in *distance education* (which by its nature seems to deny the possibility of face-to-face interaction between course members). This is a dilemma to be faced by a variety of groups aiming to enact a critical view of distance education, not just for members of the Deakin 'Curriculum Theory' course. On the assumption that the dilemma of communitarian ideals and distance education practice is of general significance, we have chosen to conclude this chapter with an exploration of the issue.

The 'Curriculum Theory' Course as an Expression of the Curriculum Problem

Our account of the first five years of the 'Curriculum Theory' course has highlighted concerns about the course which point to a confusion about expectations about the nature of distance education generally and the study of curriculum specifically. The analysis to this point has concentrated on establishing a warrant for a new perspective on the nature of the curriculum problem as a problem for people whose work is the production of curricula and, through curricula, of the social relations and social life of society. Though the course is still far from exemplary in achieving its aims, we have attempted to argue that its steps towards a collaborative, communitarian practice of curriculum critique and curriculum production are at least suggestive of models of curriculum work appropriate for a society in which people can legitimately see themselves as the producers, not just the products, of history. Our reflection on the history of the course has revealed a potential contradiction between the practice of distance education and the collaborative, communitarian practice which the course aimed to foster. We can begin our exploration of this contradiction with an extract from the Dire Straits song, 'So Far Away':

> I'm tired of making out on the telephone
> And you're so far away from me.
> . . .
> I get so tired when I have to explain
> When you're so far away from me.
> See you've been in the sun and I've been in the rain
> And you're so far away from me.[14]

In the modern world absence and presence, the concrete and abstract, are united in radically new forms. The global satellite network, new innovations in telecommunications and the spread of computer technology have collapsed the time and space boundaries that previously structured social interaction. Modern jet transport permits travel to most corners of the globe in a relatively short time. The geographic and cultural divisions between north and south, east and west have altered dramatically during the latter part of this century. This new level of social exchange has been called the emergence of the 'information society'. 'Curriculum Theory', as a distance education course, is itself an expression of the expansion and diversification of the 'information society', attenuating and straining the social relations of education as they have been understood in previous times. The new cultural situation is one in which ideas and action become radically reconstituted and produce the opportunity for new forms of social interaction *and* the need for new forms of theoretical interpretation. In what follows we attempt to sketch the outlines of an interpretive alternative.

In the 'Preface' to the Kemmis/Fitzclarence monograph for the course we wrote:

> More substantively, there is also disagreement about what aspects of contemporary social life should be represented in curricula for students to learn. Contemporary views of what should be 'in' the school curriculum reflect ideas from three different periods in recent history: ideas from a period of relatively high social consensus (the late 1950s), from the period when this consensus broke down (the 1960s and '70s), and the current period in which strenuous attempts are being made to re-establish consensus about the nature, needs and problems of society. (p. ix)

The general curriculum problem introduced here holds the clues for an interpretation of ECS 802 'Curriculum Theory'. The monograph is at pains to point out that a number of theoretical perspectives collide and confront one another in contemporary educational debate and in contemporary curriculum theorizing. But this image of contested positions actually begs the question as to which theoretical position provides the greatest interpretive power.[15] The substance of a perspective which provides a way of thinking about the curriculum problem is offered by Doug White (1987a), when he notes:

> The possibility now exists that students no longer need to be constrained by the restricted and divided curriculum of years past. The curriculum problem is that we now have to find ways in which students can be assisted to find a structure and identity which can give order and meaning to the various elements of the curriculum. That order and meaning once came from the social categories of work. In the present form of society, that source of structure is insufficient. We must turn to broader considerations of the formation of persons. (p. 4)

The 'post-industrial' or information society is constituted around the convergence of new social associations.[16] We need think no further than the course described here to understand how this new level of associations comes into being. Distance education works on an assumption of establishing and maintaining continuing contact despite the 'class' members being thousands of miles apart. The assumptions here are supported materially by the capacity to exchange information quickly and over vast distances. The long distance associations of the modern world are directly linked to the extended market relationships that stretch relationships away from the former face-to-face relations that characterized the clan and kin associations of former times, the village relationships of pre-industrial society, and the class relationships that existed in the industrial communities of the late nineteenth and early twentieth centuries. The extended market logic of contemporary Western society envelops the predominantly concrete relationships of family and neighbourhood and school,[17] and locates them in a matrix of abstracted functional relationships characteristic of the modern state and its increasingly transnational economic structures. Increasingly, in our formation as persons, we carry our sense of primary attachment to others in our families and neighbourhoods into this more abstracted realm of functional associations — for example, through informal relationships with others in the workplace, through our use of the new telecommunications media and through the identifications we make with political and cultural identities known to us only through television. The data highlighting the time that children spend watching television (and using computers) provide just one example of evidence to support this trend.

Education has become directly involved in the transformation being discussed here. Schools, colleges and universities have become an aspect of the 'information revolution', in helping to provide the skills and develop the predispositions associated with the more complex juxtaposition of abstract/concrete relationships.[18] The increasing stress on exposure to different forms of print media and computer hardware and software, coupled with the contemporary return to pedagogies of problem-solving and discovery learning, are indictors of education's role in the new level of social transformation. The changes in social relationships in education (and elsewhere in society) are not confined to the development of these new communication technologies but also appear in technologies of social and educational administration. The trend has been recognized since Weber. In bureaucratic modes of social organization and management, persons are construed not as common bearers of a shared culture and shared circumstances, but as 'individuals' dominated by the pursuit of private modes of consumption and gratification. While 'autonomy' is lauded as a primary social value, in fact people find themselve cast as objects (rather than subjects) — as employees, to be managed and controlled like other elements in production processes.[19] In his eloquent critique of the rise of modern, bureaucratized forms of consciousness and morality, MacIntyre (1981) expressed it this way: '. . . the society in which we live is one in which bureaucracy and individualism are partners as well as antagonists' (p.33).

MacIntyre argues that contemporary social life does not presuppose the sharing of forms of life or sharing of perspectives on the world characteristic of a sense of 'community'. Our moral and intellectual debates can no longer presuppose the forms of sharing on which fundamental agreements can be based, sufficient to sustain us through debate to mutually agreed conclusions. Instead, contemporary culture takes a 'marketplace' view of debate, in which people feel free to select the premises and conclusions which best suit their views and interests — and suffer the consequences in interminable disagreements. The burden of MacIntyre's argument is that we need to re-establish such forms of community. To do so, he argues, three things are necessary: (1) a sense that our social (and educational) practice are cooperatively agreed, embodying shared values and excellences, (2) a common sense of tradition against which the excellence of practice may be judged, and (3) a sense of 'the narrative unity of a human life' — the sense that a person's life can only be judged from the perspective of her or his death as having embodied a striving to enact particular values. The unity of these three features in the social life of earlier times, he argues, has been fragmented by contemporary conditions. Referring to the great theorist of bureaucracy, Max Weber, he says, 'We are all Weberians now' — meaning that our sense of being and belonging through communities in civil society has been replaced by a sense of being and belonging through the bureaucratic institutions of the modern state.[20]

It is our contention that many debates relating to the form and substance of current education practices are related to a misinterpretation or misrepresentation of the changed nature of contemporary social life. The current debate about the nature of tertiary education in the new struggle for national renovation is an example of the confusion and conflict engendered by the bureaucratized form of social life. Within the more restricted context of distance education it is essential that the radically altered nature of social life is made problematic and placed on the agenda of considerations for students of curriculum.

The 'Curriculum Theory' course, as described in this chapter, brings into question any static view of the relationship between education and society. By its practice it clearly brings into question more conventional assumptions about the relationship between the university and society. In its substance and its pedagogy it challenges the view that it is the task of the teachers of the course to present a 'correct' view (or a variety of competing but adequate views) of theory to be implemented by students of the course in their curriculum practice. Yet it must confront its own role and agency in the production of more bureaucratized and abstracted social relations.[21] The following comment in the 'Editorial' for Volume 5, Number 4 of the *Course Journal* notes the implications for the course of the kinds of social transformation we have been discussing:

> Many of the articles which have been written in this *Journal* as well as the earlier editions highlight the impact of this transformation. It is relevant for all of us to read the different articles with a strong sense of the new logic which is at work. It is here that our separate contexts and problems can help inform us of the bigger picture which is being etched on the ground on which we all stand. This approach of critical exchange is also part of a practice which maintains a sense of the ideal of education as an aspect of the cultural heritage; and not just as an appendage of the instrumental demands of the new breed of political managers. That is where curriculum issues can be debated as an aspect of long term traditions and practices in particular settings and not simply according to the quantifying logic of performance indicators. (Fitzclarence, 1987, p.2)

The changing ideas, practices and social relations of society in general can be read in the life of the 'Curriculum Theory' course, just as they can be read in other parts of social life, despite the aspirations of the course to challenge at least some of them. It would be at least uncharitable to assert that the course did not (or does not) challenge some taken-for-granted assumptions about curriculum and pedagogy (for example, by changing the role of the teacher, by establishing direct communication between students through the medium of the *Course Journal*, by taking some steps towards establishing a critical community in which students together make critical analyses of their own curriculum work and of contemporary curriculum theoretic ideas). But the very modes of relationship possible in the course are ones which bedevil contemporary social life, including the abstraction of ideas and interpersonal relationships. The need and demand for distance education is in a sense an expression of what some might see as a social pathology — the isolation of people from the sites and people in which and with whom they can become educated. We are less certain than we were when first we designed the course about whether distance education is an expression of the problem or part of its resolution. In the case of the 'Curriculum Theory' course there is a certain irony in creating a 'course community' in which members interact almost wholly through a journal, with very limited access to one another as persons,[22] and in a highly deliberate, careful, written form (without the elasticity and openness possible in conversation). The appearance of the *Journal* only four times a year also gives the interaction an attenuated, stylized quality which mitigates against the kind of 'suck it and see' interchange which helps people develop confidence and competence in critical discourse.[23]

It is not simply that the 'Curriculum Theory' course is limited in achieving its aspirations by the attenuation of relationships characteristic of distance education. It is also that, by its very operation, it models these attentuated relationships and thus creates conditions for their reproduction. To the extent that it is successful it may even encourage participants to believe that distance relationships are as 'normal' and as 'real' — even as 'critical' — as face-to-face relationships can be. There is little doubt that such relationships are increasingly typical of the abstracted social relationships characteristic of contemporary society, but the course aims to treat such relationships critically rather than to take them for granted. If such relationships are part of the means by which societies are able not only to coordinate action across vast spaces but also to keep the operation of certain economic and cultural interests invisible and thus contain the expression of critical thought and the development of solidarity (for example, in social movements[24]), then a profound question is raised for any course which attempts to creat a 'critical community' through distance education. Can such a course be 'critical' in ways which challenge the presumptions of the very means by which it is offered (distance education practices and technologies)? Can it be 'critical' in ways which reveal the ownership and control of the means of communication which make it possible? Does such a course reveal the attenuation of social relationships in technologized, bureaucratized societies, or does it simply exploit and symbolize them?

Of course, these questions do not apply to Deakin's 'Curriculum Theory' course alone. Nor do they apply only to courses with an explicitly 'critical' intent. The trends to abstraction are apparent in institutionalized education in general. What is apparent in innovation in distance education as a field (especially given its fascination for the potential of new information technologies like computer-based teaching and learning, the use of satellite communication, and the like) is the emergence of new patterns of social interaction based on the increasing acceptance of abstraction — abstraction not only in the realm of ideas, but also in our modes of social relationship (increasingly mediated by organizations and technologies of communication), and even our understanding of our own identities (for example, in terms of our roles in organizations). This trend towards abstraction requires interpretation and it requires attempts to invoke alternative practices — interpretations and practices capable of relocating us as agents in the production of our own identities, our social relationships and our society.

Our argument is that the forms of social life which previously shaped education and schooling have changed markedly. Some argue that education should 'keep up with' the shifts in our forms of social life which the changing technology of communications has wrought by mimicking and extending the new communicative forms in schooling (for example, by increased use of computers as if this were necessarily a contribution to the development of the 'information society' as a better society for all people). Others are less sanguine about such developments, seeing in them the possibility that an extension or expansion of these technologies of communication in schooling may threaten the practice of education (a practice always potentially at odds with the institutional processes of schooling), undermining the very possibility of critical thought. The problem was well articulated by Stanley Aronowitz (1977), writing about Max Horkheimer:

> In his book *The Eclipse of Reason* (1947), Max Horkheimer, founder of the Frankfurt Institute for Social Research, provided one of the most succinct formulations of the problem engendered by mass culture. According to Horkheimer, the significance of the challenge posed by the massified culture industry to civilisation as such consisted in its assault on the capacity to engage in critical thought as a meaningful form of social discourse. Horkheimer cared deeply about the content of critical thought, but with the rise of fascism he became more concerned with the spectre of the end of reason itself. In his view, the capacity of humans to distance themselves from the object in order to gain a perspective on their social world can no longer be taken for granted. The restricted language and thought codes produced by the reduction of all thought to its technical dimensions reach far into the culture, encompassing schools as well as communications, the public as well as the private spheres of discourse. It is no longer a question of whether ordinary discourse is able to deal with specific ideological and social content. As Jürgen Habermas expressed it, the new situation raises the question of the competence of people to effectively communicate ideational content. The issue is the capacity for

theoretical or conceptual thought itself. When people lack such competence, social action that transcends the struggle for justice within the empirically given rules of social organization and discourse is impossible. (p.768)

On this analysis it is inappropriate for distance educators to continue thinking about their curricula and pedagogies in terms of criteria associated with a form of education and social life that has been superseded. The challenge now appears to be to find alternative ways to think about the new social contradictions associated with the turn towards the abstract mode of ideational, social and economic exchange characteristic of contemporary social life — a trend of which distance education is manifestly a part. This requires a form of theorizing that views culture in a comprehensive sense — one that moves beyond the different kinds of interpretation noted in the 'Preface' to the course monograph (quoted earlier in this section) in which ideas about social consensus played such an important theoretical (and ideological) role. At the current historical juncture there is a need to offer a theoretical alternative to narrow, consensualist, bureaucratic and technicist approaches to thinking about education. In curriculum theory significant steps were taken in this direction by the development of reproduction theory as a means of understanding education in relation to society, at first in its 'correspondence' form (Bowles and Gintis, 1976) and later in its 'contestation' (Apple, 1982) and 'resistance' (Giroux, 1983) theory forms (which began to comprehend and explore conflict and contradiction in the reproduction of the patterns of economic and cultural life through education). In their turn certain of the key ideas and assumptions of reproduction theory which persist from the theoretical frameworks of earlier times need to be challenged. For example, ideas about the determination of the cultural superstructure by the economic base (which tended to survive in the correspondence theory of reproduction) must be replaced by more dialectical understandings of the mutual determination of base and superstructure, and there is a need to move beyond outmoded ideas about the nature and significance of social class which fail to acknowledge that the social relations of advanced capitalism are very different from the class relations of nineteenth century capitalism.

Developing such new forms of interpretation and new practices is the permanent problem of social theorizing, including curriculum theorizing. In the Kemmis/Fitzclarence monograph we argued that 'the central problem of curriculum theory is to be understood as a double problem of the relationship between theory and practice, on the one hand, and of the relationship between education and society, on the other' (p.22). Moreover, 'curriculum theories are social theories not only in the sense that they reflect the history of the societies in which they arose, but also in the sense that they entail ideas about social change and, in particular, about the role of education in the reproduction and transformation of society' (p.35). We hold the view that these are the abiding concerns of curriculum theory and curriculum theorizing. We are as aware as ever that our own theory and practice, and the reproductive and transformative relationships created by the 'Curriculum Theory' course, are as much objects for critical and self-critical scrutiny as are any other educational institutions and practices. We remain conscious that both our theories and our curricula are, and must be, both the products of their times and limited by the blindnesses and partialities of the historically bound people who develop them.

Yet the curriculum problem confronted in the early days of planning the 'Curriculum Theory' course remains fresh and compelling — the problem of making a curriculum for a course about curriculum. It is even more culturally pointed as in 1988 the course team considers the problem of remaking the course — a *distance education* course about curriculum for students whose lives are inceasingly characterized by abstracted and 'distanced' social relationships. The analysis is far from complete; the task is unfinished. Despite changing to meet its changing analysis and changing circumstances, the course team — and the students of the course — still stand at the threshold of the possibility of making a course which is what the original course team intended it to be: an introduction to the problems of theory and practice in curriculum which reveals these problems through a self-disclosing pedagogy, and a view of the substance of the course as both a product of the history of the field and a model for future practice.

Notes

1   'Course team' is the term used within Deakin University to designate the group of people involved in developing, teaching and revising a course. The composition of these groups changes over time. The group of people who originally started work on 'Curriculum Theory' is rather different from the group who are currently teaching and revising this course. The 1982-1983 course team was Lindsay Fitzclarence, Garry Gillard (Course Assistant), Colin Henry, John Henry, Stephen Kemmis (Chairperson), Robin McTaggart, Neil Pateman and Duane Saltzgaver. The 1988 course team is Michael Garbutcheon-Singh, Lindsay Fitzclarence (Chairperson), Colin Henry, Stephen Kemmis and Robin McTaggart.
2   The British arguments for the centrality of teachers in curriculum development and research built on a relatively strong existing tradition

which recognized the professional autonomy of teachers, providing a model for Australian teachers who lacked such a tradition and such recognition. In Australia the argument for school-based curriculum development was in part an argument for greater autonomy for the profession — but it quickly gathered support as increasingly well educated and politically acute teachers of the late 1960s and early 1970s expressed their resistance to the bureaucratic demands of state educational departments. The British case can be contrasted with the traditions of school-based curriculum development in the US, where the role of teachers in curriculum development and research was closely associated with the progressive education movement and teacher education in the 1930s and 1940s, and was later reasserted by Schwab following some of the major curriculum development projects of the 1970s.

3   A definition of action research is '. . . a form of collective self-reflective enquiry undertaken by participants in social situations in order to improve the rationality and justice of their own social or educational practices and the situations in which these practices are carried out' (Kemmis and McTaggart, 1988, p.5).

4   See, for example, Carr and Kemmis (1986; 1st ed., 1983); on the Frankfurt School see Jay (1973) and Habermas (1972, 1974).

5   Jean Rudduck is now Professor of Education at Sheffield University.

6   Here the course team worked on the assumption that the majority of the participants in the course would be practising teachers.

7   In this spirit of equality the course adopted a policy of non-competitive assessment. If students satisfactorily fulfilled requirements for the course, they would be granted a P* (ungraded pass); if not, they would be permitted a short time to complete requirements or resubmit work which had been assessed as failing to meet requirements.

8   It is of some significance to note that the *Course Journal* was to be made available only to students and the course team (and not, for example, to the Australian National Library which normally receives copies of all Deakin off-campus course materials). This decision was taken following consultation with the first students of the course. It acknowledged that writing 'in public', even for the relatively limited public of the course, was threatening for many students, and that extending the readership of the *Journal* would unnecessarily increase this sense of threat.

9   See, for example, Paulston (1976).

10   In more recent times the members of the course team have come to characterize this issue as the attempt to resolve the question, 'what should schools teach?'

11   After much discussion it was decided that the *Journal* should normally appear four times each year. It was regarded as desirable that there be six numbers per year to encourage a sense of community among students, which might be expected to develop from more frequent, even if less substantial, communication. In the end, however, it was decided that there should be only four because of the demands imposed upon students, the course team, the course assistant and the University's production facilities if six numbers per year were to be produced and distributed. In particular there was the problem that, if six were expected, it was likely

(given the exigencies of turnaround times) that students would have to be submitting articles for the forthcoming number of the *Journal* before they had received the previous one.

12   It is significant that this student calls for more person-to-person, if not face-to-face, contact in the course. Her comments caused the course team to review the decision to abandon the annual conference after 1984. In the end, however, the decision not to reinstate the conference stood: it seemed unreasonable to require that students from such distant locations come to Deakin for the conference.

13   In *Wilhelm Meister's Travels,* Goethe had written: 'Thought and action, action and thought, that is the sum of all [educational] wisdom . . . . Whoever makes it a rule for himself . . . to test action against thought and thought against action cannot go astray, and, if he should stray, he will soon find himself back on the right path' (Goethe, quoted by Georg Kerchensteiner in E. Hahn (Ed.), *Die Padagogik der Gegenwart in Selbstdarstellungen,* Leipzig, Felix Meiner, p.91).

14   From 'So Far Away' by M. Knopfler, on the record *Brothers in Arms.*

15   This position is inspired by a proposition advanced by Alfred Sohn-Rethel when he notes, 'The ideas of an epoch are in conformity with the socially synthetic functions of that epoch' 1978,p.5).

16   The term 'post-industrial society' was coined by the sociologist Daniel Bell (1974).

17   For an extended analysis of the trend described here see Sharp (1983, 1985).

18   See the section 'Universities: A Critical Return', in *Arena,* No.81, 1987 and 'The University and Higher Education', in *Arena,* No.82, 1988.

19   For a good account of the convergence of individualism and the bureaucratic control of production processes see the account of contemporary 'modern' social life in Berger, Berger and Kellner (1973).

20   The tensions between community and bureaucracy and between democracy and bureaucracy have long been studied by social theorists. See, for example, Etzioni-Halevy (1983), Pateman (1970) and Weber (1948).

21   In this context it is worth noting that the explicit rules for the satisfactory completion of work in the course have sometimes been described as 'legalistic' by students. Their use of the label suggests that the course has indeed touched the raw nerve of their alienation within the bureaucratized conditions of contemporary distance education.

22   The point made by Rigmor George (quoted earlier).

23   A friend, Saville Kushner, told us the old joke about the monk permitted to speak just one sentence each year. On the appointed day, moving close to the colleague whose sentence he had listened to the year before, one used his long-awaited opportunity to speak: 'Pardon?'. Perhaps the *Journal* has been a bit like that.

24   On the development and character of social movements see, for example, Touraine (1981).

Chapter 10

Democratic Curriculum Development at a Distance: A Case Study of a Curriculum Development for Youthworkers

Frances Bonning and Terry Evans

In 1986 the authors acted as consultants to several youthwork groups who were developing training kits for youthworkers on behalf of an Australian federal government department. The kits were to be used at a distance by people engaged in youthwork practice — or in the 'field' as it is often called. Funding was provided by the department under the guidance of Les Hendry who was its training consultant.[1] The department's intention was for the kit developers to spend six months developing a prototype which would then be reproduced and packaged for distribution by the end of the year.

In this chapter we focus on the curriculum development phase of one of these kits. We have chosen this kit because the youthwork agency, 'Youthaction', specifically and deliberately sought to engage the field in developing its own curriculum for the construction of a training kit to be used within that same professional group. We describe the nature and context of youthwork practice, administration and funding in Australia because these are substantially different from those of distance education, or even education in general. As consultants, it was important for us to understand youthwork practice, including the particular nature and ideologies of streetwork practice which underpinned the democratic curriculum construction process discussed here. We concentrate on the ways in which different and sometimes competing ideologies came to bear on the curriculum development of the kits and how these affected the processes and outcomes. We show how the boldness of the original democratic intentions wilted under existing and emerging bureaucratic strictures. There are several lessons to be learned by distance educators working in 'traditional' settings from Youthaction's approaches, especially those developing courses for people who are working in particular occupations, services or organizations. Such lessons are not solely positive ones, however; even (or especially?) the negative ones provide us with an opportunity to reflect critically on the bureaucratic structures surrounding our work and to change and use them to the best ends.

Youthwork Practice

In recent times we have seen the emergence of 'youth' as not merely a stage in the human life-cycle, but as an element of social life for which particular cultural features have been constructed. Increases in the legal school leaving age, changes to labour market requirements and a greater emphasis on educational certification have meant that involvement in adult work activities has been pushed back in a person's life. The growth of youthwork as a 'semi-professional' activity corresponds closely with the emergence of 'youth' as a discrete entity in society.

Changing social and economic conditions in Australia over the past two decades have resulted in concerns about high unemployment, homelessness, drug addiction and alienation amongst young people; thus the plight of the 'visible youth' in our society became a political issue. It is no longer seen as sufficient to provide a few recreational activities in an attempt to reduce vandalism or alcohol consumption. Now youthwork involves a variety of human service activities, and youthworkers require diverse skills and knowledge to meet contemporary demands.

Youthwork in Australia is a highly disparate activity; this is manifest not only in the youthworkers themselves, but also in the ideologies and approaches adopted, in the work environments and in the bureauracies which administer and fund youthwork. For example, youthworkers are employed in Community Youth Support Schemes (CYSS), in 'drop-in' centres, hostels and agencies operated by churches, service groups or local governments, and also out 'on the streets' in cafes, pool halls, bars, pinball parlours and anywhere else young people meet. Streetwork is a form of youthwork practice; streetworkers, like other youthworkers, are based at an agency or local authority, and their aim is to meet young people on their own terms, in places (hence 'on the streets') and at times which are determined by the young people themselves.

In any of these settings youthwork practice can be very demanding. Illicit drugs, alcohol, pregnancy, sexually transmitted diseases, violence, poverty, homelessness, alienation, unemployment, illiteracy and crime are all part of youthworkers' practice. For many youthworkers there is a tension between assisting young people to meet their needs and simultaneously adhering to the structures, rules and processes of the bureaucracies which employ them. Their work involves arbitration, initiative and advocacy, and there are immense difficulties in maintaining good faith with both the agencies or bureaucracies which employ them and the young people with whom they work. However, despite the need for youthworkers to possess a variety of skills and knowledge, there are no specific qualifications necessary to become a youthworker. A few youthworkers do have a youthwork qualification, and others have related tertiary qualifications in social work, welfare studies or education. However, most youthworkers are people who have previously acted in a volunteer capacity in youth organizations or who, as young people, have benefitted from association with youth workers or youth centres and continued in this line of work. A few youthworkers left school at the minimum age and have limited literacy skills.

Youthwork Training

Opportunities for youthwork training are few and far between. Federal and state government and non-government youth affairs bodies have concentrated their efforts on the issues that affect young people, on formulating policy and on funding programmes to alleviate some of the problems. In effect they have become bureaucracies with strong self-perpetuation mechanisms geared to the attraction of continuing funds. Consideration of the training needs of youthworkers is a relatively recent concern. Typically training for youthworkers is mostly 'on the job'. In particular, the non-government youthwork associations, often with church affiliations, provide information and occasional seminars and workshops. CYSS also offers training programmes, but these are generally seen as insufficient to fulfil the broad training needs of youthworkers.

When training is offered by government and non-government organizations, there are many youthworkers who are unable to avail themselves of the opportunities. Not all youthworkers are members of these organizations and receive scant information about training opportunities. Many members are outside the metropolitan areas where the youthwork bureaucracies organize most of their training sessions. In addition, youthwork programmes usually operate on tight budgets, often provided through voluntary organizations, with little, if any, money for training. Even time release to attend training is difficult because youthwork, particularly streetwork, is often crisis driven so the demands of the job prevent workers from being absent.

There are many obstacles — some of which are very familiar to distance educators — to providing a consistent and thorough training programme for youthworkers. The diversity of knowledge and skills amongst workers, the range of problems they may have to deal with, the various contexts in which they work and the disparate bureaucratic organizations administering youthwork contribute to the difficulty in devising and providing training which is seen as relevant and valuable to all youthworkers.

Our discussions with youthworkers revealed that they want their training to provide answers to the difficult practical questions they face everyday: How do I deal with the 16-year-old who consistently comes drunk to the drop-in centre and disrupts everything? What do I do if, as a streetworker, I have gained the confidence of a young person who now wants my help to shoot-up heroin? How do I cope with the strains of the job? How do I liaise with the police when there is a 'blitz on kids'? How do I develop programmes which will serve my young people, when I am constrained by local government politics or the funding agency's guidelines, and the limitations of short-term funding?

Training Youthworkers at a Distance

The heavy emphasis on practical issues, and also the value youthworkers place on informal personal contact with other workers as their primary source of information, raise some interesting pedagogical and curricular questions for any developers of in-service training kits. Les Hendry, a former streetworker, acting in his capacity as the training consultant to the federal department, was instrumental in shaping the rationale and procedures for developing the youthworker training kits. His conception of how these would address the training needs of youthworkers was influential in many curricular and pedagogical decisions, especially for the streetworkers' kit.

Les Hendry envisaged that youthworker in-service training kits would make knowledge, information and materials transferable from one individual to another or from one programme to another. The fact that youthworkers rarely met, especially nationally, to exchange information and discuss issues was of major concern to him. In his days on the streets he had become concerned at the way streetwork had developed differently in each state without recognizing what was happening elsewhere; he felt a sense in which youthworkers throughout Australia were constantly 'reinventing the wheel'. He was concerned that there was no consistency in training or even a guiding set of basic principles for streetwork/

youthwork on which people could build their practice. As a training consultant he encountered the difficulties and expense of organizing national training schemes. Mobile in-service training kits were his way of enabling people to read about each other's ideas, to think about and articulate each other's methods, approaches and practices, and to train themselves around those themes. He saw it as a way of opening up national communication channels and of developing a body of knowledge about youthwork practice.

The International Year of Youth (IYY) occurred in 1985. The Australian government designated youth as 'Priority One', and in consultation with the states nominated specific disadvantaged young people for attention: young women, young rural Aborigines, people with mental, emotional and physical disabilities and young people from non-English speaking backgrounds. With the prospect of 'Priority One' funds, Les Hendry formulated his proposed youthworker training kits around these disadvantaged young people. Street kids had not been given a special mention within the IYY policy initiatives. However, as the government was concerned about access to services, Les Hendry was able to add a fifth kit to those that were more politically expedient, on the grounds that young people who had taken to the streets for whatever reason were not going to get access to mainstream services unless youthworkers made the links.

Each of the kits was to be developed by agencies based in the field. The agencies were selected by tender, on Les Hendry's advice, and were coordinated by him until he resigned soon after the project began. He specified that distance education advice was to be provided by consultants to ensure that the kits were suitable for youthworkers with diverse educational backgrounds and from a variety of youthwork contexts.

Youthaction was the first of the kit developers to receive funding to produce a streetworker training kit over a period of six months. We were engaged as consultants a few months later along with the other kit developers. The intention was that the streetwork kit would be available for release in October 1986 as an indication of the government's concern for youth and the training needs of workers, and as advance publicity for the remaining four kits to come. This was to prove impossible, mainly because of Youthaction's ideologies relating to youth work and training, and because of the heavy dependence on voluntary effort by the federal department.

The guidelines Les Hendry devised for the kits were based on a model of training which he called 'humanistic group work'. This encompassed a pedagogy which is experiential and practice-based. He planned that through 'real-life examples', 'environment specific exercises', group discussions, workshops and role plays youthworkers would have the opportunity to think about a number of different approaches to practical issues, to rehearse responses and consider the likely consequences of various options which might apply in any given situation. The kits would also be a way of building a body of knowledge that *is* youthwork, of unlocking personal theories of youthwork through individuals reflecting on their own practices and those of others. Through these processes and through additional readings, the youthworkers would be able to make the links between theory and practice. The pedagogy of the kits would allow youthworkers control over their own learning, information would be segmented and relatively easy to comprehend in short training 'sessions' or 'modules'. It would provide for and encourage the sharing of knowledge, not only on a local or work context level, but also nationally and across the various contexts of youthwork practice.

To enable the sharing of knowledge on a national scale, Les Hendry stipulated that the kits should be 'dynamic'. This meant there should be space in each kit to add new information as it passed from worker to worker or network to network. The kits would be a means of creating dialogue between youthworkers; for example, any information added would have contact telephone numbers for follow-up discussions. Dialogue was possible through people responding to others' inclusions, by making comments or attaching a note to explain their response. The generation of new information through this process could then provide a basis on which the core content of the kits could be revised. Evaluation would be built into the kits via a diary in which people could indicate the length of time they used the kit, the circumstances in which it was used and its usefulness to them as a training resource.

The type of kit envisaged by Les Hendry — its size, its multi-media presentation and its emphasis on experiential learning — was very different from that which many youthworkers normally viewed as a 'kit'. For them a 'kit' ranged from a booklet through to a folder of 'resources' on a particular practical topic. Les Hendry wanted training kits which resembled the types of experiences and information exchange which training workshops provided. In many respects he was searching for the forms of dialogue at a distance which several distance educationists have considered (see Evans and Nation, 1988) and which is addressed by other contributors to this book.

The pedagogical and curriculum development processes embedded in the Department's guidelines to the kit development agencies were founded on Les Hendry's beliefs arising from his practice as a streetworker and youthwork trainer. They represent an example of how people try to adapt a bureaucracy's policies into procedures which are congruent with their own. In Les Hendry's case his approach to training had been shaped by his streetwork experiences.

We began our consultancy with some research into streetwork because it was necessary to understand the practical context before we provided advice on teaching about *and* through this practice at a distance. As consultants, we were privileged 'outsiders' who could discuss, question and give views about the field to the people engaged within it. For us it represented a critical process of questioning, reflecting upon and challenging our own assumptions about education and, in particular, distance education as we immersed ourselves in understanding youthwork and streetwork. Our understanding was pieced together and verified through questioning and discussing with people in the field. Some tensions within and between youthwork and streetwork unfolded as we worked with the four kit developers and the federal department. Some of these tensions were concerned with funding, administration and state/federal rivalries; others were founded on ideological differences, for example, between evangelical Christian, humanist and liberationist concerns. It is useful now to reflect on streetwork to provide the reader with a glimpse of the context through which the democratic curriculum construction process emerged.

Streetwork

> Streetworkers are not street-cleaners. Our intention is not and should not be to act as truant officers or police officers. Our job is to understand the person — where the person is coming from, not just geographically, and to help him/her reach independence. The interests of the individual are the prime motivation for streetwork involvement. (Williams, 1986, p.21)

Some streetworkers are colloquially termed 'graduates of the streets': they have never been trained, they have no formal qualifications, but they do possess a great understanding of street youth culture. Other streetworkers have more highly developed conceptual skills gained through formal qualifications, however, they usually lack the experience and understanding of street youth culture. 'Culture shock' is not an uncommon experience for these streetworkers; the reverse is true of the street graduates. A difficulty for them is in handling some of the organizational aspects of the work, such as negotiations with bureaucracies, local governments and police.

Streetworkers contact and work with young people who are often outside formal social structures such as schools, families or workplaces. A lack of social skills, educational skills and self-confidence makes some of these young people unlikely to benefit from the usual provision of services available to them. They remain generally outside existing structures and often shrink from obtaining the benefits available to them because of their concerns about dealing with bureaucracies and, in some cases, fears about certain authorities becoming aware of their whereabouts.

The streetworker needs to gain the trust and acceptance of the 'street kids', so that he or she can help create the circumstances in which these young people recognize they have the power to take charge of their own lives. Streetworkers often see their job as aiding an empowerment process through which their clients reflect on their circumstances and future prospects and begin to challenge the norms and values of their sub-culture and those of society at large. Streetworkers provide accurate information and links with other agencies (such as health and welfare), act as advocates for youth and generally offer support in the transition to adulthood. The aim is for the streetworker and the young people to work together to make realistic and viable decisions about their futures. An important requirement for this working relationship is age; in effect streetworkers have to 'retire' in their 20s because they cannot easily move in street kids' groups, the youngest of whom are about 12 years old.

The way in which Youthaction attempted to develop their in-service training kit for streetworkers is a reflection of the ideologies embedded in streetwork itself. Youthaction aimed for collective effort in sharing knowledge and experiences as a way of reflecting on and challenging existing practices. The emphasis was always on putting the learning into the hands of the workers themselves. Of central importance to Youthaction was that workers should have a strong sense of ownership of *their* kit. It was to be their creation, directly relevant to their training needs. As with streetwork, there would be no prescriptions, just other people's personal experiences, reflections and ways of working. It would be for the learners to take from each kit whatever was relevant to their personal circumstances.

The congruence between the way Youthaction and Les Hendry each envisaged the curriculum and pedagogy of the training kits is inescapable. The approach they have taken stems from an ideology which values the knowledge and experience of individuals as the major source of information. It places emphasis on communication, reflection and the sharing of knowledge in the development of professional skills so that the field as a whole can learn and grow. In a field that is said to be 'anti-academic' and 'anti-professional' the kits were a way of providing easy access to the existing knowledge and processes as a means of professional development.

A point of departure between Youthaction and Les Hendry, however, was in the volume and nature of consultations each thought necessary to produce a national kit. The guidelines which Les Hendry had created encouraged all kit developers to consult with networks throughout Australia in order to identify important issues. He wanted the developers to make 'critical decisions on the basis of their consultation about content and method', and then to produce the content of the kits themselves. To this extent Hendry viewed the developers as experts in their possession of the knowledge, skills and experience necessary to develop a kit around which youthworkers could train.

Youthaction resisted viewing themselves as experts; they believed that expertise resided with the practitioners in the field. They recognized that they had a worthwhile contribution to make but that this contribution was not superior to, or more expert than, any other youthworker's. They saw their task as one of marshalling the knowledge, experience and skills of the field in a way which was open and democratic.

Democratic Curriculum Development

Developing a training kit for streetworkers was a problematic task for Youthaction. Their usual approaches to training — as in other aspects of the work — were essentially based on an ideology and rhetoric of democracy. This involved the participants in workshops, group discussions, role-playing, etc. They eschewed notions of expertism, opting instead to facilitate equal participation and engagement with the problems and issues at hand. As we have shown previously, such approaches are consistent with the prevailing ideology of youthwork practice and especially with streetwork. However, when confronted with the task of developing a kit for use at a distance, the difficulties of maintaining the openness, involvement and democracy came sharply into focus. As consultants to the project we were concerned to recognize the demands of their kit and to help create the conditions whereby the kit could achieve their aims.

A first, major task for Youthaction was to construct the kit's curriculum framework. Pedagogical questions were rarely explicit, although, of course, pedagogical sub-texts existed from the start. The exercise can be seen as an attempt to structure democratically some knowledge about streetwork and then to aggregate this knowledge into a kit.

Youthaction established the principles through which they wanted the curriculum to be constructed. They argued that it had to emerge not from 'a mysterious guru source', but from 'the field itself, past, present and potential'.[2] The curriculum was not to be an exhaustive or complete one on streetwork practice, but was to be seen as the 'bones' on which the 'meat' would be produced through engagement with the sorts of people who would use the kit. A glimpse of the underlying pedagogical processes was afforded when Youthaction declared that they assumed 'a basic interest and enquiry exists with respect to "unattached youth"' on the part of the kit's users, which would drive them to produce the 'meat'. Youthaction saw the field as both the curriculum developers and the kit users. The curriculum of the training kit was to emerge from the field, for the field — something which was consistent with Les Hendry's view.

From the outset Youthaction sought the active participation of others in the field, first to develop the curriculum framework and then to contribute the curriculum materials. Several key people from the state streetworker network were asked to attend a weekend meeting to draft an outline of the problems, issues and topics, and 'to catalyse the process and enlist energies'. This meeting resembled a 'workshop/think-tank' on the matters surrounding streetwork from which a tentative structure to the training curriculum emerged. This structure was used for the development of a questionnaire, called an 'expression of interest sheet', to be distributed to members of the state network. However, it was recognized that the network did not include everyone statewide who might be interested in commenting on and contributing to the curriculum framework or in developing the kit itself. The inclusion of the national concerns and interests of streetworkers was required by the federal department, and so it was decided to take a 'cross-section of the national network'. This was also important for 'a wide sense of ownership of the project' — a concern often mentioned by Youthaction — and for 'accuracy'. Therefore, the 'expression of interest sheet' was to be made available to anyone who wanted it and the networks were to be used to commence the process. The project was publicized at occasional conferences and workshops and through agencies, institutions, church groups, etc.

The telephone was used to initiate contacts with people. The 'expression of interest sheets' were not posted to anyone without preceding telephone contact with Youthaction to discuss the project. Usually the contact was initiated by Youthaction, although occasionally people telephoned to ask to be involved as a result of the publicity or other personal contacts. The telephone was central to the process of developing the curriculum at a distance. Its use stemmed from youthwork practice, where the telephone is a medium for communicating problems, negotiating outcomes and obtaining information. Much youthwork is informal and 'done on the run', so the telephone, especially with its immediate, 'personal' contact, is commensurate with such practice. In addition, the telephone rather than letter was used to pursue non-returned 'expressions of interest' and to pursue offers of contributions, materials, etc.

People who received an 'expression of interest' document did so in conjunction with four other documents about the project. In total there were fifteen sheets, six of which were the questionnaire. Hence, over and above the extensive use of the telephone, Youthaction was distributing, receiving and filing large amounts of paperwork. The project office contained numerous filing boxes, a personal computer/wordprocessor, and the inevitable telephones and an answering machine. At this stage one could see the democracy being moulded into a bureaucratic form. This will not surprise distance educators for whom the rise of bureaucracy is something which they encounter in their work. Youthaction used most of its funding to employ a woman as a part-time 'liaison' person to run the office, and in effect to keep the project moving. Because the other members of the agency were only providing 'voluntary' labour, the liaison person was the one most conscious of the various bureaucratic deadlines they had set themselves or which were imposed from Canberra. The pressure on her became onerous as the magnitude of the task unfolded during the initial weeks.

The bureaucratization of the curriculum development process represents an emerging contradiction with the ideologies of streetwork practice and training. These contradictions were later manifest by the lack of response from the field, especially interstate, and only partly recovered by public and personal contacts at conferences, etc. We were told later by streetworkers that even though they agreed to participate through the initial telephone contacts, the mailed 'expression of interest' package left them with the feeling that everything was fixed and decided and that they could only respond on Youthaction's terms. In many ways this was an accurate assessment, although this was not Youthaction's intention.

The trap Youthaction had fallen into was to produce a lengthy questionnaire with categorized responses. This was accompanied by other documents which were intended for information, but left the impression that a centralized, city agency had made most of the key decisions. Streetworkers are inherently suspicious and prone to resist decisions and instructions from centralized authorities, and the agency was beginning to be seen in this light. The letter accompanying the package commenced in a friendly manner, 'thank you for taking the time to talk to us on the telephone the other day', and it suggested that 'we will attempt to keep in touch by telephone from time to time', but it concluded with the imperative that, 'due to a very tight schedule, we would appreciate if you could respond as soon as conveniently possible.' What the whole process required was time, and Youthaction simply did not have enough time if it was to conform to the funding guidelines. To some of the streetworkers this meant that there was little time and scope to participate in a process which, ostensibly at least, was endeavouring to incorporate their experiences, ideas, needs and concerns in a curriculum about streetwork.

About mid-way through the initial six months funding period it became clear that the 'responses' were coming in too slowly and were in too few numbers for the project to be completed successfully on schedule. Youthaction was in a double bind because, not only was the questionnaire their principal means of constructing democratically the streetwork curriculum framework, but also they were using it to identify people who would contribute to the curriculum materials or provide existing 'resources' for use in the kit.

Simultaneously they were becoming aware, largely through our advice, of the sort of work and problems which are encountered in preparing distance teaching materials. For example, the procedures surrounding legally reproducing copyright materials were new to the agency, and we also had difficulties in assessing where such a training kit would stand in relation to the Copyright Act (see Moore, 1986). All the traditional distance teaching considerations of educational design, layout, numbers of pages, etc. were new to Youthaction. However, we were concerned not to impose such traditions on them, rather we were critically reflecting on such traditions ourselves as we engaged the youthwork, and especially streetwork, approaches to training, curriculum and pedagogy. It was decided to seek an extension of the project deadline and some additional funds to continue employing the liaison person. In spite of strong lobbying, only some additional time was allowed. Youthaction fell into a position of trying to complete the project with less than the minimal part-time support they had relied upon previously.

The budget Youthaction had tendered for was unrealistically small; they had failed to comprehend the costs involved in preparing the type of kit required, especially in using their democratic approach to curriculum development. Their tender costing was also indicative of the extent to which voluntarism and 'favour' were part of the normal way of operating a youthwork agency. The federal department was also unclear about the likely costs of the type of kit they were specifying, and their undoubted need to keep costs to a minimum meant that they accepted uncritically a budget which was substantially insufficient. These difficulties applied to all the kit developers and also to the final production costings.

Youthwork is essentially a marginal activity on the fringe of social welfare services. However, determination and resourcefulness are often born out of such adversity, and Youthaction used these qualities to continue its task; the curriculum construction process continued slowly. It became clear that they would need to produce a greater proportion of the kit's contents than they had originally expected. They had expected to prepare little content themselves because the processes they employed would generate a wealth of material from the field. They relied on the voluntary efforts of many people not only from the streetwork field, but also more generally from academics, social welfare personnel and others. Ideologically, voluntarism is significant in youthwork practice, and Youthaction was drawing on this to fuel its democratic curriculum construction process. In practice voluntarism could not sustain the substantial additional efforts required by the project.

From senior bureaucrats in Canberra through to experienced youthwork agency managers and new recruits to streetwork there was a strong endorsement of Youthaction's approach to developing the kit. Even some of the other kit developers were impressed by their procedures and, we felt, harboured regrets that they had not used some of the same approaches themselves. However, it was also recognized that the magnitude of the task — which has more than a little to do with the broad scope of the curriculum first established by Youthaction and its initial 'think-tank' group — was beyond that which could be reasonably accommodated in the time and with the available funds. Eventually it was the democratic curriculum development process which the federal department wanted to adapt and adopt as a model for future distance education kits in youthwork. The department saw this as sufficient to satisfy their bureaucratic and political masters who were becoming anxious to have some results from their youthwork training initiatives. In some respects this represented a convenient compromise because Youthaction were quite unable to fulfil their contract with the time and money available, and the department was aware that their original costings and schedules were highly optimistic. However, the major significance for us was the readiness with which the federal department accepted the democratic curriculum construction process as a model for their future training kits. It is hard to imagine other bureaucracies administering professional training acting so readily. It was also agreed that the production of the streetwork kit itself would be into a further separate project to be funded by the department.

Democracy and Bureaucracy

Developing curricula in distance education, as in other forms of education, is usually left to the 'experts'. The experts are invariably those people who are highly credentialled in the subject matter of the discipline or topic concerned. Bourdieu (1976) has argued that academic curricula are essentially about exclusivity, selection and differentiation; not merely in the forms and levels of knowledge which they comprise, but also through the cultural dissonance which exists between the curricula and the particular learners. Whereas the curriculum development process for the streetwork kit was more open to influence and negotiation than most other forms of academic curricula, it carried with it implicit assumptions of a consensus about what streetwork is and should be, and about the processes through which the field would articulate and learn about its practice. In essence curriculum development is about making social and political choices, amongst others, and such choices will interact with the social and cultural values, skills and knowledge held by the learner. Such interaction produces conflict as much as consensus, and Youthaction, like many before it, was going to use its nascent bureaucratic power to cement the democracy when conflicts arose.

Forms of education which, like the youthwork kits, are designed for a body of practitioners often possess areas for conflict over the 'relevance' or the lack of relationship between the 'theory' being learned and actual work practices. Youthworkers, perhaps especially streetworkers, are particularly sensitive about such matters. Distance education raises the problem of setting any apparent irrelevancies between theory and practice into a fixed form which can be tangibly identified throughout the years of a course's or kit's life. At the outset Youthaction recognized these potential difficulties, especially those concerning 'relevancy' — not because they were academic 'experts' writing a course, but because they were practitioners, largely sharing the same views, who were 'funded' to develop a kit for (or rather with) their colleagues. Youthaction required contributors to articulate elements of their practices, and to some degree to theorize about them. The fact that this proved to be a slow and tortuous path for the streetworkers to follow is not surprising, given our previous explanation of their work and educational experiences.

Youthaction was mainly seeking written contributions, and most streetworkers would have found neither the time, nor felt especially disposed to write about their practice; their usual form of articulation was verbal. This raises the question of the consequences of the original 'expression of interest' package, not only in its form and content, but also in the structuring of the form and content of the required responses. Whereas the 'think-tank' had been very successful in identifying many key areas of streetwork practice and management, and the initial telephone contacts with the field had also looked promising, the form and content of the questionnaire pushed back people's enthusiasm. There was a clear need to use a different process or another form of 'expression of interest' package. Arguably the dialogue was broken after the initial telephone contact, and although subsequent telephone calls were made, they fell mainly into the style of begging reminders rather than the 'keeping in contact' originally stated in the letter to the field.

In the construction of a curriculum about streetwork practice, especially if through a process of democratic curriculum development, the contentious and conflicting issues come to the surface. There were two broad areas of difficulty which Youthaction faced: the federal department had the power, through its control of the kit reproduction process, to edit or delete matters which it found contentious; and the field itself could produce conflicting ideas and materials, for example, between the different religious and secular ideologies. The agency was prepared to argue its case in the event of difficulties with the funding authority, but recognized that the authority had the ultimate power to change the materials. However, in the case of conflicts within the field they assumed the power to arbitrate or exclude as particular circumstances arose. Ultimately the responses were so low in terms of materials that such problems were minimal, but it was clear that they were prepared to circumscribe democracy if they felt it necessary to do so. Hence the 'wide ownership' and democratic principles espoused for the kit were potentially in conflict and tension with the sense of ownership and control felt by Youthaction, and with the bureaucratic control from Canberra.

As 'traditional' distance education increases its provision of professionally oriented courses, both for intending and experienced practitioners, there are increasing reasons to recognize the depth of knowledge and the range of needs and requirements which exist in those occupations. The approach to the streetwork training kit recognized explicitly such reasons and set out to address them. The bureaucratization, or at least the form of it they employed, was not successful with the streetworkers. However, especially if modified, this approach may be more productive with occupational groups which are more bureaucratized or less antipathetic to bureaucracies than streetwork. For example, the federal bureaucracy which funded the project was most impressed by the process. It fulfilled their policy requirements, and for the bureaucrats it had the trappings of being an efficient and effective means of obtaining, collating and storing a broad, representative collection of the field's knowledge. Indeed, their enthusiasm was at one stage so unquestioning that we felt obliged, as their consultants, to provide a balanced appraisal of the process. The ideological and pedagogical implications were buried beneath bureaucratic concerns to close the files and audit the accounts. Bernstein (1979) has suggested that 'invisible pedagogies' are the most subtlely pervasive in transmitting the dominant ideology. One can only question in whose interests it was for this form of bureaucratized democracy to be imposed on all youthworker training at a distance.

For distance educators interested in using a democratic curriculum development process with occupational groups, it is clearly important to tailor the procedures to the pertaining circumstances. Such circumstances include the ideological bases of the occupational group itself as well as the practical constraints on their ability to contribute. We emphasized to the agency that it was risky to depend on voluntary contributions because the field would not understand or share in the commitment to the deadlines which existed for the various production stages of the kit. This is a perennial problem for distance educators because the deadlines for the production of course materials represent another rigid set of requirements in addition to those which already obtain in academic institutions.

We would suggest that there are benefits for distance education in the adoption of more open and democratic approaches to curriculum development for occupationally oriented courses. One of the difficulties with distance education is the static nature of courses due to the production lead times and the length of time before courses are revised or replaced. It may be difficult to build in the degree of dynamism to which Les Hendry aspired, but the Youthaction approach to the development of the curriculum structure and materials provides a contemporary statement of the matters and issues of field practice. This enables a curriculum to be formed which starts its life at the 'cutting edge' of an occupation's practice, rather than as a selection of what academics see as pertinent. The administrative and student support services in distance education may be usefully incorporated into the curriculum development process to provide the resources which Youthaction found difficult to provide. The people in these services have valuable knowledge, skills and information of their own which may be useful in, for example, contacting previous students now in occupational practice or for helping develop and distribute requests for contributions from the field. Youthaction's use of brainstorming, editorial or workshop sessions composed of practitioners and others could be used to help shape the whole curriculum development process through to the final organization and pedagogy of the course.

Such procedures for democratic curriculum development accord well with the forms of critical pedagogy discussed in other chapters of this book and elsewhere (see, for example, Freire, 1972b; Shor and Freire, 1987). The outcome is likely to be that such courses will reflect more closely the occupations which they address, and that the hoary old criticism of the lack of relationship between 'theory' and 'practice' will become redundant. Furthermore, involving an occupational group in the development of curricula about their own practice may help foster a greater critical awareness among that group as they articulate and engage in debate within a critical community of their peers.

Notes

1 'Les Hendry' and other names have been changed in the interests of anonymity.
2 These and other quotations are from documents or field notes taken by the authors during the project.

Chapter 11

When Teachers Theorize Their Practice: A Reflexive Approach to a Distance Education Course

John Smyth

This chapter has two agendas. On the one hand, I want to canvas something of the rationale behind and the experiences involved in providing a distance education course that involved primary and secondary teachers theorizing their practice. On the other hand, I want to stand back and locate my 'teaching' of that course within the broader educational crisis afflicting Australia and most other Western democracies at the moment. I have labelled this a 'reflexive' approach because what I am attempting is to engage myself in the kind of action I recommend for the teachers who undertake the 'Teachers' Theories of Action' distance education course.

Before I disclose the details of the course and the experiences of the school-based participants in it, it is important that I reflect briefly upon the wider political context of higher education in which I am implicated, and my own actions in it. It is only as I begin to realize the awesome extent to which my own pedagogy is constrained by forces that I neither fully understand nor control, that I come to appreciate fully the difficulties of my own students in trying to maintain and regain power over their teaching.

There can be little doubt that higher education in Australia, as indeed in the USA and the UK, is in deep crisis. The precise nature of that situation is extremely complex, but it is located in a wider legitimation crisis in capitalist societies generally (Habermas, 1974). Educationally speaking, there are three aspects to this. Firstly, there is a 'crisis of rationality' that takes expression in so-called 'scientific approaches' to solving perceived social and economic problems. Invariably these involve a series of constructed and artificial separations

— of facts from values, of means from educational ends, of administration from pedagogy — and the substitution of technical/rational administrative solutions to what amount to complex social questions of equity, access and distribution of society's resources. Secondly, there is a deepening 'crisis of legitimacy' as these centrally driven technologized solutions (particularly in respect of education) are justified, packaged and perpetrated in the community by recourse to the rhetoric of their supposed cost efficiency and cost effectiveness. Of course, they are nothing of the kind — there is rarely any evidence in support of such extravagant claims for enhanced centralism, and the evidence that does exist is spurious, to say the least. In taking on economistic language and methods to analyze and resolve our social problems, we are required to write off the accumulated wisdom and cultural traditions that have enabled us to resolve social problems in the past, but more importantly we have destroyed the cultural habitus that has held educational communities together. Thirdly, both of the above crises interact with one another to produce a 'crisis of motivation' as feelings of increasing alienation and powerlessness accompany the situation in which we feel that control lies 'out there', 'with them', and 'not with us in here, in this institution'. Not only does this produce a loss of meaning, identity and purpose, but more importantly it is accompanied by the imposition of forms of language and discourse that further reinforce and bolster the orientation of measurement, technocracy and managerialism.

In the context of the 'project' reported later in this chapter it is clear that higher education is at an advanced stage of dramatic collapse and transformation. It is unnecessary to engage in heavy citation here to make the point that in the USA, UK and Australia higher education is perceived by politicians, and the bureaucrats who advise them, as being primarily a device for satisfying the manpower needs of economies which are themselves in a state of progressive disintegration. With the cost cutting measures and the enforced closure and amalgamations of large numbers of institutions ('rationalization' is the official euphemism), what we are witnessing is the progressive whittling away of the autonomy that higher education teachers have had in the past, and the 'proletarianization' (Larson, 1977; Poulantzas, 1973) of educated labour in much the way that blue-collar workers were subjugated in the early stages of the industrial revolution. The evidence on this is both widespread and compelling (Meisenhelder, 1983; Beverley, 1982), and has come to characterize a range of other professional fields such as medicine, law and engineering (Derber, 1982; Meiksins, 1982). The overly simplistic argument driving this process, at least so far as higher education is concerned, goes like this:

> Because of the way in which the capitalist system in general has
> been able to ascribe the causes of our economic ills to the personal
> inadequacies of individuals (illiteracy, lack of incentive, and poor
> work habits among students), it has not been difficult to link this
> with systematic failure of [those institutions] to meet the needs of
> industry. The argument is such a compellingly simplistic one
> that it is proving almost impossible to dislodge — get students
> . . . to conform through more compliant forms of education, and
> all our economic woes will disappear. (Smyth, 1987e, p.42)

As we rush headlong into this era of economic rationalism it is clear that
not only is the content of our teaching being reshaped so as to generate
more desirable 'output', but the way in which we are able (indeed,
'required') to do that teaching is being increasingly dictated to us.
Distance education is a particularly good example. Because of the alleged
cost effective way in which this form of higher education 'delivers'
education (notice the language — we usually only deliver commodities
like newspapers, tons of uranium ore, and in the past bottles of milk) to
large numbers of widely dispersed students, it is looked favourably upon
by educational technocrats. The well embedded implication is that
learning is nothing more than another form of commodification to be
perfected, in which pre-digested knowledge is deposited in the heads of
ever-grateful consumers. What is most disturbing about this kind of
analysis is that learners are regarded as some kind of passive receptacle,
rather than active agents engaged in their own recuperation and learning.
It is interesting to speculate whether, behind this apparent endorsement
by governments of the distance mode of learning is the view that distance
education, being an individualistic and compliant way of teaching and
learning, is essentially unproblematic. It is not hard to see how
technocrats who regard knowledge as being no different from ingots of
aluminium might come to believe mistakenly that distance education is
the way to resolve the nation's reskilling problems, while at the same
time avoiding controversial social questions about whose interests are
really being served by the educational enterprise. Nothing could be
further from the truth!

As I think about the nature of the particular distance education
course to be described shortly, I can see a significant tension between the
philosophy of the course which has to do with 'empowerment' of the
participants (by which I mean giving them control over aspects of their
lives hitherto denied them), and the alleged portability of such courses, if
it were to be seriously mooted in any process of economic rationalization
that distance education courses could be taught nationally through some

university network system. The fallacy in this argument is that just because a course has a set of covers around it, it does not automatically follow that it can readily be transported (or even sold 'off-shore'). What participants (whether they be tutors or school-based) buy into in courses of the type to be described shortly is a certain philosophical and epistemological view of who generates and owns pedagogical knowledge — indeed, who has the right to lay claim to this. Like the teachers I describe later in this chapter, I feel that informed decisions about how best to engage with ideas about teaching lie at the intersection between teaching practices and the forces that are continually at work invisibly shaping those practices. Such notions do not rest easily with the dominant ideology of the instrumental transmission view of knowledge as expressed continually in the media and in proclamations and reports by politicians and bureaucrats. As those of us in distance education mode are forced more and more towards endorsing an input-output view of what education means, and as surveillance procedures in the form of performance indicators and appraisal schemes proliferate, the pressures will intensify to homogenize courses so they fit the mould of what is bureaucratically decreed as being efficient and effective by people outside teaching (based on lowest per unit cost).

What should not be lost sight of in this era of economic rationalism is that universities (or any other providers of distance education) are organized along the lines of the industrial model. Like their industrial counterparts, campus administrators are able to:

> . . . justify the Taylorization of higher education by referring to the needs of the public and the demands of organizational efficiency. Although it is at least doubtful whether academic specialization and standardization actually reduces cost without harming the quality of education and whether or not it is demanded by the public, it clearly does have the effect of increasing management's control over the working situation of faculty . . . . While the objective situation of fiscal shortfall created by the economic problems of late capitalism may force administrators to try to reduce costs and increase the efficiency of work, it allows them to do so in a manner that increases their own power at the expense of faculty. (Meisenhelder, 1983, pp.302-3)

Viewed in this way, the crisis in higher education has more to do with the centralization of power than with any alleged shortfall of funds. An example may serve to make the point. My own institution is deeply committed to providing distance education, as reflected in its act of creation which says: '. . . to provide the opportunity for tertiary education at university level to all qualified persons whether within or outside Victoria by means of external studies' (*Deakin University Act 1974,* Section 5). Maintaining a high level of personal contact with students studying in this mode, we would expect to be a high priority for any staff who regard this mode of teaching seriously. While it is clearly possible to do this, to an extent, by means of written text material, the large distances involved make it imperative that students be contacted regularly by phone, often outside normal working hours. Repeated attempts by myself over several years to have my phone converted to direct dialling access (so avoiding calls having to go through the time-consuming process of contacting a switchboard operator) have been denied. On each occasion my request has been turned down by the Buildings Manager on the grounds that any such widespread practice of this kind within the university would lead to serious budget over-runs. As I think about this now, the contradiction becomes patently clear. The reality for me in teaching in the distance mode is that I do not have anything like a modicum of control over my pedagogy — it is being dictated to me by the Buildings Branch! Where does this leave matters of professional autonomy and the like?

During the presentation of the course I teach another incident of political intrusion occurred, but with somewhat different results. It is always a problem that while distance education courses may appear to be cost efficient (a fact which I dispute), courses like the one I am involved with are heavy on intellectual engagement with the written experiences of participants, and to that extent are very costly. In response to a cost cutting directive aimed at redressing the labour-intensive nature of my course, I reduced the number of reflective written pieces required of the students by 50 per cent. My reaction was a knee-jerk one in response to the directive, even though I verbally opposed it and defended my pedagogy. The effect of my reducing the amount of structure was quite unexpected. By slicing off the amount of 'air time' I as a tutor mortgaged in this course, the participants were 'freed' to spend more time reflecting about what was happening to them as teachers. Had I not been required to react to that economic imperative, I may have continued to act in a way which was quite contrary to the intent of the course. Unwittingly, and because they were at a distance, I had fallen into the trap of treating the school-based participants in disempowering ways by imposing too much structure. Being polite, and not in my physical presence, they were reluctant to inform me of this. Unless I wanted my views to predominate, why else would I require them to interact so frequently with me and my view of the world? When I handed more control over to them, they were able to develop the kind of voice I had wanted all along. Until required to think about what I was doing I was oblivious to the fact that my pedagogy had got in the way of my message.

As I write this, another contradiction is becoming glaringly apparent to me. While the course literature and philosophy eloquently address the *socially* constructed view of knowledge, as their tutor I continue to endorse a highly *individualistic* way of working with the course participants (something I inherited from my professional history as a teacher). In thinking through what I was trying to do I can see more clearly now than at any other time in my involvement with this course what Solomon (1987) meant when he said:

> Reflection is not just deck-chair musing. . . . [It] can be an active process, and usually involves a circle of like-minded people. The ways in which we all re-explore our experiences through private reflection or social discussion is set out in the phenomenological approach to the sociology of knowledge . . . . [We] all need to hold out our ideas to other people, and receive their responses, not just to hear their criticisms and approval, but to understand better our views of the world. Lack of social conversation actually inhibits the healthy construction of personal beliefs because these only become totally clear to us when we can speak about them to others. Constructive reflection on classroom experience will require us to provide a social forum for discussion. (p. 271)

But how to develop a socially constructed view of knowledge through the distance education mode is the perplexing question. That is a matter I shall return to later: first, something about the archaeology of the course itself.

In the remainder of this chapter I want to disclose something of the ways in which experienced teachers might begin critically to interrogate their own teaching so as to locate themselves in their teaching historically, theoretically and politically. I will argue that they can only realistically do this by penetrating the habitualness of teaching, and thereby developing a critical or an emancipatory pedagogy. Unlike the teachers in McDonald's (1986) project who embarked on the process of reclaiming the theory behind their teaching through a discursive process of solidarity through face-to-face contact as they sought to raise their voices in the cacophony of what passes for discussion about educational reform, the participants in my project laboured under the burden of the 'tyranny of distance'. They were graduate students in full-time teaching positions, studying at a distance (often many thousands of kilometres) from the university and from one another. While they were precluded, therefore, from developing anything but a limited dialogue with one another, they were able to engage in a 'reflective conversation with the situation' (Schon, 1984, p.42) made possible by the abundant richness of the daily experience of teaching. In terms of the opportunity this provided to 'name their world' and to 'frame the limit situations' (Freire, 1972b), there was a certain authenticity to what was being attempted — they were active agents working to overcome the tensions between '. . . theory and practice, between authority and freedom, and . . . between yesterday and today' (Freire, 1985, p.177). That is not to say that there were no problems; there were, and I shall return to those shortly.

There are three sections. The first part deals with what I label a 'Problematic Legacy'. My claim is that it is becoming increasingly realistic to portray teachers in terms of an oppressed social group — a notion generally reserved for racial, cultural or social minority groups, notwithstanding the fact that teachers have historically been part of a power élite, at least as far as students are concerned. I argue that there has been a gradual but perceptible proletarianization of teaching as a workforce (Larson, 1977; Derber, 1982; Meiksins, 1982), in much the way that manual workers were disempowered in the early phases of capitalism. All of the hallmarks exist of an occupational group experiencing oppression and extensive deskilling. As Lawn and Ozga (1981) put it, teachers are increasingly being subjected to 'indirect rule' in which the inequality of power is concealed in a rhetoric of partnership and consensus about education. The outward appearance is given of 'decentralization and devolution, with a quasi-autonomous role for the "natives"' (p.226), but the partnership is an empty one with increasing real control over all major aspects of schooling being firmly retained and extended by centralized educational authorities.

In the second section I present a case for an 'Openly Ideological' view of teaching, in which teachers might begin to see how to transcend the technicalities of their teaching so as to view the practicalities as part of a broader constructed social and moral reality. The shift is from a preoccupation with 'how to' questions to a concern with 'why' questions about their teaching. The teachers I work with use a journal (Holly, 1984) to create a *narrative* (or text) of their teaching as a basis for a dialogue that aims to assist them to locate their pedagogy, historically, culturally and politically.

Finally, in 'Teaching against the Grain' some anecdotal evidence is presented as to what has been achieved in a distance education Masters course entitled 'Teachers' Theories of Action'. Illustrations of what occurs when teachers conceive their teaching in this novel kind of way are canvassed, and some attempt is made to arrive at a reflexive understanding of what can reasonably be achieved in working in this critical way. I conclude by reflecting upon the nature of my own pedagogy in working with distance education students in these ways, and try to be clear about the extent of my own implication in entrenching the very notions that course was supposed to critique and supplant.

A Problematic Legacy

The essence of my argument is that the conditions of the professional lives of primary and secondary teachers will continue to degenerate in the way they have in the recent past (as evidenced in increased moves to extend centralist control through curriculum guidelines, courses of study and forms of teacher appraisal) unless teachers begin 'critically' to confront their work in ways that enable them to open up new intellectual challenges and frontiers. My claim is that there are ways of finding these 'frontiers' *within the act of teaching itself,* but they involve regarding teaching as a political activity (Stevens, 1987). What this means is that the starting point lies in teachers theorizing their own practice in ways that involve them in coming to see how their own understandings have become limited and distorted by non-educational forces, such as institutional structures and political constraints. It also means coming to recognize the extent of their own unwitting involvement in acquiescing to those forces. I like Greene's (1986a) way of putting it when she said: '. . . [we have to] burrow through the taken-for-granted, the conventional, the genteel . . . [if we are to] . . . be released from internal and external constraints . . . and leave [our] own thumbprints on the world' (p.432). How often do we hear earnest and hardworking teachers respond, when challenged as to why they do something the way they do: 'It's the only way, under the circumstances'. What this amounts to is an expression of hopelessness and powerlessness in which teachers feel somebody else is 'calling the shots'. What is needed is an approach in which things previously taken for granted are seen as problematic. Becoming 'critical' about teaching, and the social theories that support it, amounts to teachers moving away from narrow 'how to' questions, that have a limited utilitarian agenda, to 'what and why' questions, that regard techniques not as ends in themselves but as part of broader valued educational purposes. Construed in this way, teacher initiated theory about teaching becomes a form of cultural critique (Marcus and Fischer, 1986) in which teachers acquire a capacity for collective self-understanding of the political struggles involved in bringing about changes.

But theorizing and reflecting about the commonplace nature of what is normally taken for granted can be an unnerving experience. As Simon (1985) noted, such a dialectical encounter brings into contention the very nature of existing social relationships in teaching, and to that extent may be difficult to live with. Before teachers can decide what they might want to do differently, they first have to figure out '. . . why things are the way they are, how they got that way, and what set of conditions are supporting the processes that maintain them' (Simon, 1984, p.380). Construed this way, teachers engage *themselves* in a critique of existing practices that Simon (1985) labels as being 'transformative' in respect of three interrelated moments:

> First, . . . [it] views knowledge as socially produced, legitimated and distributed and seeks to make explicit the ways in which such production, legitimation and distribution take place. Second, knowledge is apprehended as expressing and embodying particular interests and values, implicating issues of power and ethics in all expressions of knowledge. Third, seeking to negate the 'objective' nature of knowledge and forcing the educator to confront the relation between knowledge, power and control . . . action that would alter the distribution of power and increase the range and scope of possibilities for individually and collectively defined projects. (p.1119)

Having said all of this, it is not difficult to become increasingly disillusioned and sceptical about what currently masquerades as 'change' in our schools and school systems. With all the chest-beating about educational 'reform' at the political level, we could be mistaken for believing that something of consequence in improving the lives of teachers and students was occurring — regrettably, this is not the case. What we have instead of meaningful reform in our schools is the rehearsal of actions that amount to worn-out and bankrupt solutions to the alleged problems confronting schools. There is a seemingly endless parade of calls for a return to the basics, demands for an increase in academic standards, an extension of testing, and moves for the removal of incompetent teachers. All of this is supposed to occur through measures designed to achieve improved quality control, efficiency and effectiveness in our classrooms. Unfortunately, none of these technical solutions addresses the *real* problem in our schools, which is not a crisis of *competence,* but rather a crisis of *confidence* which has its roots deep in the social and cultural dimensions of what schooling and learning are about.

Current attempts at educational reform have, therefore, failed largely because teachers as the major 'actors' have been largely excluded from the action, except as benign respondents to the agendas formulated by others. Teachers have had a long history of having been treated as the 'objects' of other people's supposed reforms (Scheffler, 1968; Hartnett and Naish, 1980; Bullough, Gitlin and Goldstein, 1984). The answer to perceived teacher malaise is seen as lying in measures aimed at increasing the rigour of teachers' work, in testing them more, in sending them 'back to school' and requiring that they work longer hours.

Central to all of these reform efforts is the nature of the relationship between theory and practice in teaching — one of the least understood and most contested notions in education. To continue to talk of 'closing and bridging the gap between theory and practice' (McCutcheon, 1985; Wadd, 1982) is to misconstrue the form of that relationship and to legitimate and perpetuate a historical division of labour between those who 'know about' and those who 'do' teaching — between so-called educational experts and teachers. Carr (1980) claims that despite substantial efforts to explain how theory should relate to practice, '. . . nothing seems to have changed . . . teachers cling to an image of theory as incomprehensible "jargon" that has nothing to do with their everyday problems' (p.60). For their part, people outside schools have become impatient at the '. . . ignorance, apathy or indifference of teachers' (Carr, 1980, p.60). It does not help either to talk in terms of moving away from a 'discipline-based' view of theory to 'problem-based' or 'integrated' approaches as ways of attempting the theory-practice rapprochement. The separation still exists, and indeed is built in to the very conceptualization of what is meant by theory — endeavours of this kind amount to no more than cosmetic attempts to avoid challenging and ultimately eliminating the dubious assumptions on which the distinction itself exists (Carr, 1980).

Speaking of the constructed separation of theory from practice in teaching, Berlak and Berlak (1981) cite the perspective of some academics that 'the experts in teaching are not teachers but scientifically-trained administrators, or educational scholars who study schooling scientifically' (p.235). What this amounts to, according to Berlak and Berlak, is a low status group (teachers) being subordinated to and dominated by another (researchers and administrators). Rowbotham (1981) goes as far as to claim that there is a class-related issue of power attaching to the notion of theory in which the working class has a deeply rooted suspicion and distrust of matters theoretical based on '. . . a defense against being made to feel ignorant and humiliated by intellectuals' use of theory' (p.85). Whatever its basis, the idea that teachers are only capable of dispensing the 'soft human virtues of patience, understanding and idealism' (Berlak and Berlak, 1981, p.235), and are incapable of rigorous and disciplined thinking about their own work, is a viewpoint that deserves to be countered in the strongest possible terms.

To be set against negative claims like these is the argument made by Kohl (1983) about the need for teachers actively to assume the responsibility for theory making (and theory testing), or accept the fact that these will be made for teachers by academic researchers and others only too willing to fill the vacuum. Kohl (1983) claims that this will be inevitable if teachers bargain away their educational power by giving up their responsibility as intellectuals. In his opinion: 'When teachers fail to develop and use educational theories . . . they open the door to stifling curriculum proposals devised by stodgy academics with no real sense of what goes on in the classroom' (p.28). He bases his claim on the view that there are always movements afoot committed to taking power away from teachers and placing it in the hands of one kind of special interest group or another. The problem with this, as Stenhouse (1983) was at pains to point out over some years, is that the nature of outsiders' knowledge is vastly different in nature and intent from that of teachers.

> The provisional knowledge created in the educational academy may be seen as a second order curriculum of knowledge about educational practice offered to teachers and potentially to students. Knowledge expressed as generalizations, more or less reliable, contributes to the teachers' and the students' understandings of the world in which they have to act. However, few such generalizations offer guidance as to how to act since they cannot by definition as generalizations take account either of the professional biographical development of teacher and student or of the crucial contextual and temporal variables. (p.212)

Thus we need to be careful about discussion that aims at dichotomy, particularly when issues of the relationship of theory to practice are involved. The fact is that we live in a world in which there are forces continually at work seeking reductionist and separationist ends under the rubric of rationalization and efficiency. Another way of viewing this same process is in terms of the disempowerment and dependency created in one group, while at the same time enhancing the power, independence, prestige and status of another.

There have been a number of distinct phases in the recent attempts to reform schools that exemplify the above discussion. Butt (1984) claims that initial attempts were of a kind that relied on outside 'experts' designing curricula to be implemented by teachers, with schools, school systems and teachers being bypassed in order to develop technological solutions to the 'best' forms of pedagogy and curriculum. Within this scheme teachers were reduced to the level of technicians with little scope for their own '. . . ideals, intentions or style' (Butt, 1984, p.3). Scheffler (1968) summed up the scene in the 1960s, and little has changed two decades later:

> It has, indeed, become increasingly fashionable in recent years to construe the teacher's work as that of a 'minor technician' within an industrial process, the overall goals . . . (of which are to be) . . . set in advance in terms of national needs, the curricular materials pre-packaged by the disciplinary experts, the methods developed by educational engineers — and the teacher's job . . . just to supervise the last operational stage, the methodological insertion of ordered facts into the student's mind. (pp.5-6)

In many ways the attempt at teacher proofing represented '. . . the low point in the history of pedagogical innovation' (Butt, 1984, p.3), based as it was on the implicit assumption that teachers were not competent or to be trusted to implement the new curricula. The proponents of this scheme sought to devise simple 'how to do it guides' that would ensure teacher compliance to a methodology deemed superior to any that teachers could devise on their own. Apple (1983a) claims that in the United States, and we could claim the same for Australia:

> . . . during the late 1950's and 1960's, there was rather strong pressure from academics, capital, and the state to reinstitute academic disciplinary knowledge as the most 'legitimate' content for schools. In the areas of mathematics and science, especially, it was feared that 'real' knowledge was not being taught. A good deal of effort was given to producing curricular programs that were systematic, based on rigorous academic foundations, and, in the elementary school material in particular, teacher proof. Everything a teacher was to deal with was provided and prespecified. (p.614)

Given the considerable autonomy teachers have always had behind the classroom door, it was not surprising that this exercise in 'teacher proofing' failed rather dismally. Apple (1983a) expressed this in these terms:

> . . . when the material was introduced into many schools, it was not unusual for the 'new' math and the 'new' science to be taught in much the manner as the old math and old science. It was

altered so that it fit into both the existing regularities of the institution and the prior practices of successful teaching. . . . [This] is at least partly tied to the resistance of a female work force against external incursions into the practices they had evolved over years of labor. (p.615)

. . . the 'mere' fact that the state wishes to find 'more efficient' ways to organize teaching does not guarantee this will be acted on by teachers who have a long history of work practices and self-organization once the doors to their rooms are closed. (p.616)

As I have argued elsewhere (Smyth, 1987a, 1987b), teaching is fundamentally different from industrial processes in that teachers are not working with inert materials that respond according to some predetermined rules. Rather, students are continually engaging in dialectical encounters with their teachers, and through this coming to create and share in a common culture.

After unsuccessful attempts to change the curriculum materials, effort was directed at remedying the perceived defects in teachers that prevented them from implementing the new curricula. The solution was seen to lie in 'in-servicing' teachers so that they could acquire the new skills and behaviours necessary to use the new curricula. The rationale was that 'you need to change the people before changing the structures'. This strategy was based on the unsubstantiated presumption that teachers had deficiencies that could be rectified through 'one shot' in-service workshops. It was too simplistic a view, destined to a similar fate to teacher proofing the curricula. More recent reform moves have concentrated on attempting to 'sell' teachers on innovations and develop a sense of 'ownership' of ideas through action research and school-based curriculum development. The notion was that teachers would experiment with new ideas, try them on for size, iron out problems and develop their own new ones. As Butt (1984) notes, even here there were still unanswered questions:

. . . questions about insider/outsider relationships . . . . How much power does the teacher have? How far can developer intentions be adapted? Does it still remain a manipulative device aimed at implementing other people's intentions, overcoming teacher resistance and gaining commitment through compliance. These questions keep coming back to haunt us. (p.6)

As a partial explanation of these occurrences, Apple (1983b) argues that since Western societies have a history of being caught up in fiscal crises, it becomes easy to provide mass education in commercialized packages, with mass produced materials becoming *de facto* mechanisms for effectively exercising centralized control over schools, and in the process intensifying and trivializing the nature of teachers' work. Schools, therefore, become politicized and contested sites as teachers are deskilled and '. . . robbed of their creativity and initiative' (Dow, 1985, p.215).

An Openly Ideological View of Teaching

Those of us in higher education who work with teachers (including those who work in the distance education mode) are not entirely blameless in contributing to the distortion of the school reform process that has occurred in recent times. In pushing the 'school/teacher improvement' bandwagon for our own ends, we have become blinded to the fact that this is based on the business management model of technical rationality which is concerned primarily with 'compliant action'. As Greene (1986b) put it, the argument in respect of schools goes thus: '*If* we have the proper knowledge base, *if* we become more rigorous, *if* we pay more heed to content and less to method, *if* we underwrite merit and mastery, *if* we enlist more experts . . . we will solve what are largely technical problems and will no longer be at risk' (p.70). What Greene (1986a) is saying is that simplistic views like this overlook the fact that we live in a palpably deficient world in which there are '. . . unwarranted inequities, shattered communities, [and] unfulfilled lives' (p.427).

What is required instead is the kind of critique that Giroux and Freire (1987) argue for that involves an '. . . unmasking of the lies, myths and distortions that construct the basis for the dominant order' (p.xii). But it is more than just an unmasking process: '. . . it [is] also a form of practical learning that involve[s] listening to the experiences of others, promoting a capacity for self-criticism, and using such criticism as the basis for developing programmatic discourses for building alternative hopes and realizable visions' (p.xii). The intent behind such critical research and analysis is a shift of emphasis away from practices that focus on how teachers 'measure-up' towards assisting them to look instead at how particular forms of domination have become 'natural' and unquestioned through the social relationships they endorse in their teaching lives. Pagano (1987) expressed it nicely when she said that in their professional lives teachers are no different from other people in that they can be '. . . satisfied with all sorts of intolerable situations. An education should equip us to recognize the intolerable and to act against it' (p.121). She points out that unless teachers engage in the kind of moral discourse that enables them critically to reflect upon and simultaneously explore both the 'emancipatory' as well as the 'enslaving' possibilities of educational practice, then those practices '. . . become fact[s] of nature to be managed scientifically' (p.119).

What all of this amounts to is a major shift in emphasis; from a concern with what Freire (Bruss and Macedo, 1985) calls the 'pedagogy of the answer' to the 'pedagogy of the question'. The pedagogy of the question involves practice that:

> . . . forces and challenges the learners to think critically and to adopt a critical attitude toward the world. It is a pedagogy that enables the learners to break the chains of alienation imposed on them by the mechanistic nature of their daily routine. The pedagogy of the question requires that learners distance themselves from their bureaucratised daily existence, while they become more and more aware through reflection of the mythical facts that enslave them. Unlike the pedagogy of the answer, which reduces learners to mere receptacles for pre-packaged knowledge, the pedagogy of the question gives learners the 'language of possibility' to challenge the very constraints which relegate them to mere objects. . . . [The] pedagogy of the answer . . . lacks any profundity of thought and cannot stimulate and challenge learners to question, to doubt, and to reject. (p.8).

As Greene (1973) put it, a critical pedagogy of teaching amounts to working actively against an 'unthinking submergence in the social reality that prevails' (p.269). She claims that if teachers wish to present themselves as actively engaged in critical thinking and authentic choosing, then they '. . . cannot accept any "ready-made" standardized scheme at face value' (p.269). Unless *teachers* problematize their teaching, then they cannot expect *students* 'to pose the kind of questions about experience which will involve *them* in self-aware inquiry' (p.269). What I am suggesting, therefore, has implications extending considerably beyond teachers merely being articulate about, or theorizing, their practice along the line of 'this is what works for me'. In particular, there are important moral and ethical questions about the nature of educational research, and who has the right, and under what circumstances, to engage in educational enquiry. At stake also is the ideological nature of that enquiry, its relationship to the distribution of power and how such enquiry can contribute to a more just and equitable world through a redistribution of power. The real agenda in this 'openly ideological research' (Lather, 1986a) is transforming rather than supporting the status quo. Such efforts are emancipatory in the sense in which Misgeld (1975) draws upon Kant's use of that term, namely a freeing '. . . of man

[sic] from a state of self-imposed tutelage, of incapacity to use his [sic] own intelligence without external guidance' (p. 24). What I am referring to here is really a socially constructed view of knowledge that is out of the hands of experts and specialists, and which resides with those who might otherwise be regarded as being dispossessed. Such a view enables people to become 'subjects' rather than 'objects' and to examine their circumstances to see not only the tensions and contradictions that exist, but how these came to be historically. This 'situated' view of teaching (Greene, 1986b) is in marked contrast to traditional 'impositional' (cf. Dunkin and Biddle, 1974) views of knowledge about teaching.

What I am arguing for, and what I have proposed elsewhere (Smyth, 1987c), is a 'liberating' view of teaching that frees teachers from dependence upon conventional axioms about teaching and the habitual taken-for-grantedness that unconsciously characterizes teaching. To talk of teaching in such 'praxis-like' terms (Lather, 1986b) and to construe it dialectically is to jettison the dominant, hierarchical and instrumentalist approaches, and to posit in their place a view that is more inclusive of what might be considered oppositional viewpoints about teaching and learning. This dialectical perspective would involve participants in self-formative processes whereby they are able analytically to reconstruct accounts of their own histories, while locating themselves in it, and being able to see how elements of the professional past live on into the present. Such a dialectical view of teaching (Smyth, 1987d), therefore, focuses on the specifics of teaching and on the social and political ends towards which it is directed, so that teaching can be seen as part of a broader social purpose. It is not difficult to construe this as a form of theorizing, or a way of making sense of the world. Theorizing, in the sense in which I employ that term, occurs as teachers come to understand what they know about their teaching (through the collection of data), and out of this create new and informed meanings about what that information reveals to them about why teaching is the way it is, and why they personally endorse those particular meanings. Theorizing, in the way I use the word, makes sense to people because the 'larger issues are embedded in the particulars of everyday life' (Lather, 1986a, p. 11). Theory does not have to be 'applied' to practical situations because there is no separation of one from the other. The relationship between theory and practice is therefore a dialectical one, such that theory emerges out of practice, and practice is informed by theory. Without wanting to put too fine a point on it, Inglis (1985) captured the salience of this 'sense making' or theorizing process:

> Everybody has a set of theories, compounded maybe of fact and
> value, history and myth, observation and folklore, superstition

and convention, but these theories are nonetheless intended to explain the world . . . and discover and confirm its meanings. Most of all, those who refuse all theory, who speak of themselves as plain, practical people, and virtuous in virtue of having no theory, are in the grip of theories which manacle them and keep them immobile, because they have no way of thinking about them and therefore of taking them off. They aren't theory-free; they are stupid theorists. (p.40)

None of this is to suggest that critical enquiry comes easily for teachers. Indeed, it is an intriguing question as to whether teachers can engage in the kind of systematic, deliberate and fundamental questioning of their teaching that is being suggested. For Shor (1980) the major impediment to critical thought is the comforting and soothing nature of everyday life itself. The way we lead our lives, he argues, militates against us asking searching questions about how or why things came to be the way they are. In Shor's (1980) words: '. . . most people are alienated from their own conceptual habits of mind. How come? Why don't masses of people engage in social reflection? Why isn't introspection an habitual feature of life? What prevents popular awareness of how the whole system operates, and which alternatives would best serve human needs?' (p.47). Critical thought is difficult to enact for four main reasons, as outlined by Shor (1980): 'reification' — the spectator approach to life, accepting the situation for what it is; 'beating the system' — remaining frozen in the system while fighting for illusory power; 'pre-scientific thinking' — ascribing causes to human nature; and 'mystification' — where *individuals* are blamed for *their* failure in a society which allegedly offers everyone opportunity.

Implicit in this inability to question the system and the models of authority that support it is the fact that people become coopted into supporting their own oppression. They become conditioned into '[policing] themselves by internalizing the ideas of the ruling élite' (Shor, 1980, p.55). In effect they develop an overpowering aspiration to 'resemble the oppressor, to imitate him, to follow him' (Freire, 1972b, p.38). They become trapped into believing that the way out of their oppression is to treat others around them in the dehumanizing way they themselves are treated (in some quarters called 'horizontal violence'). They cannot see that they have internalized the ways of thinking and acting that caused them to be the way they are. There are also structural impediments and constraints at work here, but as I have argued elsewhere (Smyth, 1986), to say that the conditions of schooling totally frustrate reflection, is to beg the question. Berlak (1987) put the same point, when she said '. . . the construction of an emancipatory pedagogy need not wait upon a more nurturing context, but may, in fact contribute to its creation' (p.5). Despite what might seem like some formidable barriers, like Berlak (1987) I happen to believe that the difficulties to emancipatory teaching are surmountable. In a real sense it is the engagement in the process of unpicking the forces that constitute the dominant ideology that is of crucial importance in ventures of this kind.

Teaching against the Grain

In working to develop programmes that aim at empowering teachers I have learnt over the past few years that it is one thing to talk about liberating and emancipatory pedagogies, but it is quite another to *do it with teachers*. In this I find myself in the quandary Sirotnik and Oakes (1986) alluded to, when they warned that '. . . the scholarly presentation of an idea is one thing; doing it is quite another.' As they candidly admit of their own work, '[We] will clearly be taking "scholarly risks" as we attempt to apply rather transcendental visions in less than utopian circumstances' (p.55). I am mindful too of Giroux's (1981) cryptic comment that '. . . the goals of emancipation are not like shopping lists that one draws up before going to the supermarket; they are goals to be struggled for in specific contexts, under specific historical circumstances' (p.220).

The notion of empowerment (which is rapidly becoming an overused and perhaps even a meaningless term) has to do with teachers actually taking charge of aspects of their lives to which they have been prevented from gaining access in the past (Fried, 1980a). It involves an active critique and an uncovering of the tensions that exist between particular teaching practices and the larger cultural and social contexts in which teaching is embedded. Willis (1977) expressed it in terms of the social actors themselves reflecting upon, challenging and refuting, rather than accepting, the structural conditions which envelop their lives. There is a sense, too, in which people embark on a process of *becoming different* by thinking critically and creatively, so as to pursue meanings that enable them to make increasing sense of the world in which they live. As Mishler (1986) put it, empowerment entails a shift in the balance of power as participants move *beyond* the description of the 'text', to embrace the possibilities of action: 'To be empowered is not only to speak one's own voice and to tell one's own story, but to apply the understanding arrived at to action in accord with one's own interests' (p.119).

There is a preparedness no longer to accept things the way they are, but to see instead '. . . patterned inequalities, institutional power, ideologies [and] . . . the internal dynamics of how a system works, and for whom the system is not functional' (Everhart, 1979, p.420). My argument is that teachers are only able to reclaim the power they have lost to those outside classrooms if they place themselves in critical confrontation with their problems. Empowerment has less to do with '. . . a handing down of knowledge . . . [and is more like] a partnership, a mutual sharing of ideas, intuitions and experiences (Fried, 1980b, p.30). In Greene's (1986b) terms this means '. . . a sense of agency is required of . . . teacher[s]' in which they can '. . . become challengers, when they can take initiatives' and in which schools become 'places in which spaces are created in which worthwhile questions can be asked' (p.73). For most teachers this is in stark contrast to the 'delivery of services' mentality created by centralized bureaucratic educational authorities which insist on presenting the educational world in terms of '. . . one rank of people (service delivers) who have been trained and hired to treat the rest. They diagnose our problems, assess our needs, and then provide us with anything from a prescription to an entire program to fix what's lacking, or leaking, in us' (Fried, 1980a, p.4). Simon (1987) expressed the essence of empowering teachers:

> . . . it literally means to give ability to, to permit or enable. When we hear the word empowerment used in education, it is usually being employed in the spirit of critique. Its referent is the identification of oppressive and unjust relations within which there is an unwarranted limitation placed on human action, feeling and thought. Such limitation is seen as constraining a person from the opportunity to participate on equal terms with other members of a group or community to whom have accrued the socially defined status of 'the privileged' 'the competent'. . . . To empower is to enable those who have been silenced to speak (p.374).

According to Anderson (1987), beyond an ill-defined and rhetorical call for teacher empowerment there have been few indicators as to how teachers themselves '. . . can reflect on the structural conditions that inform their practice' (p.14). It is that I want to turn to now.

If consciousness raising is about teachers becoming aware of their own alienation and coming to recognize the nature and sources of the forces that keep them subjugated, then as Harris (1979) says, this has to start with *them* sketching out the contours of actual lived situations, and posing problems about those concrete situations. This process of 'distancing' themselves from classroom events and processes can be difficult and perplexing for teachers. As MacKay and Marland (1978) found, classrooms present such a rapidly changing kaleidoscope of events that it is difficult for teachers to obtain stable images of themselves and of the interactive part they play in the creation of those events. Before we can engage teachers in untangling the complex web of ideologies (Berlak, 1987) that surround them in their teaching, we first need to get them to focus on those manifestations of their teaching that perplex, confuse or frustrate them; that is to say, the practicalities of the 'here-and-now' that teachers pride themselves in being so vitally concerned with.

If teachers are going to uncover the nature of the forces that inhibit and constrain them, and work at changing those conditions, they need to engage in four forms of action with respect to their teaching, each of which can be represented as a question:

1 Describe . . . what do I do?
2 Inform . . . what does this mean?
3 Confront . . . how did I come to be like this?
4 Reconstruct . . . how might I do things differently?

Describing . . . what do I do? This is where teachers begin to develop 'a third inner eye' on their teaching. They use a journal, or a diary, as a way of accumulating a written account, as evidence of what is happening in their teaching. Many of them find this quite strange to start with; others have been keeping a professional journal for years. The advantage of a written account is that it provides a basis for revisiting and for sharing experiences, that are all too readily forgotten. Having to write also requires that they be clearer about what was actually happening. By focusing on describing incidents they find annoying, perplexing or puzzling, they are able to highlight the elements — the 'who', 'what', 'when' and 'where'. The description does not have to be long and involved, nor does it have to be in academic language. Indeed, it is important that they use their own language. If they can describe the incident in their own language, then they have made an important start both in owning and analyzing their teaching. As Mishler (1986) put it, empowerment involves 'social actors' being able to find and speak their own 'voices', and '. . . one of the significant ways through which individuals give meaning to their experiences is to organize them in narrative form' (p.118). The rationale is that it is necessary first to have teachers create a text as a prelude to them problematizing their teaching — if they are not able to be articulate about the elements of their teaching, then they are unlikely to develop the kind of dialogue that will enable them to see how their consciousness was formed in the first place, and be even less likely to challenge and to change it. Such records are usually done 'after the event', usually at the end of the working day as the teacher casts his/her mind back over the day.

Sometimes these descriptions can be very brief and to the point; at other times they can be more expansive; and sometimes they go beyond mere description into being somewhat speculative. Here are three examples of teachers' journal entries:

> John didn't finish his work again today. I must see that he learns to complete what he has begun. (Tripp, 1984, p.28)

> Yesterday was Friday again! Friday Bloody Friday. It's the third Friday that I've *had* those year 7's — emphasis on the *had* . . . I am the principal of a primary school of 150 kids. I've just come from a smaller school of 50 kids; had been there for 5 years. Kids were beautiful . . . independent, reliable, self-directed, self-motivated. Great. Now, after 20 years of teaching I meet 21 year 7's, half of whom act like caged bastards. God I've been angry. . . . [Took] them for a lesson intending to get to know them and do some social learning activities. I'd told them to work in small groups on a task — read a story and answer some questions. They did everything but. Roamed around, talked about everything else, annoyed the class next door, drew and coloured-in . . . I couldn't believe it. I'd been so used to asking year 7's in previous years to do so and so, and they would; but not this mob.

> Using my theory of social learning and group development as a guide, I tried to explain my *modus operandi* and why I was doing it this way. Half of them wouldn't even listen. I asked them several times to sit down. Because I didn't know them by name, I walked over to the offenders and said: 'Excuse me, but I would like you to sit down so I can tell you what I would like you to do'. Some complied with my request. After almost pleading for co-operation, I did my block and yelled at them. That got their attention, but it is not the way I tend to operate.

> I was teaching a year 10 maths class in which we were doing Pythagoras' geometrical application. I decided to feign forgetfulness and hand over responsibility for the conduct of the lesson to the students so they could help one another. They found the notion of the teacher sitting down among them as a student disarming. A suggestion from a student that drawing on the blackboard was necessary was taken up, so Darren was asked whether he would take up the chalk. While the intention had

been to get a volunteer, the direct cue to Darren, on reflection, was loaded with covert teacher power. It seemed to Darren to be a directive, and while he did proceed to the blackboard, his initial drawings were an inadequate representation, but eventually he came up with one without assistance from me. . . . When he was asked to explain, Darren faltered, about half-way through. . . . The students were surprised when no real help was forthcoming from me as the teacher.

In each of these instances the teacher has engaged with an incident that is significant to him/her: in the case of John something to be fixed up; in the case of the year 7s an intense frustration on the part of the teacher and an inability to adjust to a new group; and with the year 10 maths group an unexpected reaction by students to a different teaching strategy. By getting teachers to start with descriptions of their own practice, and using these as a basis for discussion, it is possible to avoid consciousness raising slipping directly into a form of 'intellectual imperialism' (Harris, 1979) in which outsiders provide answers to questions that are non-issues for teachers. Teachers need not only to discover those things they 'thought they knew, but [which they] now realise they need to know' (p.175). In Shor's (1980) language they have to 'extraordinarily re-experience the ordinary'. It is only by 'naming' their world (Freire, 1974), in the sense of concretely describing those elements of it that alienate and confuse them, that some basis exists for teachers to begin to reconstrue actions in ways that amount to changing them. The intent, therefore, is to get teachers to see that the social settings they inhabit are not given, immutable and unchangeable, but that they offer '. . . problems that can be solved, or "limit-situations" that can be transcended' (Fay, 1977, p.220).

Describing the 'situatedness' of concrete instances of their teaching enables teachers to begin to reverse the view that there is somehow a set of universal laws as to what constitutes 'good teaching'. It is to begin to counteract what Shor and Freire (1987) describe as the 'amputation' of teachers from the lives and realities they are supposed to be working with in the process of teaching. One of the tragedies of the teacher education enterprise is that it somehow succeeds in promulgating a view that the act of teaching can exist separately and apart from the lives, cultures, aspirations and problems of teachers and students. It is these practices, and the social processes they encapsulate, that form the 'situated pedagogy' (Shor and Freire, 1987) that has to be described and analyzed.

Informing . . . what is the meaning within my teaching? Having captured some limited descriptions of those aspects of their practice that perplex them (although they may not be clear about the reasons for their unease), teachers need to be invited to revisit the descriptions and start the process of 'untying the text' (Young, 1981). Obviously it is not enough simply to have described something — it may be the beginnings of understanding, but on its own it is not informative as to the principles that lie behind the action. To that extent the action remains in the realm of the mystical — caused as it were by vague, magical forces that teachers do not really understand or control.

What is really occurring here is that teachers are theorizing about their teaching — unpicking, as it were, the broader pedagogical processes that lie behind their specific actions. What they come up with is a kind of 'local theory' (Tripp, 1987), that is not universal, but which nevertheless seems to be embedded in the particular incident they have described. It may not be generalizable at all; but it may be important in situationally explaining something. In terms of the earlier cited descriptive examples of teaching:

John and the unfinished task
Here the teacher was able to see that what lay behind her journal entry about John was a belief, a theory about teaching, that had to do with a sequential mode of learning — this task must be finished first, because it is a prerequisite to the one that is to follow.

Year 7 kids on Fridays
This teacher found that he was trying to put into effect a theory that says: learning cannot occur unless students are paying attention so they can hear directions. He was prepared to pursue that theory to the point of verbal violence, if necessary. The students, on the other hand, seemed to be displaying a different set of values and beliefs (a theory) about learning; namely, that they had the right to communicate with one another and dictate what went on in class, and the teacher was powerless to change that. What they were expressing was a form of opposition to what they saw as the teacher's exercise of hierarchical control, despite his claim to be doing otherwise.

Year 10 maths class
When he stood back from his described incident, the teacher was able to see that he held a theory about peer learning, albeit a somewhat naive one because of the way it failed to acknowledge that the students come to class with a long history of expectations about what they see as likely to happen. They hold certain views about who has a right and a duty to impart knowledge. What the teacher

overlooked here was the fact that students cannot always readily cope with quick, unexpected and dramatic shifts in power, especially if they have been socialized in particular ways.

What teachers are seeking to do here is to inform their classroom practices; that is to say, to theorize or look for some broad explanatory principles that lie behind their actions. They are not looking for universal laws of teaching, or for the existence of what the experts claim to be true about teaching; rather, the search is for 'local theories' (Tripp, 1987) that help the teacher to make sense of particular situations and moments they encounter. This is to put a somewhat different complexion on the contested notion of theory.

The intent, then, is for teachers to see the embeddedness of local theories (Tripp, 1987) in the normal act of teaching (Smyth, 1987c) — something they tend to have difficulty with because of the mythology surrounding the positivist notion of the enforced separation of theory from practice. When they are able to get behind the habitualness and taken-for-grantedness of what they do, they have a measure of control and ownership over what counts as knowledge about teaching. Carr (1982) makes the point more generally:

> [There is] a deeply ingrained image of educational theory as a miscellaneous collection of maps, guides, itineraries and rule-books produced in some far-off land and then exported to the 'world of practice' so that its inhabitants can understand where they are, what they are doing and where they are supposed to be going. What this image conceals, of course, is not only that these consumers have themselves produced and already possess a map of their situation, and rules and guiding principles about what they are trying to achieve; it also disguises the fact that since these theoretical products are the outcome of non-educational activities, they will always reflect the use of non-educational concepts and categorizations and so re-draw the map of the 'real world of education' in non-educational ways. (p.26)

What is at issue here is the political question of who defines and articulates knowledge about teaching. Historically teachers have been led to believe that they have only a benign part in this. Their acquiescence is not altogether surprising, given the ideology of oppression that lies behind hierarchical regimes of teacher evaluation and supervision. The broader argument is well put by Carr (1982):

> Once it is conceded that to undertake a practical activity like education, involves engaging in some recognisable set of

practices, and once it is acknowledged that these practices are not
. . . free from theoretical preconceptions, then it becomes
apparent that 'educational theory' is not something that is created
in isolation from practice and then has to be 'applied',
'implemented' or 'adopted' through a 'sustained effort' on the
part of the two reluctant parties. 'Education' is not some kind of
inert phenomenon that can be observed, isolated, explained and
theorized about. There are no 'educational phenomena' apart
from the practices of those engaged in educational activities, no
'educational problems' apart from those arising from these
practices and no 'educational theories' apart from those that
structure and guide these practices. The only task which
'educational theory' can legitimately pursue, then, is to develop
theories of educational practice that are intrinsically related to
practitioners' own accounts of what they are doing, that will
improve the quality of their involvement in these practices and
thereby allow them to practise better. (p. 26)

If it were not true that teachers have ways of making sensible and
intelligible quite complex aspects of their teaching, then teaching would:

. . . have to be some kind of mechanical behaviour performed by
robot-like characters in a completely unthinking way. But
teaching is not like that. . . . [Teachers do have a] 'way of
thinking' that provides the theoretical background against which
teachers explain and justify their actions, make decisions and
resolve real problems. Anybody engaged in teaching, then, must
already possess some 'theory' which guides their practices and
makes them intelligible. (p. 1)

An inescapable part of theorizing is, therefore, its transformative
potential — the kind of critical questioning that challenges taken-for-
granted assumptions and practices, and brings about changes in the way
practice itself is experienced and understood (Carr, 1980).

The other issue that teachers have to be prepared to question has to
do with 'causation', or how they came to hold these theories about
teaching.

Confronting . . . how did I come to be this way? It is at this point in
working with teachers that difficulties can arise; after being asked to
'describe' and to be clear about what it is that 'informs' their teaching,
teachers are then asked to move outside themselves, and indeed, outside
their comfortable world as they know and experience it. In a word, they
are asked to *confront* themselves. Asked why teachers would deliberately

want to make their lives uncomfortable in this way, I respond in terms of Harris' (1979) maxim that: '. . . the more ignorant one is, and the more one is satisfied in one's ignorance, the more easily one can be exploited by those less ignorant' (p.166). Philosophically the problem has to do with managing the dilemma of how to: '. . . both respect the rationality of social actors and their way of constructing meaning while at the same time address[ing] the contradictions and distortions created by social structures' (Anderson, 1987, p.8).

What I invite teachers to do is to seek to 'locate' or 'situate' their practices, beliefs and assumptions about teaching in a broader cultural, social and political context. By that I mean engaging in critical reflection about the assumptions that underlie their methods and classroom practices. They are asked to see their teaching not as isolated technical procedures, but as historical expressions of shaped values about what they consider to be important about the nature of the educative act. They are invited to write about their own biography and how they feel this has shaped the construction of their values, and in turn how social and institutional forces have been influential. They are asked to confront their previously described local theories of teaching through the lenses of a series of guiding questions:

> What do my practices say about my assumptions, values and beliefs about teaching?
> Where did these ideas come from?
> What social practices are expressed in these ideas?
> What is it that causes me to maintain my theories?
> What views of power do they embody?
> Whose interests seem to be served by my practices?
> What is it that acts to constrain my views of what is possible in teaching? (Smyth, 1987c)

It is here that teachers are being asked to 'problematize' their teaching and to ask questions about the 'social causation' (Fay, 1977) of their actions. It is where they are required to untangle and re-evaluate the taken-for-grantedness of habitual practices. Breaking into this con-structed mythology is not easy, as Berlak (1987) indicated: '. . . it would be hard to over-estimate the difficulty of the challenge, the complexity, and the enveloping nature this net of taken-for-granted ideas presents for those who want to encourage independent thought in classrooms — and outside of classrooms as well' (p.7).

Following through with my previously cited examples, the teachers concerned were able to confront themselves and their teaching in the following ways:

John and his incomplete task

When this teacher was able to share her journal item with a group of colleagues, she was able to see that there was more to it than just a problem to be solved; in fact, there was a series of other questions:

> why doesn't John finish his work?
> why should he finish his work?
> how does John see the tasks demanded of him?
> are the tasks of the right kind, quality and quantity? (Tripp, 1984)

Rather than asking 'how can I get Johnny to finish his work?', she was able to see that a more important question was, 'why must Johnny finish his work before going onto the next task?' In a sense, it was her own unquestioned professional history as a successful teacher that prevented her from asking the why questions — she had become fixated at the how level. Asking the simple question WHY AM I DOING THIS?, can produce some quite startling answers. In the case of John's unfinished work it can be argued:

> In everyday life outside the classroom we continually leave unfinished what we have begun, so how is it that we are in a position of having to enforce upon these students the rule that they must finish one thing before they can go onto the next. Where did that rule come from, and when is it necessary? (Tripp, 1984, p.28)

The issue, therefore, transcends the individual teacher and has a lot to do with the hidden curriculum of social control in schooling. As Tripp argues, for reasons of orderliness and the general smooth and efficient running of the school, it is desirable that teachers have students complete tasks in a linear fashion. There may be little or no educational rationale for this requirement.

The Pythagoras case

The teacher was able to reflect on this incident and see more clearly the nature of the power relationships involved in his own teaching, and the fact that what he was doing was going against an established norm. Even when he tried this, he was sensitive to the feelings of uncertainty as students tried to adjust to the new kind of risk-taking and exposure that was involved.

Year 7 kids on Fridays

On other occasions, teachers struggle with little apparent success in trying to see the nature of their own implication in processes in which they are 'caught up'. This teacher was unable to see how his own actions were inextricably bound up in perpetuating a particular power relationship with his students, despite the fact that he thought he was actually divesting power to students. He was also unable to see the nature of student opposition for what it really was — an expression of their unwillingness to submit to what they saw as a thinly veiled authoritarian form of control, dressed up as democratic intent. As his words below indicate, while this teacher had some success in seeing the more general point about the historical domination of students by teachers, he was still blind to the contradiction in his own practice:

> It seems to me that it's always been the practice for teachers to 'bark' orders at students, just as if they were in the army . . . . It's the way teachers have spoken to students ever since schools began; it's never been questioned . . . I believe that asking students for cooperation . . . goes hand in hand with an explanation of why the request is being made. This gives children more information to go on when they make their choices about cooperating or not . . . .
> [And later] . . . it seems I am the person with the power in that I have decided what the class is going to do, but I am willing to 'give the power away' to the students by negotiating what I intend to do. What I am saying is that I hold the power, because I am making decisions about how I want the students to behave while I tell them my intentions for the lesson. But *then,* they have the power to renegotiate the activities.

In large part the difficulty facing each of these teachers is their cultural upbringing that involves the belief that schools (and what transpires within them) are objectivist, neutral and apolitical. This can be a difficult view to dislodge, especially in a context where it is being continually reinforced and massaged by a 'scientific' and management pedagogy (Giroux, 1985) view of schooling. Because the notion of social critique is so foreign to teachers, what they end up doing is either of two things: they often (metaphorically) turn the blowtorch on themselves in quite self-denigrating ways that reveal enormous guilt feelings at the way they do things; or they seek to rationalize and justify their practices on the basis of what they consider to be the perceived needs of children or the communities which schools exist to serve. In both cases the result is the same: an unwillingness to confront the systematic way in which their teaching has been dictated to them by others outside schools.

For example, what is exemplified in the case of the year 7 teacher and his students is a kind of conforming and acquiescent failure to challenge the trajectory of history; it amounts to a fatalistic, metaphorical throwing up of the hands, that says, 'things have always been this way'. This particular teacher has not become empowered because he has been unable to elicit or respect '. . . the integrity of the cultural informant's [own] constructions' (Anderson, 1987, p.5), in this case that of his students. Had he been able to understand the year 7s on their terms, he would have been able to see that their '. . . apparently irrational behaviour takes on a certain rationality [even predictability]' (p.5), where 'social learning' means genuinely democratic relationships among students, not some version of social engineering that teachers try to engender. But, to be fair to the teacher, there is also a rationality to his apparently irrational behaviour. What we can see here is the difficulty teachers encounter in trying to sort out the overlapping complexities of Willis' (1977) school norms — the 'official' (what the institution says are its statements of purposes), the 'pragmatic' (how they speak about the 'official' and the 'pragmatic' in the staffroom and with colleagues). As Anderson (1987) put it, the interpenetration of these presents a teacher with an '. . . inchoate social reality from which he or she must extract a rationale for his or her actions. The practitioner, then, cannot be blamed for possessing contradictory goals and rationales which he or she uses in different contexts . . .' (pp.11-12).

It is against this kind of philosophical background that I try to get teachers studying in the distance education mode to see why it is that the social, cultural and political structures around them have unwittingly caused them to come to regard as 'natural' and 'unquestioned' the ideas they have about teaching. I ask that they see their teaching practices as social constructions of reality, and even misrepresented constructions at that, on some occasions. Their resistance to this is not altogether surprising. They are not simply being asked to discard a few false beliefs; they are being asked to confront a '. . . set of interrelated illusions about human needs . . . about what is good and of value, and about how one should act in one's relations with others to achieve these things' (Fay, 1977, p.214). As Fay (1977) notes, the systematic, shared and deeply rooted nature of these illusions means that dislodging them is extremely difficult: 'This is because giving up such illusions requires abandoning one's self-conceptions and the social practices that they engender and support, things people cling to because they provide direction and meaning in their lives' (p.214).

Sometimes they can see these contradictions in varying degrees, and sometimes they are able to talk about their own confusion in trying to come to some kind of reconciliation so as to live with the incoherence. Speaking of his endeavours to 'negotiate' the content of the curriculum with his students, one of the teachers captured the dilemma in which he found himself, when he said: 'I am negotiating from the position of wanting the other party to see reason. . . . Be reasonable, see my way!' He went on to reveal the feelings of powerlessness and the way in which he felt trapped by social forces he neither controlled nor understood: 'I don't have any desire to exert control over others, but it is an inherent part of my practice (as I've seen from this project). [But] more and more I am feeling the influence of the accountant mentality of "politicians". More and more decisions are being made about schooling by people who are not part of the schooling scene.' The tragedy for this teacher, and countless others like him, lies in the kind of social relationships he is forced to endure in the workplace and in the way these are unwittingly reproduced in his pedagogy and in the relationships he develops with his students. While dimly aware of the contradiction, he seemed incapable of seeing a way out: 'As the teacher I see myself as a creator of the appropriate learning environments *which will encourage kids to construct the knowledge the teacher has planned* . . . I still tend to be the teacher and the giver of information' [my emphases].

In a more general sense, while teachers are becoming increasingly 'proletarianized' (Poulantzas, 1973; Derber, 1982) in terms of losing control over their teaching, they are also increasingly caught up as part of a 'power élite' with respect to their students. Speaking of his own biography, one teacher was able to locate himself historically in relation to his opposition to the Vietnam War and his support for other traditionally oppressed social groups during the 1960s. He was also equally open about how individual competitiveness and upward social mobility had thwarted his ideals and caused them to become twisted and tarnished in the intervening period:

> All of these social phenomena seemed to me to indicate that something was wrong with the traditional authority structures. This, combined with my school experience (rigid, hierarchical, privileged, private school) . . . [caused me to leave] the place angry and rebellious, and made me an enthusiastic radical. [But now] I am part of the structure that I once daubed with slogans; survival has become a priority . . . .

It was a sad reflection on the state in which he found himself that this same teacher claimed to have '. . . found it difficult to achieve the level of political analysis called for [in this project] . . .' and of having '. . . struggled without much success to identify the nature of the ideological domination at work in the school'. Clearly, he had travelled much further than he was able to give himself credit for.

There can be little doubt that teachers' notions of professionalism and teacher autonomy actually get in the way of the process of confrontation. Grace (1978), for example, found that teachers held a view of themselves and their work as lying largely outside social and political structures, and to that extent they were relatively immune from analyzing them. The teachers in his research : '. . . were able to maintain this position with conviction because *control* of their activities and, consequently, *notions of a 'dominant order' or of a 'controlling apparatus' and of the necessity for struggle against it were insubstantial in their consciousness, whereas notions of autonomy were real and actual'* [emphases in original] (pp:216-17). Grace's (1978) argument is essentially that in teaching there is a considerable inertia that prevents teachers from challenging the network of invisible controls (examination boards, curriculum guidelines, community pressures on teachers to achieve results, etc.) that have come to envelop teaching. When controls over teaching were more visible and obvious (at least in Australia), it was much easier to challenge such obvious practices as inspection. The game seems to have changed quite dramatically with control over the work of teachers becoming much less obtrusive but no less potent. The problem with the apparently benign and unobtrusive nature of these controls is that teachers *can* be deluded into developing a mistaken belief as to the true limits of their own autonomy. As one teacher said of her freedom, 'If I'd rather use a different worksheet or create a worksheet of my own, as long as it meets the [mandated] objectives, I feel free to do that'; while another said, 'The objectives are spelled out, but they are left open-ended enough so that you can approach them from any angle you want' (Bullough, Gitlin and Goldstein, 1984, p.349). Bullough, Gitlin and Goldstein (1984) argue that this is symptomatic of the very nature and power of technocratic values in shaping the consciousness of teachers. The ideology is one that '. . . takes the form of a hierarchy controlled by seemingly benign, value-neutral, progressively wiser experts who will settle all our moral, political, social, and educational problems by applying some variation of the production model of efficiency' (p.349).

Teachers have come to accept the ideology of professionalism believing that the construct of professionalism was a '. . . first line of defence against pedagogic and cultural imposition' (Grace, 1985, p.8). This 'ethic of professionalism' (Grace, 1985), or 'licensed autonomy' (Lawn and Ozga, 1981), has been accompanied by a belief by teachers that the political has no place in classrooms or schools. In practice this has meant an unreal detachment by teachers from the political and economic agendas of the state and an 'avoidance of the controversial [in the] naive belief that "being political" is "being socialist"' (Grace, 1978, p.249). With the shift of control over teaching from a '. . . visible, prescriptive and centralised system to an essentially invisible and diffuse mode' (Grace, 1985, p.11), and the disappearance of the 'malevolent invader' from their classrooms, teachers have not been quick to grasp the significance of the shift in the locus of control:

> This invisible control is constituted, among other things, by the activities of examination boards and their definitions of valid knowledge; by the constraints of the work situation; and, crucially, by what 'being a good teacher' and 'being a professional' are taken to imply. These controls are invisible to the majority of teachers in so far as they form part of the taken-for-granted and unchallenged social world within which they operate (Grace, 1978, pp.217-18).

Reconstructing . . . how might I do things differently? It was Freire (1972b) who said, 'reflection without action is verbalism, and action without reflection is activism.' His point is surely that there must be an *active* dimension to empowerment, for without that we never move beyond the mere speculative. My earlier claim about the need for teachers to start with the concrete lived reality is not based on convenience; rather, by starting with reality we are able to work on it, see its limits and hence begin to overcome it (Shor and Freire, 1987, p.107). Because of the way our culture accommodates us to working in unthinking and unquestioning ways, and because we have come to accept as 'natural' the ways we teach and the social relationships we develop with our students, we tend to accept as bearable forces around us which are really quite intolerable. This happens because of the way in which teaching is construed as being a technical process that only requires fine-tuning in order to achieve predetermined educational objectives. When viewed in this light, teaching becomes a form of 'single-loop' (Schon, 1983) learning in which questions about the ends to which actions are directed and whose interests are being served are actively denied as being issues. Double-loop learning (Schon, 1983), on the other hand, involves contesting the variables that govern the way we teach, and opening up for contestation and debate crucial issues about the politics, the ethics and the morality of that teaching. Part of the difficulty in uncovering these alternative courses of action is that they are shrouded by such complex networks of forces that they are not always easily penetrable.

Here is an example of a teacher that describes how he began to problematize his teaching by speculating about the courses of action he needed to adopt to change the wider structures that surrounded him. He relates an incident in which he called the class to attention, gave them permission to proceed with a 'set' assignment, and what happened when a student came to him with a 'puzzled look' on his face:

S: Mr . . . . What's the answer to number five?

T: [referring to the question] What is meant by the texture of the soil?

S: I don't know, that's why I'm asking you.

T: Well, . . . you should be able to find the answer to this question. Have you read the information sheets I gave you when the assignment was handed out?

S: No.

T: What about searching through your notes on soil texture? Have you done that?

S: No.

T: Well you should refer to your notes first, read them through and then if you don't understand something come and see me. [student left still looking puzzled]

The teacher then proceeded to analyze what had happened, his own aspirations for his students and his implication in this little incident:

Why do I maintain a situation where student participation, negotiation and construction of learning is minimized? Why do I continue with non-negotiable forms of teaching and learning processes? If I expect my students to assume increasing levels of responsibility for their own learning, then surely I must begin to allow them to participate in deciding how they are expected to learn.

His explanation carried him a stage further into pursuing questions he had not even thought about in his teaching. Certainly his thinking about his school has undergone a major reconstruction, and we would imagine this to be a prelude to actions he might adopt. His analysis, and the way in which he was able to see that his actions were not the consequence of personal shortcomings, begins to provide him with some avenues for action. He put it in these words:

. . . the school's current practice of rank ordering students through competitive assessment means that some students are locked out of future life options. Those who succeed are being rewarded for their compliance in following the rules which have been laid down by the community and endorsed by the school.

My school demands that the quality of a student's work be judged. Why then do I allow such a requirement to pervade classroom life in such a manner that it discourages learning for some of the students I teach?

. . . my practices are constrained within the philosophical constraints laid down by the . . . values of the school. One of the goals of the school is to provide an ordered, structured environment so that learning and willingness to apply effort to worthwhile tasks is facilitated. I may ask myself, who decided which tasks are worthwhile? Why do I expect the full attention of students when addressing them? Why do I demonstrate to the students my ultimate power over the classroom? The answer is becoming more and more apparent. The accepted political order within the school makes it that way.

The established political order of the school dictates the curriculum. It decides what is taught and where resources are allocated, even down to the timetable allocations. The same political order restricts students from being involved in any meaningful decision-making within the school.

> Why are the students excluded from decision-making?
> What kinds of decisions should they be involved in?
> Why do I expect my students to gracefully accept decisions being handed down to them?
> Why are students precluded from possessing an effective power within this school?

Reconstructing teachers' practices is not something that can readily be done in a thirteen-week part-time course. Nevertheless, if there is a shift in the questions teachers ask, from the 'how to' to the 'why' kind, then some significant strides will have been made.

Some Reflections on Our Own Pedagogy

The major difficulty of this 'project' (used here in the sense in which Greene (1985) uses that term to refer to the identification of 'something we want to bring into being', p.13) was its inability adequately to grapple with how to empower teachers to break out of the 'culture of individualism' (Hargreaves, 1982) that is so characteristic of teaching. If anything, the pedagogy of the course, involving as it did university staff interacting with *individual* students (who were experienced teachers) via the written and spoken word, served only to reinforce tacitly the already existing notions of individualism in schools. In part this can be explained by the tyranny of distance, but more importantly it seemed to have to do with a certain inertia or unwillingness by us to challenge the very structures surrounding the course itself and the way it was delivered to students. Thus ideas that were meant to empower teachers in terms of unmasking their taken-for-granted ways of operating actually did little more than provide a sophisticated gloss of modernity. Instead of getting teachers socially to construct the meanings attaching to their teaching by critical debate and dialogue with one another, by working with them on a one-by-one basis we provided endorsement for forms of alienation and fragmentation that have long characterized teaching.

In this we were acquiescing to the dominant individualistic and competitive culture within institutions of higher learning by selectively transmitting certain cultural competencies to our students, while actively ignoring others. Although we had departed from Freire's (1972b) banking notion of educating our students by not relying on 'regenerative' (Everhart, 1987) forms of knowledge, it was still as if we had to prove a point to our academic colleagues by not departing too radically from the ways in which we engaged our students with the central ideas of the course. In Denscombe's (1980) terms there was a well hidden pedagogy within our own teaching in which we were saying one thing, while actually doing another. It was true that there was very little 'content' in the course we provided. We were providing a process by which teachers were able to describe, analyze and confront their own teaching. Nor were the course participants competitively ranked or assessed in their performance. But by engaging with students individual- ly (even though we *recommended* that they share with their colleagues in their schools) we were still acting in ways that endorsed a mindset that predisposed teachers '. . . to understand their work in individualistic ways' (Sachs, 1987, p.88).

In engaging our students within the limits of the distance education mode and the non-negotiable credentialling function imposed by the university, we were trying as their tutors to enact a role of 'critical friends' (Ingvarson, 1986). While we were not there to rank or rate them (and we had gone to considerable lengths to spell out the nature of our non-competitive assessment criteria for the course), there was still considerable scope for us to react and respond to their written pieces as supportive colleagues as they worked their way through the project. There can be little doubt that on occasions even the most diplomatic posing of tentative questions on our part aimed at getting the participants to politicize their teaching (or at least to see it in a political light) was greeted less than enthusiastically by some participants who wanted to continue to cast us in a traditional supervisory and inquisitorial light. To that extent, regardless of what we did or said, we had difficulty in living down the history of the practices and reputations of what a university course should be about, as well as how tutors should act.

We also had another history to struggle against as well, and it had to do with the alleged non-political nature of schooling. Stevens (1987) summed this up nicely:

> The view that politics and education are autonomous activities and areas of discourse is entrenched in educational theory. The related assertion that politics and teaching are similarly distinct attracts wide support among politicians, teachers, educational theorists, and, last but not least, parents. Teachers are told with increasing force to keep their politics out of the school and the classroom. A stronger version of this assertion holds that politics should be excluded entirely from the curriculum; teaching is defined as a limited set of specific professional 'duties' which teachers are employed to carry out.
>
> At the same time teachers [and] schools are required to accept increased political interference and pressure from central authorities as to what and how they teach. These are brought about by financial restrictions on spending and by direction towards the establishment of a vocationally-oriented curriculum at the expense of the humanities, one of the few remaining areas which allow for social criticism. Those who protest most loudly when teachers introduce progressive initiatives into the curriculum or act collectively within their organisations to combat class, race or gender prejudices, seek nevertheless to impose their own political choices (p.75).

Having some 'distance' from the sites and the people involved enabled us as 'outsiders' to be responsive to the often obscure but highly politicized nature of much of what passes as teaching in a manner that may not have been possible had we been closer to the action. Having at least some degree of geographic detachment allowed us to see the issues embedded in the journal entries in a way that was often quite impossible for the participants themselves. Because we had access to their journals (and they held the final power of veto over how much they wanted to share with us), we were still able to develop a sense of closeness and intimacy with what was happening.

Yet despite these advantages, we were still plagued with the question of ownership. Although the narrative texts as created by the course participants through journalling were clearly owned by them, it was much less clear who owned the *issues* generated from those texts when we intervened as critical friends in seeking to get them to situate or locate those described practices in wider social, cultural and political contexts. We were engaged in something that bordered on the manipulative, although at the time we saw ourselves as merely posing questions that had to be asked. Perhaps we were too sensitive to that and should rest content with the belief that unless teachers are given some assistance in developing processes that enable them to unmask the forces that are controlling them, then they will be exploited as they have always been in the past.

In a curious twist of fate as we approach the second year of this course offering, its continuation is under a cloud. The forces of economic rationalism, efficiency and effectiveness are rampant in the university, and while no one is actively working to close the course, it is clear that we are being required to tailor our pedagogy to suit the economic climate. Course participants are being urged as part of the austerity move to develop stronger alliances with one another as critical friends, sharing journals and reacting to one another's work. It may be that the kind of solidarity we wanted our teachers to develop in the first place may come about for very different reasons — well, that's the hope, anyway!

In our original conceptualization, if there was any sense in which there was a communitarian aspect to what we were trying to get our teachers to do, it was to see their own teaching as 'social practices' (Bourdieu, 1977) that are culturally, historically and politically located. In other words, if teachers can see that the actual forms of their teaching amount to more than mere technical acts that have a constructed and quite deliberate history or genealogy, then they may be able to see how it is that they have come as a professional group to appropriate some ideas, while at the same time disavowing or denying others. This was to acknowledge C. Wright Mills' (1970) point that an '. . . individual can understand his experience and gauge his own fate only by locating himself within his period' (p.12). By asking pointed 'why' questions rather than exclusive 'how to' questions, they may also begin to see how those practices have been shaped and determined by forces outside schools. That is to say, it is through the 'historical' that they can begin to develop a sense of the 'political'. While some may be less optimistic than we were about what is possible (Barton and Lawn, 1981), it was our intention to develop a perspective in which '. . . biography and history, individuals and society, are linked' (Pollard, 1987, p.55).

PART 3

A CRITIQUE

Planning Committee who played a key role in the propagation of these ideas, for example, Norman MacKenzie, who was also a member of the original Council, and at the time held the post of Director of the Centre for Educational Technology at the University of Sussex (Ferguson, 1975, pp. 15-16). Those people also played a key role in the related area of teaching methods.

Crucial to any understanding of the OU's teaching methods is a recognition of its conceivers' views that it was to be a 'university of the air'. As Harold Wilson imagined it, there would be a combination of radio and television broadcasting, based around 'teaching films' like those produced by *Encyclopedia Britannica,* combined with correspondence techniques he had observed in the Soviet Union (MacArthur, 1974, pp. 3-4). The OU gave 'educational technologists' an ideal opportunity to show their wares: they could move from the marginal position they occupied in conventional institutions into the mainstream of course development and production. At OU they seized this opportunity and triumphed.

The Planning Committee concluded that it was 'neither practically possible nor pedagogically sound to rely on broadcasting as the major teaching method' (Ferguson, 1975, p. 15). Its report again established foundations which were accepted by the Vice-Chancellor and the founding staff as the basis upon which to build. Perry sums this up succinctly:

> There were to be specially written correspondence texts sent to the student through the post and these were to be integrated with television and radio broadcasts transmitted on open circuit. The specially constructed teaching materials would refer to set text books and to additional background reading lists. Students would be required to undertake written assignments which would be marked by a 'correspondence tutor' and this activity was seen as a method of teaching as much as a method of assessment of performance. In addition students would be required to attend short residential summer schools and would be offered, optionally, the opportunity of meeting a counsellor (and later a tutor) and other students at one of a network of local study centres. Each course would end with a final examination to be held in local examination centres. (Perry, 1976, p. 76)

The key organizational structure for the production of course materials is the Course Team. Each team consists of 'three groups of staff: academics, educational technologists and the BBC production staff' (Perry, 1976, pp. 83-4). The team has complete responsibility for the course and is always chaired by an 'academic' who is finally responsible to the University for the course. The academics are responsible for 'content', the educational technologists for advice on course design and materials development (especially print) and the BBC staff for production of the radio and television programmes. In practice there has often been much overlap, considerable mutual interchange of ideas and occasional acrimony (Perry, 1976, pp.92-6).

The OU teaching system assumes a large number of students, most of whom will enrol in courses with large enrolments. It is organized as a large information production and distribution system. This applies to the course materials which are produced using models adapted from magazine publishing and electronic media production. It is worth emphasizing the adaptations which have taken place, especially regarding printed materials. In effect, the University has created a new form of educational publishing (MacGibbon, 1974). Other institutions, such as the UNE, had used correspondence texts for some time, and in a sense provided the OU with models to emulate; however, the OU radically developed these models with a unique concentration of intellectual resources — the academics, the educational technologists, the graphic designers and other print technologists. This system emerged in the circumstances, there was no attempt 'to deliberately plan' a 'particular method of publishing', problems were tackled 'as they happened to arise' (Perry, 1976, p.97).

The University's use of 'regional staff' and part-time tutors was a bold and significant innovation. The system of teaching which emerged from the combination of the course materials, correspondence tutors, face-to-face tutors, summer schools, computer marked assignments and examinations was extremely comprehensive. It was a synthesis of many pedagogies extant in higher education, primary and secondary schooling, existing forms of distance education and educational publishing and broadcasting. The integration of 'outside academics' into the system had the important benefit of enhancing 'the reputation and status of the university in the academic world' (Perry, 1976, p.113).

Educational technology had a considerable influence on the development of the teaching methods of the OU. Consequently, the University can be seen as a pre-eminent example of the 'instructional industrialism' we mentioned earlier. However, this approach has not dominated the OU's teaching methods completely. Perry's reflections on the emergence of the system demonstrate the serious attention which was paid to the educational technologists, but there is clear evidence that other methods were adopted to 'balance' the system. The clearest reflection upon this comes within a well-known article, 'Distance

Teaching: A Contradiction in Terms?', written by a senior member of the OU's regional staff, David Sewart (1983). His particular concern was the possible overemphasis upon 'teaching packages' in the University. 'There is,' he suggested, 'a beguiling temptation to assume that the problems of teaching at a distance can all be solved by the production of an as yet merely hypothetical perfect package of material' (Sewart, 1983, p.48). The burden of his discussion surrounds an analysis of the type and frequency of assistance students need from counsellors and/or tutors in a system which has very well designed study materials. The balance should never swing totally towards a teaching package, he concludes, and there must always be appropriate forms of 'human services' available. In concluding his discussion he outlines an instructive model of teaching:

> If we consider the variety of teaching and learning processes we might see at one extreme the continuous face-to-face dialogue between one teacher and one student, a totally supportive learning situation. Further along the spectrum we find the conventional primary schools in which the authoritative figure of the teacher provides a continuous contact throughout the day with a group of students. Much further along the spectrum we find a traditional university teaching system in which the authoritative figure of the teacher appears only occasionally and the students are more independent in their learning situation. At the other end of the spectrum we find a pure system of teaching at a distance in which the student is learning at a distance from those who have prepared the material and learns at his own pace, where ever he wishes to study. The Open University, like conventional universities, falls somewhere between the two ends of the spectrum, although it is clearly further towards the end of pure distance teaching. (Sewart, 1983, p.60)

Sewart's analysis provides us with just one example of many of the contributions which have been made to debates over teaching methods which have emanated from the OU. Mary Thorpe has offered a recent discussion which returns to Sewart's themes (Student Research Centre, 1986). The OU journals, *Teaching at a Distance* and its successor *Open Learning*, have published many articles, letters and discussions which reviewed and debated the University's teaching processes; they have also encouraged contributions from distance educators elsewhere. The OU took teaching methods out of the higher education closet! In doing this it has had a significant impact upon curriculum development and teaching practices in distance education internationally. Many institutions were set up according to the 'Open University model', while in established institutions examples of its practices have been influential. The OU still provides the richest single source of curriculum development and pedagogical practices in the field of distance education.

David Harris' (1987) recent book, *Openness and Closure in Distance Education,* deserves our special attention. Using a thoroughly comprehensive range of research methods, including intensive interviews, documentary analysis and participant observation, Harris offers an insider's detailed description of the impact of educational technology upon OU teaching practices. He proceeds from a perspective within 'critical theory', and shares much common intellectual ground with us. We endorse, particularly, his constructive criticism of educational technology, which recognizes its positive achievements along with its serious shortcomings. Harris' concentration upon the OU and his glossing of its style and methods as distance education *per se* are both understandable and unfortunate. Since his book is essentially about his study of the OU, it is to be expected that it will concentrate heavily upon it. However, it is regrettable that he did not engage in more substantial comparisons with other institutions involved in distance education in the United Kingdom and internationally. The other recent collections, *Open Learning for Adults* and *Open Learning in Transition*, offer more detailed comparisons within the United Kingdom, but make little reference to international examples. Further developments in these areas are required.

The UNE and OU provide us with two contrasting models of teaching practices commonly adopted by institutions embarking upon distance education. The former represents a conservative approach which adapts conventional university teaching techniques; the latter requires the espousal of various techniques from the warehouse of educational technology. In rejecting both approaches we would caution against ignoring the valuable lessons each has taught. The adaptive model has often solved problems associated with academic credibility quite pragmatically; its practitioners also have a very good record in providing services to students, especially those of a 'non-academic' kind. We have canvassed the achievements of the educational technology model in detail above. But one must be reiterated, despite its obvious nature: the OU has made a careful consideration of teaching practices legitimate in distance education particularly and higher education more generally. Educational technology, 'OU-style', has effectively provided the damning critique of the adaptive approach. We do not wish to add to this. Our objective is to criticize educational technology and to offer a critical discussion of some ideas which constitute the bases for alternatives.

Elsewhere we have referred to the adoption of educational technology in distance education as *instructional industrialism* (Evans and

Nation, 1987). We are concerned that this approach is founded upon theories of learning which induce teaching practices which treat students and teachers as 'objects', passive receivers of advice and knowledge. We wish to pursue this general line of argument here, with particular reference to the development of printed and audiovisual course materials; we call this process 'text production'.

We find it inescapable that the nature of text and text production and reproduction processes are central to instructional industrialism. Other media are common in distance education but often they can be interpreted as texts or as emanating from textual forms and structures. Often such media can only be interpreted and understood by distance students alongside the printed texts of their courses. Most distance educators talk of 'writing', rather than 'preparing' or 'teaching' their courses, yet the writing process — in particular the forms of writing traditional to distance education — has a powerful shaping influence over the teaching strategies they use. Beyond the teaching strategies, the 'writing' of courses has profound effects on the nature of the students' learning experiences and on the relationships, or lack thereof, between themselves, their teachers, their institutions and their students' organizations. The alienation typified in highly divided labour practices in industrial production, especially with 'outworkers', is not, superficially at least, dissimilar to that foreshadowed in the orthodox approaches to distance education, although we realize that many distance teachers would reject or abhor such outcomes of their practices.

The production of distance education course materials may resemble industrial production, but essentially this observation distracts us from questioning the social relations of distance education production as text and knowledge production. Although we recognize the importance of print production processes in structuring the nature of teaching and learning in distance education, we argue that all forms of text and text production help to shape the conditions of teaching and learning at a distance (Evans, 1989). The processes through which texts are produced, as distance teaching materials, are shaped by the structural properties of those texts. In this way the language, rules, codes and means of interpretation embedded in particular textual forms shape the ways distance teachers engage in producing their text. The knowledge production of distance education is shaped and mediated by and through the forms of text production which constitute distance educational practice.

The expansion of distance education in recent years has led to the institutionalization of particular forms of text production as conventional distance education practice. Archer (1982) has observed that as educational systems expand they undergo 'structural elaboration' conditioned by the preceding structural properties. In the case of distance education, we suggest, distance education systems have developed increasingly elaborate structures based in the previous establishment of behaviourist models of learning mediated by forms of text production. Nowadays teachers in a distance education institution need to engage with and largely conform to these elaborate structures. These structures shape practices of teaching and learning which are far removed from 'good' face-to-face educational practices, especially those which are democratic and concerned with transformative learning experiences (Mezirow, 1981). The separation of teacher and student, the dis-empowerment of students from making decisions about their own learning, the requirements of production schedules, postal dispatches and the many other aspects of working in distance education, spin an intricate web around the teacher in distance education.

Teachers have varying degrees of autonomy and power over what they teach (curriculum) and how they teach (pedagogy). The distance teacher's autonomy and power are both circumscribed and enhanced by the context of distance education. In effect, both curriculum and pedagogy are structurally prefigured by the institution. However, the nature of the prefiguration is such that students are structurally confined to dominated and alienated positions within the distance teaching-learning relationship. In order to explain these points it is necessary to reflect on the basic 'raw material' of distance education. Ironically, whereas education is seen typically, as Bernstein argues (1982), as a site or context of knowledge production, the processes and structures of distance education are overlaid with those features of material (industrial) production mentioned previously. In fact, the knowledge production of distance education is tightly linked to forms of text (material) production which help reproduce and legitimate the dominating/dominated dichotomy between teachers and students.

Distance teachers use their temporal and spatial autonomy from their students to select and shape the knowledge which the students must learn for success. Through their use of 'industrial' teaching practices, distance teachers regulate the forms of discourse in which the students can engage. Bernstein observes that 'in the production/reproduction of discursive resources we have sets of specialised categories (such as teachers) and sets of specialised practices' (1982, p.312). Accordingly, the social relations which exist between teachers and students are constituted by and in the specific practices between them, for example, through the assessment of work or in tutoring by telephone. Bernstein recognizes that it is the 'insulation' between the categories (distance teachers and students) which is important, not only for their own maintenance and reproduction, but also for the maintenance and reproduction of the power relations between them. In distance education, we would suggest, the insulation is substantively produced by 'distance', that is, the temporal and spatial separation between teacher and student (Evans, 1989). However, this is not to imply that such 'distance' creates the relations of power between teachers and students, rather it 'insulates' teachers from students and assists in the maintenance of the power relations between them.

Bernstein (1979) has also been concerned with the ways in which educational knowledge is 'classified' and 'framed' to reflect and reproduce class relations, and in the ways 'class relations generate, distribute, reproduce and legitimate distinctive forms of communication, which transmit dominating and dominated codes' (1982, p.312). In distance education the classification and framing of educational knowledge are communicated through forms of text which signify the power relations we have discussed previously. We contend that it is these forms of knowledge and communication, and the processes through which these are enacted, which need to be analyzed in distance education. Contemporary distance educational practice is fundamentally about these aspects of knowledge and communication, yet they are rarely subjected to critique.

Wexler has focused on a socially critical analysis of knowledge. He argues:

> knowledge can be analysed as a process of transformation. It is made by a series of transformative activities which end at the point where knowledge is a recognizable commodity. The end point, the labelling of activity as knowledge, and the process of transformation which leads to that, is socially patterned. The source of knowledge, human labor, the transforming activities which constitute it, and the definition and distribution of the product are socially variable. (1981, p.280).

For distance teachers, whether as individual practitioners or in course teams, their principal activity is 'labelling' or even 'packaging' knowledge as course curricula. The social relations involved in and expressed through their transformative processes are usually invisible to the students. As an example, one only has to consider knowledge being 'packaged' for two different curricula on 'the family' by distance teachers with different ideological positions such as radical feminist and Christian fundamentalist. Through such 'packaging', knowledge about 'the family' is transformed into curricula in radically different ways from the respective ideological positions. Several years of students' discourses within each curriculum will be fundamentally shaped by the socially and ideologically patterned knowledge they engage. Distance education, as we have argued previously, typically allocates little power or space to students to create their own discourses within a curriculum, therefore, they may have little option but to conform to a substantial degree or fail.

The ways we use text in distance teaching close students' discourse. The forms of text and pedagogical approaches used in distance teaching are monologic; dialogue is seen as impossible because of 'distance' (Evans and Nation, 1988). However, Wexler, drawing on the work of Eco, points to the possibilities of 'closed' or 'open' texts (rather like Barthes' 'readerly' and 'writerly' texts):

> The open text invites participation. It refuses the assumption of a reproduction of fixed forms as the basis of expression and communication. The open text . . . is a process of activity rather than a dead object. . . . Texts can be open to the continuing work of transformation, which is a form that teaches activity rather than passive consumption as its message. . . . The presentation of ambiguity, of a text which remains unexhausted even after systematic interpretation grids are placed over it, 'structurally prefigures' a world of indeterminacy, of possibility. (Wexler, 1981, p.289).

Can we really push distance education along this path? To do so would require a critical enquiry into the power relations of the process of distance teaching, followed by drastic changes in distance teaching and learning processes and relationships. There are three broad outcomes of such critical enquiry: (1) the changes would not take place because the interlocking structures of education, society and economy would readily snuff it out; or (2) forms of superficial change would take place which keep the critically inclined in a state of false consciousness created within the social, educational and economic structures; or (3) a form of continually contested debate and change would occur wherein students and teachers critically appraise the educational, social and economic structures and make various inroads into them in the form of modification and change. As a consequence of changing the power relations of distance education the students would become collaborative developers of their own courses through critical reflection.

The instructional industrialists have failed to recognize and encourage the autonomy of adults over their own learning. It seems as if, after their own years of directed schooling and higher education, many distance teachers assume that other people need to be guided, checked, cajoled and tested throughout their adult learning. As Brookfield argues, volumes of research evidence show that adults are self-directed and self-motivated in their learning. He concludes that 'many adults are, apparently, devising and conducting much of their own learning, without assistance from professional educators, and doing so mostly to their own satisfaction' (1984, p.68). This is a crucial point: many people, men and women of different social classes and ethnic backgrounds, pursue their own learning to their own satisfaction and interests. Their learning may be around a hobby or sport such as fishing, philately, car racing or needlecraft; or it may be directed to a particular event or problem in their lives, for example, having a first child, building a house, resisting a local development or understanding diabetes; or it may concern involvement in a religious, trade union, political or other group. In each case adults pursue their own learning and develop expertise which they then share with others — the networking of women's groups or environmental organizations are complex and formal examples of such shaping, but often it may be just between friends, relatives or colleagues in an informal manner. Adults' learning decisions in distance education institutions are affected by various concerns and interests, however, their engagement with formal education does not mean that they have lost their quest for self-directed learning. Indeed, enrolment could represent a culmination of their desire to learn. However, distance education generally assumes otherwise, and immediately stops the 'practical and conceptual heart of self-directedness in learning' which 'is the control over the learning processes and curriculum content exercised by the learners themselves' (Brookfield, 1984, p.69). Distance education uses its textual, curricular and pedagogical processes to marginalize and dissolve the self-directedness of people's learning, and confines them to a system of learning which reflects and aids the reproduction of the ideological and structural conditions of society.

Mezirow has argued that an adult educator often 'blindly helps a learner blindly follow the dictates of an unexamined set of cultural assumptions . . . and . . . relationships' (1981, p.20). Mezirow presses for education to lead toward 'perspective transformation' whereby a learner identifies and understands the 'real problems involving reified power relationships rooted in institutionalized ideologies' (1981, p.18). From this position learners acquire and construct new meaning perspectives which transform their understanding of their own psychological histories and lead them to critical appraisals of the prevailing social, political and economic conditions. For Mezirow the end and means of perspective transformation in adult education are the recognition and enhancing of the learners' capacities for self-direction.

Recognizing and enhancing students' capacities for self-direction in distance education is tantamount to recognizing the power that people have as agents to shape and control their own destinies and the social conditions which surround them. This means recognizing the centrality of human competence, together with what Gibson sees as 'the essential reciprocity of individual and society, event and structure' (1984, p.136). It is worth considering Gibson's structural analysis of education a little further because he helps to make some links between educational, literary and social theory which are pertinent to distance education. Gibson suggests that structural analysis in education can be 'concerned with four elements: structures of competence, structures of social organization, structures of thought and structures of feeling' (1984, p.137). We have already argued that human competence be recognized through our quest for the recognition and encouragement of self-direction and autonomy in distance students. Likewise we have pointed to those structures of social organization within and without distance education institutions which powerfully shape the ways distance teachers ('competent humans') are able to teach their students. However, Gibson pulls structures of thought and feeling into focus, and thereby encompasses the contribution of the notable theorists. Structural analysis of the ways people develop and use their thought processes are interwoven in educational theory and practice. Jean Piaget has been the supreme influence in this regard; although adult educators would be less aware of his work, it is arguable that the influence of Piagetian ideas has pervaded all educational practice, especially in our ideas about the logical sequencing of intellectual development in courses.

Structures of feeling are brought into Gibson's structural analysis of education principally through the work of Raymond Williams. As Gibson states, Williams 'has spoken often of its [the concept of structure of feeling] elusiveness and defiance to easy definition' (1984, p.61). In essence, structures of feeling represent the relationships between one's emotional, affective and perceptual processes and one's social experiences and actions. They recognize that in any given social engagement the individual's understanding and activities are partly structured by their feelings at that time. In so doing they emphasize an element of 'human agency', to use Giddens' term (Giddens, 1984), in arenas of social engagement such as education, and in the structuration of social life through institutions such as education.

Gibson suggests that his four elements — structures of competence, structures of social organization, structures of thought, and structures of feeling — need to be brought to bear in the structural analysis of education to shape the questions we pose about educational settings.

Drawing from Gibson (1984, p.13), we might pose questions about distance students' engagement with a particular course such as: What sorts of structures of thought and feeling do the students use and exhibit in their assignments and teletutorials? What social structures constrain and enable their actions? How do they exhibit their particular personal characteristics and understandings to achieve their own ends? In true structuralist fashion the researcher (as distance teacher) is being challenged to engage critically his or her practice at the occasion it occurs; to stop and think, and through so doing to change future practice.

This leads to the notions of reflection, reciprocity and reassessment which, for us, provide important links between distance education practice and social theory. In taking Gibson's view of the importance of competence and reciprocity what we are embracing is a view of social life which recognizes what Giddens calls its essential 'recursiveness'. For Giddens social structures do not represent pre-existing and reified cultural edifices to which all people are bound to pay homage in the form of slavish, automatic obedience. Rather, social structures are constructed, interpreted and reconstructed by people through time. These structures envelop social life and pattern social behaviour but do not determine it. Individuals have varying degrees of power to resist, reinterpret and reconstruct social structures, but such power is constrained as well as enabled by social structures. Giddens talks of a 'durée' of social life as a 'flow of intentional action' (1984, p.8) by individuals with their own particular competencies. Distance education forms part of the 'durée' of social life in that it embodies the structural properties we have discussed earlier which are brought about and mediated by and through the 'intentional actions' of the people concerned.

In recognizing the recursive properties of social life we are also recognizing the reciprocity which Gibson argues is fundamental to structural analysis. In our view recognizing these properties as important to both Giddens' social theory and Gibson's structural analysis provides us with theoretical bases to propose the notion that reflection on distance educational practices should be located in such bodies of theory. We are arguing a case for the evaluation of distance educational practices to be informed not only by a notion of reflection on those practices, but also by an understanding of the relationships between agency and structure. Mezirow (1981) is one of several people who have sought to develop such an approach drawing on the work of Habermas (e.g., Carr and Kemmis, 1986). However, Mezirow concentrates on a critical theory of adult learning which, as we have discussed earlier, leads to a transformation in the meaning perspectives of the people concerned. For Mezirow perspective transformation acknowledges 'the central role of critical reflectivity' in adult learning. Hence critical reflectivity occurs where people reflexively monitor their social actions by critiquing them against and through their understanding of the structural conditions of social life, and thus change their actions and thereby those structural conditions. In distance education this means reflecting on one's practices in terms of the structural elements and bases discussed previously, and changing those practices accordingly. The process of critical reflection is continuous and leads to a set of transformatory practices through which students (and teachers) become competent, self-directed learners. The process of critical reflection is not just about distance teachers reflecting on their practices but is also about critical reflections in distance education. In this sense both distance teachers and students are engaged in a reciprocal teaching-learning/action-reflection process which leads to each other's understanding of themselves and the social conditions of their existence. Freire (1976b) uses the term 'conscientization' to describe a form of dialectical relationship between a 'consciousness of reality' and a 'critical attitude' which leads to transformative actions to change the circumstances of oppression.

For many distance educators the process of critical reflection in the teaching-learning relationship may seem fanciful. Indeed, Freire himself, who constructed his forms of adult education in difficult circumstances, argues that his ideas about teaching are utopian. He declared that, 'if we are not utopian we will easily become bureaucratic and dehumanizing' (1976b, p.225); we would argue that this is precisely what is happening in distance education: it is becoming bureaucratic and dehumanizing. In Freire's terms we need to make distance education 'liberating' not 'dominating'.

Many who stand with us in the tradition of critical reflexivity are concerned with abstract theory and they often express themselves obscurely. We do not dismiss them for this, rather, we acknowledge their intellectual support. Our objectives, however, are more practical. We hope this chapter offers the beginnings of a useful critique of instructional industrialism, some ideas worth following up and some new theoretical connections. We want it to be a part of broader attempts to theorize in this field — a field crying out for more workers. Above all we want to orient theory to practice, we want this book to be read, discussed and used in this light.

Bibliography

ANDERSON, G. (1987) 'Towards a critical ethnography of educational administration', paper presented at American Educational Research Association Conference, Washington.

APPLE, M. (Ed.) (1982) *Culture and Economic Reproduction in Education*, London, Routledge and Kegan Paul.

APPLE, M. (1983a) 'Work, gender and teaching', *Teachers College Record*, 84, 3, pp.611-28.

APPLE, M. (1983b) 'Conrolling the work of teachers', *Delta*, 32, pp.3-15.

ARCHER, M.S. (1982) 'Theorising about the expansion of educational systems', in ARCHER, M.S. (Ed.) *The Sociology of Educational Expansion*, London, Sage.

ARGER, G. (1987) 'Promise and reality: a critical analysis of literature on distance education in the Third World', *Journal of Distance Education*, 2, 1, pp.41-58.

ARONOWITZ, S. (1977) 'Mass culture and the eclipse of reason: the implications for pedagogy', *College English*, 8, pp.768-74.

BARTHES, R. (1973) *Mythologies*, London, Paladin.

BARTHES, R. (1982) *Camera Lucida*, London, Fontana.

BARTON, L. and LAWN, M. (1981) 'Back inside the whale', *Interchange*, 3, 4, pp.2-26.

BELL, C. and ENCEL, S. (Eds) (1978) *Inside the Whale*, Rushcutters Bay, Pergamon.

BELL, C. and NEWBY, H. (Eds) (1977) *Doing Sociological Research*, London, Allen and Unwin.

BELL, D. (1974) *The Coming of Post-Industrial Society*, London, Heinemann.

BERGER, P., BERGER, B. and KELLNER, H. (1973) *The Homeless Mind: Modernization and Consciousness*, New York, Random House.

BERLAK, A. (1987) 'Teaching for liberation and empowerment in the liberal arts: towards the development of a pedagogy that overcomes resistance', paper presented to the American Educational Research Association Conference, Washington.

BERLAK, A. and BERLAK, H. (1981) *Dilemmas of Schooling: Teaching and Social Change*, London, Methuen.

BERNSTEIN, B. (1974) *Class, Codes and Control, Volume 1*, London, Routledge and Kegan Paul.

BERNSTEIN, B. (1979) *Class, Codes and Control, Volume 3*, 2nd ed., London, Routledge and Kegan Paul

BERNSTEIN, B. (1982) 'Codes, modalities and cultural reproduction', in APPLE, M.W. (Ed.) *Cultural and Economic Reproduction in Education*, London, Routledge and Kegan Paul.

BEVERLEY, J. (1982) 'Higher education and capitalist crisis', in DERBER, D. (Ed.) *Professionals as Workers: Mental Labor in Advanced Capitalism*, Boston, Mass., G.K. Hall.

BOLTON, G. (1986) 'The opportunities of distance', *Distance Education*, 7, 1, pp.5-23.

BOURDIEU, P. (1976) 'Schooling as a conservative force: scholastic and cultural inequalities', in DALE, R. *et al.* (Eds) *Schooling and Capitalism*, London, Routledge and Kegan Paul, pp.110-17.

BOURDIEU, P. (1977) *Outline of a Theory of Practice*, Cambridge, Cambridge University Press.

BOWLES, S. and GINTIS, H. (1976) *Schooling in Capitalist America: Educational Reform and the Contradictions of Economic Life*, Philadelphia, Penn., Temple University Press.

BROOKFIELD, S. (1984) 'Self-directed learning: a critical paradigm', *Adult Education*, 35, 2, pp.59-71.

BRUNDAGE, D.H. and MACKERACHER, D. (1980) *Adult Learning Principles and Their Application to Program Planning*, Ontario, Ministry of Education.

BRUSS, N. and MACEDO, P. (1985) 'Towards a pedagogy of the question: conversations with Paulo Freire', *Journal of Education*, 167, 2, pp.7-21.

BULLOUGH, R., GITLIN, A. and GOLDSTEIN, S. (1984) 'Ideology, teacher role, and resistance', *Teachers College Record*, 86, 2, pp.339-58.

BUTT, R. (1984) 'Curriculum implementation, classroom change and professional development: the challenge for supervision', paper presented to the Canadian Society for Study in Education Conference, Guelph.

CARR, W. (1980) 'The gap between theory and practice', *Journal of Further and Higher Education*, 4, 1, pp.60-9.

CARR, W. (1982) 'Treating the symptoms, neglecting the cause: diagnosing the problems of theory and practice', *Journal of Further and Higher Education*, 6, 2, pp.19-29.

CARR, W. and KEMMIS, S. (1986) *Becoming Critical: Education, Knowledge and Action Research*, 2nd ed. (1st ed. 1983), Geelong, Deakin University Press, and Lewes, Falmer Press.

CLEARY, L. (1983) 'Correspondence to course team members', *Curriculum Theory Course Journal*, 1, 5.

COMBER, B. (1983) 'Writing back to writers: a tertiary experiment', *English in Australia*, 66, pp.55-9.

CONNELL, R.W., ASHENDEN, D.J., KESSLER, S. and DOWSETT, G.W. (1982) *Making the Difference*, Sydney, George Allen and Unwin.

DAVIES, G. (1979) *The Future of External Studies at the University of Queensland*, internal report to the University of Queensland.

Deakin University (1987) *Deakin University Programs Handbook 1988*, Deakin University.

Deakin University Act 1974.

DENSCOMBE, M. (1980) 'The work context of teaching: an analytic framework for the study of teachers in classrooms', *British Journal of Sociology of Education*, 11, 3, pp.278-92.

DERBER, D. (1982) *Professionals as Workers: Mental Labor in Advanced Capitalism*, Boston, Mass., G.K. Hall.

DOW, G. (1985) 'Curricular reforms that were "caught not taught" in Australia', *Journal of Curriculum Studies*, 17, 2, pp.215-26.

DUNKIN, M. and BIDDLE, B. (1974) *The Study of Teaching*, New York, Holt, Rinehart and Winston.

EDGAR, D. (1980) *Introduction to Australian Society*, Sydney, Prentice Hall.

ETZIONI-HALEVY, E. (1983) *Bureaucracy and Democracy: A Political Dilemma*, London, Routledge and Kegan Paul.

EVANS, T.D. (1985a) '"Participation and Equity": some problems in the relationship between Australian Government policy and access to higher education through the distance education mode', paper presented to the University without Walls International Council Conference, London.

EVANS, T.D. (1985b) *ECS 802: Curriculum Theory: Some Notes on an Evaluation*, Deakin University Distance Education Unit.

EVANS, T.D. (1988) 'The dance of distance education: theories of time-space in relation to distance education', paper presented to the International Council for Distance Education 14th World Conference, Oslo.

EVANS, T.D. (1989) 'Fiddling while the tome turns: reflections of a distance education and development consultant', in PARER, M. (Ed.) *Development Design and Distance Education*, Churchill, Centre for Distance Learning, Gippsland Institute.

EVANS, T.D. and NATION, D.E. (1987) 'Which future for distance education?', *International Council for Distance Education Bulletin*, 14, pp.48-53.

EVANS, T.D. and NATION, D.E. (1988) 'Dialogue in distance education', paper presented to the International Council for Distance Education 14th World Conference, Oslo.

EVERHART, R, (1979) 'Ethnography and educational policy: love and marriage or strange bedfellows', in BARNHARDT, R. *et al.*, *Anthropology and Educational Administration*, Tucson, Ariz., Impresora.

EVERHART, R. (1987) 'Understanding student disruption and classroom control', *Harvard Educational Review*, 57,1, pp.77-83.

FACUNDO, B. (1984) *Issues for an Evaluation of Freire-Inspired Programs in the United States and Puerto Rico*, Rio Pedras, Puerto Rico, Alternatives.

FAY, B. (1977) 'How people change themselves: the relationship between critical theory and its audience', in BALL, T. (Ed.) *Political Theory and Praxis: New Perspectives*, Minneapolis, Minn., University of Minnesota Press, pp.200-33.

FERGUSON, J. (1975) *The Open University from Within*, London, University of London Press.

FITZCLARENCE, L. (1987) 'Editorial', *Curriculum Theory Course Journal*, 5, 4, p.2.

FORSTER, A. and KING, B.S. (1985) 'A South Australian perspective on student support', in CASTRO, A.S., LIVINGSTON, K.T. and NORTHCOTT, P.H., *An Australian Casebook of Study Centres in Distance Education*, Geelong, Deakin Open Education Monographs, Deakin Universty.

FOSKETT, D.J. (1962) *The Creed of a Librarian*, London, Library Association.

FREIRE, P. (1972a) *Cultural Action for Freedom*, Harmondsworth, Penguin.

FREIRE, P. (1972b) *Pedagogy of the Oppressed*, Harmondsworth, Penguin.

FREIRE, P. (1974) *Education for Critical Consciousness*, London, Sheed and Ward.

FREIRE, P. (1976a) *Education: The Practice of Freedom*, London, Writers and Readers.

FREIRE, P. (1976b) 'A few notions on the word conscientization', in DALE, R. *et al.* (Eds) *Schooling and Capitalism*, London, Routledge and Kegan Paul.

FREIRE, P. (1985) *The Politics of Education: Culture, Power and Liberation*, South Hadley, Bergin and Garvey.

FRIED, R. (1980a) *Empowerment vs. Delivery of Services*, Concord, N.H., New Hampshire State Department of Education.

FRIED, R. (1980b) *Learning in Community: An Empowerment Approach*, Concord, N.H., New Hampshire State Department of Education.

FROMM, E., (1960) *Fear of Freedom*, London, Routledge and Kegan Paul.

GEORGE, R. (1986a) 'A critical look at critical theory', *Curriculum Theory Course Journal*, 4, 3.

GEORGE, R. (1986b) 'ECS 802: a critical experience', *Curriculum Theory Course Journal*, 4, 3.

GIBSON, R. (1984) *Structuralism and Education,* London, Hodder and Stoughton.

GIDDENS, A. (1979) *Central Problems in Social Theory,* London, Macmillan.

GIDDENS, A. (1984) *The Constitution of Society,* Cambridge, Polity Press.

GILLARD, G. (1981) 'The implied teacher-student dialogue in distance education', in CRUMP, P. and LIVINGSTON, K. (Eds) *ASPESA Forum '81 Papers,* Supplementary Volume, pp.12-21.

GIROUX, H.A. (1981) 'Pedagogy, pessimism and the politics of conformity: a reply to Linda McNeil', *Curriculum Inquiry,* 11, 3, pp.211-22.

GIROUX, H.A. (1983) *Theory and Resistance in Education,* South Hadley, Bergin and Garvey.

GIROUX, H.A. (1985) 'Teachers as transformative intellectuals', *Social Education,* 49, pp.376-9.

GIROUX, H.A. and FREIRE, P. (1987) 'Series introduction', in LIVINGSTONE, D. *et al.* (Eds) *Critical Pedagogy and Cultural Power,* South Hadley, Bergin and Garvey.

GOETHE, J.W., *Werke,* Book VIII, *Wilhelm Meister's Wanderjahre,* 2, 9, Hamburg, Wegner.

GOSSAGE, H. (1983) 'From stepping stone to millstone', *Curriculum Theory Course Journal,* 1, 4.

GRACE, G. (1978) *Teachers, Ideology and Control: A Study in Urban Education,* London, Routledge and Kegan Paul.

GRACE, G. (1985) 'Judging teachers: the social and political context of teacher evaluation', *British Journal of Sociology of Education,* 6, 1, pp.3-16.

GREEN, R. (1983) 'News and notes', *Curriculum Theory Course Journal,* 1, 4.

GREENE, M. (1973) *Teacher as Stranger,* Belmont, Wadsworth.

GREENE, M. (1985) 'Teacher as project: choice, perspective, and the public space', paper presented to the Summer Institute of Teaching, Teachers College, Columbia University.

GREENE, M. (1986a) 'In search of critical pedagogy', *Harvard Educational Review,* 56, 4, pp.427-41.

GREENE, M. (1986b) 'Reflection and passion in teaching', *Journal of Curriculum and Supervision*, 2, 1, pp.68-81.

GRUGEON, D. and THORPE, M. (Eds) (1987) *Open Learning for Adults*, London, Longman.

HABERMAS, J. (1972) *Knowledge and Human Interests*, London, Heinemann.

HABERMAS, J. (1974) *Theory and Practice*, London, Heinemann.

HAMPDEN-TURNER, C. (1970) *Radical Man*, London, Duckworth.

HARGREAVES, D. (1982) *The Challenge of the Comprehensive School*, London, Routledge and Kegan Paul.

HARRIS, D. (1987) *Openness and Closure in Distance Education*, Lewes, Falmer Press.

HARRIS, K. (1979) *Education and Knowledge: The Structured Misrepresentation of Knowledge*, London, Routledge and Kegan Paul.

HARTNETT, A. and NAISH, M. (1980) 'Technicians or social bandits? Some moral and political issues in the education of teachers', in WOODS, P. (Ed.) *Teacher Strategies: Explorations in the Sociology of the School*, London, Croom Helm.

HOLLY, M. (1984) *Keeping a Personal-Professional Journal*, Geelong, Deakin University Press.

INGLIS, F. (1985) *The Management of Ignorance: A Political Theory of the Curriculum*, London, Basil Blackwell.

INGVARSON, L. (1986) 'With critical friends, who needs enemies?' in FENSHAM, P. *et al.*, *Alienation from Schooling*, London, Routledge and Kegan Paul.

JAY, M. (1973) *The Dialectical Imagination: The History of the Institute for Social Research and the Frankfurt School, 1923-1950*, Boston, Mass., Little Brown.

JEVONS, F. (1984) 'Distance education in a mixed-mode institution: working towards parity', *Distance Education*, 5, 1, pp.24-37.

KEEGAN, D. (1986) *The Foundations of Distance Education*, London, Croom Helm.

KEMMIS, S. with FITZCLARENCE, L. (1986) *Curriculum Theorizing: Beyond Reproduction Theory*, Geelong, Deakin University Press.

KEMMIS, S. and MCTAGGART, R. (1988) *The Action Research Planner*, 3rd ed., Geelong, Deakin University Press.

KEMMIS, S. *et al.* (Eds) (1983) *ECS 802 Curriculum Theory Study Guide*, Geelong, Deakin University Press.

KIDD, R. and KUMAR, K. (1981) 'Coopting Freire: a critical analysis of pseudo-Freirean adult education', *Economic and Political Weekly*, 16, 1-2, pp.27-36.

KOHL, H. (1983) 'Examining closely what we do', *Learning*, 12, 1, pp.28-30.

KOZOL, J. (1977) *The Night is Dark and I am Far from Home*, New York, Bantam.

LARSON, M. (1977) *The Rise of Professionalism*, Berkeley, Calif., University of California Press.

LATHER, P. (1986a) 'Issues of data trustworthiness in openly ideological research', paper presented to the American Educational Research Association Conference, San Francisco.

LATHER, P. (1986b) 'Research as praxis', *Harvard Educational Review*, 56, 3, pp.257-77.

LAWN, M. and OZGA, J. (1981) 'The educational worker? A reassessment of teachers', in BARTON, L. and WALKER, S. (Eds) *Schools, Teachers and Teaching,* Lewes, Falmer Press.

LAZARRE, J. (1981) *On Loving Men,* London, Virago.

LOVETT, T. (1975) *Adult Education, Community Development and the Working Class,* London, Ward Lock.

LUNDGREN, U. (1983) *Between Hope and Happening: Text and Context in Curriculum,* Geelong, Deakin University Press.

MACARTHUR, B. (1974) 'An interim history of the open university', in TUNSTALL, J. (Ed.) *The Open University Opens,* London, Routledge and Kegan Paul.

McCUTCHEON, G. (1985) 'Curriculum theory/curriculum practice: a gap or the Grand Canyon', in MOLNAR, A. (Ed.) *Current Thought on Curriculum,* Alexandria, Association for Supervision and Curriculum Development, pp.45-52.

McDONALD, J. (1986) 'Raising the teacher's voice and the ironic role of theory', *Harvard Educational Review,* 56,4, pp.355-78.

MACDONALD, B. and WALKER, R. (1976) *Changing the Curriculum,* Melbourne, Macmillan.

MACGIBBON, H. (1974) 'The OU publishing operation', in TUNSTALL, J. (Ed.) (1974) *The Open University Opens,* London, Routledge and Kegan Paul.

MACINTYRE, A. (1981) *After Virtue: A Study in Moral Theory,* London, Duckworth.

MACKAY, D. and MARLAND, P. (1978) 'Thought processes of teachers', paper presented to the American Educational Research Association Conference, Toronto.

MACKIE, R. (Ed.) (1980) *Literacy and the Revolution: The Pedagogy of Paulo Freire,* London, Pluto Press.

MARCUS, G. and FISCHER, M. (1986) *Anthropology as Cultural Critique: An Experimental Moment in the Human Sciences,* Chicago, Ill., University of Chicago Press.

MEDVEDEV, Z. (1987) *Gorbachev,* Oxford, Blackwell.

MEIKSINS, P. (1982) 'Science in the labor process: engineers as workers', in DERBER, C. (Ed.) *Professionals as Workers: Mental Labor in Advanced Capitalism,* Boston, Mass., G.K. Hall.

MEISENHELDER, T. (1983) 'The ideology of professionalism in higher education', *Journal of Education,* 165, 3, pp.295-307.

MEZIROW, J. (1981) 'A critical theory of adult learning and education', *Adult Education,* 32, 1, pp.3-24.

MILES, M. (1959) *Learning to Work in Groups,* New York, Teachers College.

MILLS, C.W. (1970) *The Sociological Imagination,* Harmondsworth, Penguin.

MISGELD, D. (1975) 'Emancipation, enlightenment, and liberation: an approach toward foundational inquiry into education', *Interchange,* 6, 3, pp.23-37.

MISGELD, D. (1985) 'Education and cultural invasion' in FORESTER, J. (Ed.) *Critical Theory and Public Life,* Cambridge, Mass., Massachusetts Institute of Technology Press.

MISHLER, E. (1986) 'Meaning in context and the empowerment of respondents', in MISHLER, E. (1986) *Research Interviewing: Context and Narrative,* Cambridge, Mass., Harvard University Press.

MODRA, H.M. (1979) *The Adult Literacy Method of Paulo Freire and an Examination of Its Relevance to Continuing Education for Public Librarians,* BSocSci Minor thesis, Royal Melbourne Institute of Technology.

MODRA, H.M. (1984a) 'Political literacy: a new agenda for library education?' *Libraries: after 1984: Proceedings of the 22nd Biennial Conference of the Library Association of Australia,* Sydney, Library Association of Australia.

MODRA, H.M. (1984b) '. . . But librarianship is not about politics!', paper presented to the Public Libraries Section Pre-Conference Seminar of the Library Association of Australia 22nd Biennial Conference, Brisbane.

MODRA, H.M. (1986) *The Short March: Social Responsibility in Australian Librarianship 1970-1983,* MEd thesis, Monash University.

MOORE, L. (1986) 'The Australian Law of Copyright and its application to distance education', *Distance Education,* 8,1, pp.18-37.

MORRISON, D. (Ed.) (1988) *Mikhail S. Gorbachev,* New York, Time.

MULKAY, M. (1985) *The Word and the World,* London, Allen and Unwin.

NATION, D.E. (1985) 'I'm sorry to bother you at home, but you said we could ring . . .', paper presented to the International Council of Distance Education 13th World Conference, Melbourne

NATION, D.E. (1987a) 'Assisting students to learn sociology at a distance', in MILLER, A.M. and SACHSE-AKERLIND, G. (Eds) *The Learner in Higher Education: A Forgotten Species?* Sydney, Higher Education Research and Development Association.

NATION, D.E. (1987b) 'Some reflections upon teaching sociology at a distance', *Distance Education,* 8, 2, pp.190-207.

OAKLEY, A. (1984) *Taking It Like a Woman,* London, Flamingo.

PAGANO, J. (1987) 'The schools we deserve. Review of Goodlad's, *A Place Called School', Curriculum Inquiry,* 17, 1, pp.107-22.

PAINE, N. (Ed.) (1988) *Open Learning in Transition: An Agenda for Action,* Cambridge, National Extension College.

PATEMAN, C. (1970) *Participation and Democratic Theory,* Cambridge, Cambridge University Press.

PAULSTON, R.G. (1976) *Conflicting Theories of Social and Educational Change: A Typological View,* Pittsburgh, Penn., University Center for International Studies, University of Pittsburgh.

PERLS, F. *et al.* (1973) *Gestalt Therapy: Excitement and Growth in the Human Personality,* Harmondsworth, Penguin.

PERRY, W. (1972) *The Early Development of the Open University,* Bletchley, Open University.

PERRY, W. (1976) *Open University: A Personal Account by the First Vice-Chancellor,* Milton Keynes, Open Univesity Press.

PETRIK, J. (1987) 'Commentary on Women's Theological Center', in EVANS, A.F., EVANS, R.A. and KENNEDY, W.B. (Eds) *Pedagogies for the Non-Poor,* Maryknoll, N.Y., Orbis Books.

POLLARD, A. (1987) 'Reflective teaching — the sociological contribution', in WOODS, P. and POLLARD, A. (Eds) *Sociology and Teaching: A New Challenge for the Sociology of Education,* London, Croom Helm.

POULANTZAS, N. (1973) *Political Power and Social Classes,* London, New Left Books.

POYNTER, G. (1983) 'Two points for starters', *ECS 802 Curriculum Theory Course Journal,* 1,2.

RICH, A. (1972) 'When we dead awaken: writing as re-vision', *College English,* 34, 1, pp.18-25.

ROBERTS, D. (1984) 'Ways and means of reducing early student drop-out rates', *Distance Education,* 5, 1, pp.50-71.

ROGERS, C. (1961) *On Becoming a Person,* Boston, Mass., Houghton Mifflin.

ROWBOTHAM, S. (1981) 'The women's movement and organizing for socialism', in ROWBOTHAM, S., SEGAL, L. and WAINWRIGHT, H. (Eds) *Beyond the Fragments: Feminism and the Making of Socialism,* Boston, Mass., Alyson Publishers.

SACHS, J. (1987) 'The constitution of teachers' knowledge: a literature review', *Discourse,* 7, 2.

SCHEFFLER, I. (1968) 'University scholarship and the education of teachers', *Teachers College Record,* 70, 1, pp.1-12.

SCHON, D. (1983) *The Reflective Practitioner: How Professionals Think in Action,* New York, Basic Books.

SCHON, D. (1984) 'Leadership as reflection-in-action', in SERGIOVANNI, T. and CORBALLY, J. (Eds) *Leadership and Organizational Culture: New Perspectives on Administrative Theory and Practice,* Urbana, Ill., University of Illinois Press, pp.36-63.

SCHWAB, J.J. (1969) 'The practical: a language for curriculum', *School Review,* 78, pp.1-24.

SEWART, D. (1982) 'Individualising support services', in DANIEL, J.S., STROUD, M.A. and THOMPSON, J.R. (Eds) *Learning at a Distance: A World Perspective,* Edmonton, Athabasca University.

SEWART, D. (1983) 'Distance teaching: a contradiction in terms?' in SEWART, D., KEEGAN, D. and HOLMBERG, B. (Eds) *Distance Education: International Perspectives,* London, Croom Helm, pp.46-61.

SHARP, G. (1983) 'Intellectuals in transition', *Arena,* 65.

SHARP, G. (1985) 'Constitutive abstraction and social practice', *Arena,* 70.

SHEATH, H.C. (1965) *External Studies: The First Ten Years,* Armidale, University of New England.

SHOR, I. (1980) *Critical Teaching and Everyday Life,* Montreal, Black Rose Press.

SHOR, I. (1986) *Culture Wars,* Boston, Mass., Routledge and Kegan Paul.

SHOR, I. and FREIRE, P. (1987) *A Pedagogy for Liberation: Dialogues on Transforming Education,* South Hadley, Bergin and Garvey.

SIMON, R. (1984) 'Signposts for a critical pedagogy': a review of Henry Giroux's *Theory and Resistance in Education', Educational Theory,* 34, 4, pp.379-88.

SIMON, R. (1985) 'Critical pedagogy', in HUSEN, T. and POSTLETHWAITE, N.T. (Eds) *International Encyclopedia of Education Research and Studies, Volume 2,* Oxford, Pergamon Press, pp.1118-20.

SIMON, R. (1987) 'Empowerment as a pedagogy of possibility', *Language Arts,* 64,4, pp.370-82.

SIROTNIK, K. and OAKES, J. (Eds) (1986) *Critical Perspectives on the Organization and Improvement of Schooling,* Boston, Mass., Kluwer-Nijhoff.

SMITH, D. and SIMPSON, C. with DAVIES, I. (1981) *Mugabe,* London, Sphere.

SMITH, P. and KELLY, M. (Eds) *Distance Education and the Mainstream: Convergence in Education,* London, Croom Helm.

SMITH, W.A. (1976) *The Meaning of Conscientizacao: The Goal of Freire's Pedagogy*, Amherst, Mass., University of Massachusetts, Centre for International Education.

SMYTH, J. (1986) 'Clinical supervision: technocratic mindedness, or emancipatory learning', *Journal of Curriculum and Supervision*, 1, 4, pp.331-40.

SMYTH, J. (1987a) 'Leadership enabling teachers to become "transformative intellectuals"', *The Australian Administrator*, 8, 3, pp.1-4.

SMYTH, J. (1987b) 'Teachers-as-intellectuals in a critical pedagogy of schooling', *Education and Society*, 5, 142, pp.11-28.

SMYTH, J. (1987c) *Rationale for Teachers' Critical Pedagogy: A Handbook*, Geelong, Deakin University Press.

SMYTH, J. (1987d) 'Cinderella syndrome: a philosophical view of supervision as a field of study', *Teachers College Record*, 88, 4, pp.567-88.

SMYTH, J. (1987e) 'A critical pedagogy of classroom practice', paper presented to the Ninth Curriculum Theorizing and Classroom Practices Conference, Dayton.

SOHN-RETHEL, A. (1978) *Intellectual and Manual Labour: A Critique of Epistemology*, London, Macmillan.

SOLOMON, J. (1987) 'New thoughts on teacher education', *Oxford Review of Education*, 13, 3, pp.267-74.

STENHOUSE, L. (1975) *An Introduction to Curriculum Research and Development*, London, Heinemann.

STENHOUSE, L. (1979) 'The problem of standards in illuminative research', *Scottish Educational Review*, 11, 1, p.7.

STENHOUSE, L. (1983) 'The relevance of theory to practice', *Theory into Practice*, 22, 3, pp.211-15.

STEVENS, P. (1987) 'Political education and political teachers', *Journal of Philosophy of Education*, 21, 1, pp.75-83.

STUDENT RESEARCH CENTRE (1986) 'The human dimension in Open University study', *Open Learning*, 1, 2, pp.14-17.

TOURAINE, A. (1981) *The Voice and the Eye: An Analysis of Social Movements*, Cambridge, Cambridge University Press.

TRIPP, D. (1984) 'From autopilot to critical consciousness: problematising successful teaching', a revision of a paper presented to the Sixth Curriculum Theory and Practice Conference, Bergamo.

TRIPP, D. (1987) *Theorising Practice: The Teacher's Professional Journal*, Geelong, Deakin University Press.

TUNSTALL, J. (Ed.) (1974) *The Open University Opens*, London, Routledge and Kegan Paul.

WADD, K. (1982) 'What theory into practice'? *Educational Review*, 34, 3, pp.219-28.

WALKER, D. (1970) 'A naturalistic model for curriculum development', *School Review*, 80, pp.51-65.

WEBER, M. (1948) *From Max Weber*, Ed. by G. Gerth and C.W. Mills, London, Routledge and Kegan Paul.

WELCH, A.R. (1980) 'Ideology, sociology and education', *Australian and New Zealand Journal of Sociology*, 16, 2, pp.71-81.

WEXLER, P. (1981) 'Body and soul: sources of social change and strategies', *British Journal of Sociology of Education*, 2, 3, pp.247-63.

WHITE, D. (1987a) 'Curriculum priorities', working paper, State Board of Education, Melbourne.

WHITE, D. (1987b) *Education and the State: Federal Involvement in Educational Policy Development,* Geelong, Deakin University Press.

WILLIAMS, J. and WILLIAMS, M. (1987) 'A student-operated support network for distance learners', *International Council of Distance Education Bulletin,* 13, pp. 51-64.

WILLIAMS, N. (Ed.) (1986) *A Year on the Streets,* Perth, Perth Inner City Youth Service.

WILLIS, P. (1977) *Learning to Labour: How Working Class Kids Get Working Class Jobs,* Farnborough, Saxon House.

WILLMOTT, G. and KING, B.S. (1983) 'Programme development in distance education', paper presented to the Australian and South Pacific External Studies Association 6th Biennial Forum, Toowoomba.

WOOLF, V. (1975) *A Room of One's Own,* Harmondsworth, Penguin.

YOUNG, M.F.D. (Ed.) (1971) *Knowledge and Control: New Directions for the Sociology of Education,* London, Collier Macmillan.

YOUNG, R. (Ed.) (1981) *Untying the Text,* Boston, Mass., Routledge and Kegan Paul.

ZUBRICK, A. (1985) 'Learning through writing: the use of reading logs', *Higher Education Research and Development Society of Australia Newsletter* 7, 3, pp. 11-12, 24.

Index